## Designed to Blossom Resou:

*A friendly place for Human Design enthusiasts
wanting to expand their understanding, deepen their experiment
and receive compassionate guidance—integrating humanistic psychology,
the Gene Keys and more.*

## IT'S TIME TO SUPPORT & REFINE
## YOUR INNER WISDOM KEEPING!

ROSY ARONSON, PHD

Seal Pup
PRESS
Berkeley, CA

For permission requests, write to the publisher, addressed "Attention: Permissions Coordinator," at the address below.

Seal Pup Press
PO Box 138
Berkeley, CA 94701
sealpuppress.com

Writing and design by Rosy Aronson
Cover design by Kim and Rosy Aronson
Muse Consulting and Editing by Pam DeLeo, LMT
Key words and concepts related to *The Spectrum of Consciousness* by Richard Rudd's *The Gene Keys*, Gene Keys Publishing © 2009

Author's Note: *The Designed to Blossom Resource Book offers information about the Human Design system through my uniquely creative, eclectic and psychologically-integrating lens. Should you become interested in learning more about Human Design, please check out* **Designed to Blossom: A Creative Workbook and Foundational Course in Human Design** *and the additional resources provided at the end of this workbook/course. Information provided in this Resource Book may not reflect the official stance of Jovian Archive, Inc. and its certified analysts (though they have my deep respect).*

Ordering Information: **Designed to Blossom: A Creative Workbook and Foundational Course in Human Design** is available on Amazon and wisdomkeepers.net.

For the online version of the self-study course, go to: designedtoblossom.com

*Designed to Blossom* Resource Book/ Rosy Aronson, PhD—1st Edition
ISBN: 978-0-9970230-7-7

**Also by Rosy Aronson**

*Designed to Blossom Foundational Course and Creative Workbook in Human Design*
*(Full color and Black & White Edition)*

*Walking a Fine Line: Becoming a Professional Wisdom Keeper in the Healing Arts (Paperback Edition)*

*The Wisdom Keepers Oracle Deck (Full Color, and Black & White Limited Edition)*

*The Wisdom Keepers Inner Guidebook (Paperback Edition)*

*64 Faces of Awakening (Artwork)*

*The 64 Faces of Awakening Coloring Book*

*64 Faces Projects (Global Outreach)*

*A Tale of Serendipity (Part One of The Wisdom Keepers Adventure Tales Series)*

# Praise from Designed to *Blossom* Enthusiasts!

"*Designed to Blossom* is a unique experience that will set you on the right track, rejuvenate you, reconnect you with the intimate parts of yourself, allow you to forgive yourself, discover the hidden cultural patterns that limit and define you. Cataclysmic, re-knowing. Rosy will love you like you've never been loved before, accept you as you've never been accepted before. Rosy is a tour de force, her insight, her imagination, her connection with the deepest parts of you will enable you to paint with words, to draw in the colors of life, to reconnect with your passion, to be more than you've ever thought you could; to draw when they told you not to, to sing when they told you not to, to believe when they told you not to, to flourish when they didn't think you could. Rosy and *Designed to Blossom* are a priceless gift. Give yourself the gift of a lifetime."

*~Yasmin, Writer*

"Rosy's *Designed to Blossom* Course opened a portal of creative self-discovery that I never thought possible. It provided a supportive container while I explored my inner terrain, enabling my process to unfold in a playful and magical way. I felt an inner dance of shadows and light as it weaved together a tapestry of my truth and authenticity, shedding layers of old conditioning while enhancing my gifts. Rosy trusted me, the process, and her loving presence was felt throughout my journey. She didn't waver, and slowly through this amazing process, I learned, and continue to learn, that *anything is possible*. I will always feel grateful for Rosy, her presence, her Program and the sacred container it provided."

*~ Judith Snyder, Holistic Licensed Therapist, Certified Yoga Teacher and LifeForce Yoga ® Practitioner, Lover of Creativity, Play, and Sacred Movement.*

"A true Human Design master is part knowledge-expert, part artist, part therapist, part facilitator. Rosy is all of these and more. The promise of Human Design is to shift the 'stuck places' and experience relief, new freedom, a sense of possibility and/or transformation. With compassion, rigor and an amazing capacity to track the complexity of experience, Rosy was able to offer me a very accessible framework and in-the-moment tools that help me make choices more easily, express myself more authentically and experience a sense of aliveness and alignment that are unprecedented in my 56 years (and ohh, so many therapy sessions!)."

*~Susan Strasburger, RPT, PhD, Integrative Coaching and Counseling, Living with Presence*

"Playing with Human Design and Rosy was one of the most encouraging, affirming, enlightening and fun experiences I've ever had. This System of discovery acknowledged who I am based on how I was designed before any of this crazy world's conditioning got in the way. It changed my life to start seeing myself through truth-glasses rather than cultural, societal, familial or trauma-based ones. Human Design was the perfect prescription to help correct my self-vision and move me toward 20/20. My gratitude abounds…"

*~Anissa Matthews, Purveyor of Passions and Worshipper of Life*

"As a magical mentor, coach, artistic midwife, and celebrator of what's blossoming in an individual, Rosy Aronson has cleared the dust from my eyes and set my feet on solid ground time and time again. She has a gift to see deep into one's soul and usher us into our greatness. I would not be this currently 'blossomed,' and constantly still blossoming version of myself without her acute wisdom and generous joyful support. I would encourage anyone wanting to step more fully into the highest version of herself to experience Rosy Aronson and *Designed to Blossom*. Rosy is a magically inspired, creative, and powerful force of nature on our planet at this time!"

*~Jenny Karns, author, healer, creator of Remembering Our Magic Telesummit: A Healing, Empowering, and Global Peace Project*

"Rosy Aronson's *Designed to Blossom* Course was the perfect intro into Human Design. She distilled Human Design's complexity into fun, accessible, lessons and practices that helped me start living my design and trusting myself in new ways. We continued to work together in a coaching relationship that has expanded beyond Human Design. But I look at the work we did together in the *Designed to Blossom* Course as the foundation of our work, where I began learning how to trust my generator belly response rather than my mind. Over time this practice has transformed my life by releasing me from pressures and those nagging 'shoulds' that weren't serving me. Human Design can feel overwhelming and complex. If you're looking for a fun, interactive, and creative approach to learning it, I highly recommend you consider the *Designed to Blossom* Course!"

*~James Alexander, Truth Seeker, Writer, and Spiritual Coach*

"Rosy possesses the rarest sort of genius, and she puts it to still rarer use. Part supportive counselor, part wise interpreter of the soul, part clear-eyed intuitive, Rosy is the sort of ally in life I wish everyone could experience. The whole world would be the better for it. In a world where, it seems, only the most conventional and obvious skills and life paths are encouraged, her commitment to naming and supporting subtler gifts and needs is vital. I'm always touched by her insight, empathy, and boundless understanding."

*~Siona van Dijk, Writer, Facilitator, Clinical hypnotherapist and Literary Dilettante*

"Rosy is a lighthouse, illuminating the way for those who seek knowledge of self. She is like a compass guiding you back home, and once there, can never stray away again. I was looking for a Human Design facilitator through the internet and I found Rosy's name. I was immediately attracted to her energy and spent several days researching Human Design. I have participated in the *Designed to Blossom* Course and worked with Rosy privately for quite some time, and I have to say she really is one of the most dynamic women I have ever met. Her intelligence, professionalism, passion, integrity and expertise are exceptional. She has a gift of combining all her wisdom and knowledge into her work. Thanks to Rosy and this course, my life has blossomed, and through an understanding of my design, I have become more empowered."

*~Sandra Rojo, Certified Wellness, Health and Life Coach, and Healer*

"Rosy is not only an expert on Human Design but a true artist in the way she personalizes the work and gives it voice. I have invested in many workbooks and coaches for personal growth and development and my experience with Rosy was by far the most valuable for what I learned and could immediately apply to all aspects of my life, relationships and business. Until understanding my Human Design I tended to make things so much harder than they needed to be. With Rosy's guidance, I was able to start to trust my rhythms and ways, and have had incredible gifts appear in my life. Just thinking of my sumptuous Human Design experiences with Rosy brings sunshine, flowers, and fresh air into my being! She is a sparkling gem. I cannot recommend Rosy's work highly or deeply enough!"

*~Karyn Amore, Catalyst and Muse for Your WildSexyFree Life*

"Learning about my design from Rosy was an amazing experience of being fully appreciated and praised for all the parts of myself and life experiences I held in contempt and judgment. Not just facts and figures, but the way Rosy interpreted and delivered the Human Design information is what was so impressive and therapeutic to me. Very powerfully, intuitively, empathically, compassionately and so joyfully, Rosy told me the story of myself; introducing me to my long lost Truest Self. Rosy completely reframed my perspective regarding my life's journey, purpose and accomplishments. I discovered I was more on track than I thought and very creatively fulfilling my Life Purpose mission. Not only am I right where I'm supposed to be but ahead of the curve in many ways. For the first time in my life I am able to accept and fully embrace my creative ingenuity and allow 'not knowing' and trusting the unfolding of life's process to be my Muse rather than my Nemesis. Thanks, Rosy. You are truly an amazing gift to all the lives you touch."

*~David Scheel, natural Empath and Change Agent, facilitator of True Self Re-membering and Embodiment*

"Rosy and the *Designed to Blossom* Course changed my life in a profound way. The brilliant creative exercises engaged me at a deep level, and passed the chatter of my mind. I've been in therapy for years, explored several spiritual paths, studied many systems of self-understanding, and had many different kinds of Readings. I had actually received a Human Design Reading by someone else, but the information was dry and lifeless. Rosy makes Human Design deep, alive and juicy, full of love, respect and humor. I had been anorexic for decades when I started the *Designed to Blossom* Course. While doing an exercise that focused on my body, I drew a tiny stick figure behind prison bars. Looking at that drawing, a deep, unknown desire to free that stick figure arose inside me! For the first time in 40 years, I felt ready to let go of my anorexia. Of course, the letting go didn't happen overnight. But the profound shift in consciousness that I experienced in the *Designed to Blossom* Course, set me on the road to true recovery. I am now fully recovered and feeling fully alive and in my body, at last, which I now experience as beautiful! I consider my connection to Rosy and the *Designed to Blossom* Course to be one of the blessings in my life."

~*Jackie Goodman, a whole, free, alive human being*

"This Human Design information can be confusing. But, shared with someone rooted in Love and Integrity such as Rosy, it begins to open, maybe…unfold…who we are. Working with Rosy, I just felt recognized…that's me, described in a new language! It comforted me, revealing an inner guide and self-trust I had never really dared to rely upon. Listening, I relaxed into who I am, and found myself…loving…the uniqueness of me! My relationships immediately took on more fullness. I came to this planet with the unwavering belief that each person has everything they need already 'installed.' Human Design is a way to discover what we have within, and how it can be reached and expressed to give shape to the life we live."

~*Brett Diethert, Imaginist, dreamer, poet, writer*

"I'll tell you now of Rosy, Compassionate and Wise—
Who's always in my Corner, Exposing all the Lies
That I in Years of Living Believed about my Self.
She Gently and with Humor Uncovers all the Wealth
That's been Hiding in the Basement under Years of Self-Neglect.
While Vacuuming and Dusting, she showed me—Self-*Respect!*
The Journey is Ongoing, and my Blossom's Just Begun
To Open, and to Fragrance the World with Joy and Fun.
What lies ahead is Foggy, a World yet Unexplored.
Technology seems Baffling, but I am Moving Toward
A Place that will be Perfect for my Projector Soul
To Flourish and to Open as an Integrated Whole.
How rare a find is Rosy! Her virtues know no end,
A Coach and Guide and Counselor, and my Eternal Friend!"

~*Margaret Blackburn, Mother, Grandmother, Wife, Teacher, Energy Worker, Musician, Author (and Angel)*

This book is dedicated to the many brave, trusting and devoted **Designed to Blossom** participants
and all of the people who've followed my work with Human Design over the years.
Because of their sincere experiments and essential questions,
I am able to bring this Resource Book to you.

Deep Gratitude to…

Ra Uru Hu, who channeled the Human Design transmission,
turned it into an easy-to-understand system, and made it accessible to people all over the world.
He believed that this profound material was meant to evolve, expand and awaken the planet
through the unique, creative and empowered voices of its students.

Richard Rudd, whose profound journey into Human Design
led him down the evolutionary rabbit hole.
He emerged an open-hearted heretic and offered us the *Gene Keys*.

*Abide not with dualism*
*Carefully avoid pursuing it;*
*As soon as you have right and wrong*
*Confusion ensues and mind is lost.*

~ Zen Koan


*The wound is the place where the Light enters you.*

~ Rumi

# Table of Contents

## PETAL 3: OBSERVE YOUR ENERGY FLOW
*(Take a gander at your magnificent Blossoming body!)*

## PETAL 4: SYNTHESIZE YOUR PARTS!
*(Enjoy the best of both worlds: your innate gifts and your beautiful receptivity)*

## PETAL 5: SUPPORT YOUR LIFE!
*(Your Inner Wisdom Keeper's Unique and Trusty Truth Compass)*

## PETAL 6: OPEN UP TO YOUR PATH
*(Gain a new perspective on your purpose)*

# My Story

From the day I burst out of my mother's womb ("like gangbusters," as she likes to say), I've been a creative, intuitive, 'highly-sensitive' type who inevitably blundered her way down unbeaten, non-linear (often incomprehensible) paths… while unfortunately, judging myself all the while.

Again and again, I've found myself flying in the face of personal, cultural, even spiritual conditioning. I have moved from one country to another, and have gone 'back to school' so many times I can't even count—each time, shaking up the entire foundation and identity that came with the first education and resulting career. I can't even count how many licenses I've ultimately rejected or thrown out, after going through the entire (INTENSE!) education, because in the end, I felt the call for greater freedom. (And believe me, that hasn't been easy, because along with those licenses, come status, open doors and a society that 'gets' you!)

Like many of us Westerners, I was raised to believe that I needed to know (up in my head) who I was, where I was going, why I was going there, and how I planned to get there.

I thought it a 'human prerequisite' to find a service or professional identity that could be intelligibly talked about at dinner parties. (A prerequisite I never managed to fulfill.) I can say with great sincerity that I really do know something about the pain and the gifts that accompany the unbeaten path.

I also know what a bright yet deeply conditioned mind can do to a person who isn't meant for the cookie-cutting business, who is simply trying to find her own way in life.

## Just to make it more interesting…

Like so many young girls, I also learned at a very early age that to be a good girl, a good daughter, sister, friend… to be a 'safely successful woman,' I had to sacrifice my needs and hold back my power so that others could get their needs met, and ultimately shine.

You could say I spent the majority of my childhood and early adulthood twisting myself into pretzels—trying to be impressively focused, creative and successful… endlessly supportive, giving and selfless… WHILE swallowing my feelings, hiding my gifts and avoiding competition at all costs.

## Empathy—a Blessing and a Curse!

My ability to empathize and help others, to intuitively tune into the needs and desires of the **WE** (whether 'the WE' was my family, friends, community, organization or institution I was a part of, or the whole world/cosmos) became both a blessing and a curse.

On the one hand, these abilities reflected my deepest core knowing (not just belief) that we are truly all connected, and that when we meet the needs of others, we're ultimately meeting our own needs. In the end, there's no difference. We're all ONE.

On the other hand, (and in this paradoxical world of ours, there is usually 'an other hand!'), my We-orientation became one of my main life challenges—a protective shield, survival strategy and wound-based identity all wrapped up in one. It kept me burying my own needs and feelings, perceiving my boundaries as dangerous, and either giving in to outer pressures and ignoring my self-preserving and non-linear instincts, or following my unique-self-celebrating and non-cookie-cutter instincts… and feeling like a failure.

*Makes me realize how much I owe my sanity (and BLOSSOMING!) to two things:*
*the Creative Process and Human Design.*

While the creative process preserved my spirit, and helped me befriend the unknown, it was an enthusiastic encounter with Human Design (and beyond as in the *Gene Keys*!) that grounded—and ultimately allowed me to fully embrace—my authentic life. One of the biggest gifts I received from my work with Human Design is that it helped me learn how to put something ELSE in charge of my life than my mind.

Even though my mind isn't at the helm anymore, SOMETHING IS. There is something I can turn to when I feel completely flooded, overwhelmed and overstimulated. There is an authority inside of me, a TRUTH compass, that is consistent and reliable and oh-so-helpful.

It is my hope that this *Resource Book* will be a place for you to feel increased permission to be who you are, and to discover and honor the (sometimes paradoxical) gems of your own life journey.

Love,

*Rosy*

# INTRO

Over the years, I've been blessed with the opportunity to field a plethora of questions from enthusiastic, bright and curious students of the **Designed to Blossom** Course (A Creative Workbook and Foundational Course in Human Design) and followers of *The Bloom Blog*.

In this *Designed to Blossom* Resource Book, I've gathered together responses to many of these wonderful questions for easy reference. It gives me great pleasure to offer this resource to anyone who has:

- explored Human Design elsewhere, but is interested in a creative, compassionate, relational and psychologically-grounded way of working with this powerful system

- longed to bridge Human Design with Richard Rudd's the *Gene Keys*, and Rudd's and Pitzal's *Integral Human Design* (IHD)

- already purchased the *Designed to Blossom* online course or Creative Workbook and would love some extra guidance and support

**My unique way of holding and working with Human Design**

- I hold an essentially collaborative—and paradox-friendly—world view. On the one hand, I believe many of us can benefit greatly from learning how to listen to and live in alignment with our unique 'Authorities' (according to Human Design). On the other, I believe that in the end we're all here to live from our hearts. You'll notice throughout this Resource Book that I share different perspectives on Human Design, some seemingly contradictory. This is an evolving field of study. There as many 'takes' on the system as there are people practicing it. I invite you to stay open to differing viewpoints, trust in your own unique experience, and join the conversation. We need your unique perspective and voice.

- I embrace a multicultural perspective and incorporate the expressive arts and a philosophy of creativity into my teaching. I tend to be very permission-giving when it comes to the experiment—not offering a lot of rights and wrongs—just opportunities to learn.

- While I love the Human Design system, I hold it lightly…as I hold all systems lightly. I don't see it as the only road to self-knowledge or authentic living. I see it as an unusually precise and practical 'authenticity tool' that has the potential to benefit many people. I also see it as a system that can cast a pretty potent shadow when clung to with too much mental rigidity.

- I also hold Human Design gently. I tend to have a lot of compassion for people, so I do my best to introduce an attitude of softness, patience and forgiveness when supporting people through their personal Human Design experiment.

● Though *Designed to Blossom* and this *Resource Book* are by no means official courses in the *Gene Keys* or *Integral Human Design*, I do incorporate a *Gene Keys*-friendly lens into all that I teach. I don't see Blossoming Bodygraphs as static, unflinching charts, doomed to a single mode of expression. I see them as living maps, here to be explored, experienced and expressed in a variety of ways, through the most 'shadowy' of frequencies, to the most service-oriented, to the most awakened. So much depends on the person, their life experience, their unique circumstance, and their forever-evolving level of maturity and wisdom. Ultimately, I see Human Design as a map that can be incredibly empowering for a period of time in a person's life, until that map is no longer necessary.

● Some believe that Human Design and Psychology (or therapy) are like oil and water; they don't mix. I feel differently. As someone with an extensive background in psychotherapy, I've found—especially when it comes to the 'de-conditioning' process—that a compassionate, integrative and psychologically-infused perspective is often necessary for a Human Design experiment to bear healthy fruit.

● Many people I work with tend to be service-oriented. Because of this, one of my central intentions is to help people find a healthy balance between self-empowerment and service-to-others, and to get comfortable in that wonderful (sometimes elusive) zone of interdependence—where we get to simultaneously enjoy our autonomy and our shared interconnectivity. I'm especially interested in exploring how a healthy individuation process can help each of us find our most fulfilling way of contributing to the whole.

# A Deeper Intention

One of my deepest intentions with *Designed to Blossom* Resource Book is to provide people with a safe place for authentic sharing and experimentation. I find few things more inspiring than supporting people who are on their growing edge, or more fulfilling than playing a positive part in their blossoming. In all that I offer, I remain committed to learning, living and teaching the following sacred balance:

● *providing others with both a safe, holding environment and an experimental, freeing one*
● *affirming our interconnectedness while promoting individuation and respect for boundaries*
● *nurturing spirit and intuition while instilling a sense of psychological/cultural/political meaning and context*
● *and finally, facilitating the journey home to the body, not necessarily 'fixing' problems, but helping people to learn how to meet life head on with vitality, and to respond to life's challenges with creative grounding.*

Ultimately, I believe it is the creative relationship between people that feeds, heals, stretches and pushes us inwards, through and beyond ourselves. To support someone in coming alive, in not only discovering their true nature but daring to live it out, is a deeply spiritual act.

As a healer, artist and teacher, I often find that *what's in the way, is the way*. Mistakes (as long as they're not too big!) not only free up the energy (in the Human Design experiment), they act as sacred portals. They open doors to unexpected genius, to moments of revelation and intimacy that could never be intentionally constructed with egoic will power.

As Stephen Nachmanovitch writes in his fantastic book *Free Play: Power of Improvisation in Life and the Arts*, "The troublesome parts of our work (*and relationships!*), the parts that are most baffling and frustrating, are in fact the growing edges. We see these opportunities the instant we drop our preconceptions and our self-importance." In such rare yet glorious healing moments, my clients and I manage to "let go of some impediment or fear, and boom—in whooshes the muse. We feel clarity, power, freedom, as something unforeseeable jumps out of us." We connect more deeply, more honestly, and become aware of the mutual, circular nature of our relationship, the divine alchemy set in motion by our mere togetherness.

It goes without saying that I tend to my work with Human Design with integrity and compassion. I do my utmost to provide a perspective that uplifts, connects and respects people, their individual paths and beliefs, as well as our shared environment. I invite in spirit, empathy and presence, and embody a deep trust in my students' essential capacity for self-actualization. Eliminating pain and anxiety are not always possible, or even desirable. Instead, I open myself up to difficult feelings, stretching myself and those whom I serve in a way that connects us to our humanness and points us towards a more authentic existence.

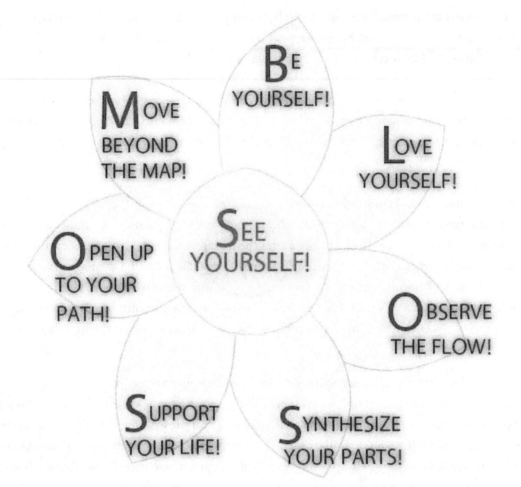

# SEE Yourself

## *Entering the Heart of the Flower*

# *HOW WILL I KNOW IF HUMAN DESIGN CAN BE HELPFUL TO ME?*

SEE
YOURSELF!

Usually, a system is most helpful (and 'Truth-full') when it comes at a time, and in a form, that is particularly suited to a person.

A transformative alchemy between 'giver,' 'receiver' and 'system' is enhanced when the *system* is coming through a *giver* whose innate intuition (and capacity to impart their unique form of wisdom) is genuinely activated through that particular form.

While I obviously love Human Design and have experienced its empowering impact on myself and countless others over the years, I could imagine a telephone book being just as transformative a divination tool, if its delivery was imbued with love and wisdom, if the *teacher/giver's* intuition was profoundly inspired by the telephone book, and if the *receiver* was particularly open to receiving a spiritual transmission through a telephone book!

I don't mean to minimize Human Design, or any system for that matter. I actually believe that there are aspects to the form of Human Design that address the living art of self-trust in ways that I haven't encountered in other systems. I certainly wouldn't have dedicated as much of my adult life to the exploration and teaching of Human Design as I have, if I didn't love it. I'm also not here to idealize, magnify or defend it either.

- Do you feel drawn to Human Design?
- So far, is what you're learning intriguing you? Inspiring you? Challenging you in ways that feel stretching and healthy?
- Are you curious to see what happens if you try trusting a different kind of wisdom inside of you than you're used to?
- Can you put some of your favorite identities and opinions about yourself on hold, at least for a little while?
- Is this a good time in your life for an experiment?
- Can you do your best to stay as non-attached to the outcome as possible?

If you get a 'yes' to these questions, chances are Human Design will be useful to you. At the very least, it'll be a fascinating life experience. At the most, it'll change your life for the better and leave you feeling a lot more relaxed, free, grounded and aligned with your truest nature.

# IS HUMAN DESIGN ACCURATE?

So many people have asked me over the years how I know that Human Design is an accurate system, or how I know that a certain part of their design has any truth to it.

During the earlier stages of my learning process, I felt the pressure to provide them with a technical explanation or 'evidence' they wanted.

Over time, I shared more personally about my own experience, since really, that's the only evidence I have. For example, I shared how learning about my Profile helped me trust the essential usefulness of the system over the years, in a very subtle but lovely way. Both my husband and daughter share my Profile, and I can really feel a resonance between us that is quite different than what I've sensed and witnessed in other families.

I shared that sometimes, the best way to sense a 'rightness' or truth in something (like the Profile in Human Design) is taking time to notice a certain resonance or parallel in people who share common Human Design aspects. Perhaps you notice that people with a given Profile or Type, share a certain way of interacting with the world, of experiencing and expressing their vitality, or a tendency to play out particular roles in life.

Another potential revealing exploration is to notice how people with shared traits impact you differently than people who don't have those aspects and vice versa. For this kind of personal research project to bear reliable results, it can take years.

Today I find it helpful to encourage people to see certain aspects of the Human Design chart from a more archetypal perspective. For instance, when we look at a Gate, Channel, or Line, (whether they're considered to be part of our Definition or not), it's good to remember that we all have the potential to experience and express all of them. Perhaps we experience certain archetypes in slightly different ways, in varying proportions or with differing levels of specialization. In the end, we can all grow and learn from exploring and finding our unique relationship to the whole kit and caboodle.

This is probably why my Human Design path led me to delve deeply into Richard Rudd's archetypal approach to the 64 Gates of Human Design, through the *Gene Keys*, and ultimately, to make this universal wisdom available to even more people through the development of the *Wisdom Keepers Oracle Deck*.

Now I can comfortably say that I have no idea if any of this is 'right,' accurate or applicable to all people. I no longer worry about whether I can convince anyone or not.

In the end, as someone who's explored many paths throughout my life, I find value in a system or synthesis when it has a permission-giving, relaxing, empowering or transformative impact on me, and on enough others, to make it worth exploring further.

# WHAT IF I DON'T RELATE TO A PART OF MY DESIGN?

While the majority of people I've worked with generally relate easily to the big picture of their designs, it's very common for people not to relate to all aspects. There are parts of *mine* I still don't relate to!

Just for starters, know that it is perfectly normal and healthy for you—or anyone studying this system— *not* to instantly relate to everything you learn about how you're designed.

It's actually essential that you don't just swallow whole everything you learn. When you try to squeeze yourself into a mold that doesn't fit, you run the serious risk of allowing Human Design to become yet another unhelpful conditioning force in your life—pressuring you to be, act and identify with something or someone other than who you are.

## That said, as a general rule:

If you hear something about your design, and you have a lot of resistance to it, I invite you to stay curious. Sometimes, the more strongly we feel the need to reject something, the more likely it is reflecting a 'shadow' aspect of our being, one worth looking into.

I recommend that you try the 'description/strategy/quality' on for a while. Even if it doesn't fit ultimately, you're likely to gain some wonderful lessons from this process of exploration.

## Another thing to keep in mind:

Sometimes the '**Red**' aspects of our designs reveal aspects of our nature that we're not so aware of. I know many Generators, Projectors, even Manifestors, for example, who feel like Reflectors, because all of their Definition is below ground.

When it comes to these less-easy-to-access parts of us, it can be helpful and interesting to ask the people who know us well (and whom we trust) whether they can see a certain tendency in us. Perhaps your friends, family, colleagues or mentors are seeing something that you're not seeing.

(For an alternative perspective, see *The 'Black and Red' isn't so 'Black and White'* in Petal Three.)

Feel free to let anything go...

If an aspect of your design keeps feeling 'not right'—in a neutral way, then I say just let it go.

You may find yourself relating to it some months or years down the line. That happened to me, and to many of the clients I've worked with. Human Design can take a long *long* time to fully understand and integrate.

I also encourage you not to reject the whole Human Design kit and caboodle, just because some of it doesn't fit. There's likely, at the very least, a sweet baby in that experimental bathwater!

# THE POTENTIAL TRAP OF LABELING

People are exploring Human Design together all over the world, in all sorts of learning and community forums. I've noticed that each of these forums has its own culture. While for the most part, the Human Design community is full of well-intentioned and caring people, I have noticed that in some situations, there can be a rather 'fixed' way of communicating about Human Design. ("This is how it is.") This tendency can unfortunately bleed into 'people labeling' and a somewhat judgmental tone. ("This is who you are.")

As human beings, we can feel uncomfortable with the unknown, complexity, and the fact that we truly are so different from others. It is easy to feel insecure when we don't have something concrete to identify with, or when we aren't able to put the people of our lives into definable, predictable boxes.

Labeling and judging are common traps that we humans fall into when learning a system.

The truth is that we are each beyond description. We can't be reduced, simplified or fit into a little box. We are who we are, regardless of what anyone tells us or sees in our Bodygraph. The various elements of our design can point towards an essential pattern or current, pulsating at the core of our life. Learning about this pattern can help us feel into it. When we can feel into it, we can surrender to a more flowing existence. We cannot only understand, but ultimately embody what it is to live a more authentic self. However, the pattern is not us. Our Bodygraphs are not us. No element of our Bodygraphs (not our Types, not our Authorities, not our Profiles) could possibly reflect all of who we are. We are all highly unique, forever-evolving beings. Let's not forget that.

Unfortunately, when we learn a system like **Human Design**, and we forget to honor the mystery in each other, we can end up using the system to reduce our own, and each other's magnificence, as opposed to celebrating it. We lose touch with our empathy.

## An Interesting Paradox

On the one hand, it may be true that before encountering Human Design, we were missing out on a core piece of information about who we are and how we're designed to operate in the world. On one level, we were walking around as Not-Selves or under the constant and unconscious sabotaging influence of our conditioning.

At the same time, we may be doing our True Selves (and each other) a disservice when we say that we had no clue who we were before we met Human Design, or that everything we did or explored before consciously living according to our Strategy and Authority meant nothing, or was deeply misguided.

Chances are, if you've been drawn to this Resource Book, you're a great example of someone who has brought wisdom and maturity to your Human Design explorations, especially if you're able to remain true to your own experience, even in the presence of a "Human Design conditioning field!"

Conditioning can be tricky business. It can get increasingly subtle and more 'spiritual looking.'

## A Good Thing to Keep in Mind

When you learn something, and it makes you trust yourself less, feel less free, or inhibits your capacity to open your heart more fully (to yourself and someone else), chances are a less-than-healthy conditioning message has snuck into an otherwise empowering lesson.

# HOW DEEP SHOULD I GO?

For me, the greatest gift of Human Design is a *practical* one. It offers people an everyday practice that can be deeply liberating.

When Human Design supports someone in spending less time agonizing over decisions in their mind, it's working. That said, when Human Design is studied more than practiced (which is easy, since it's such a vast, detailed and fascinating system), it can become an out-of-control mental quagmire.

There are people (like me!) who feel called to delve deeply into the system. Some spend decades studying all of the layers beneath the Gates, specializing in fascinating aspects of the Human Design world, like

PHS, the Dream Rave, and more. When they're aligned with their nature, deep study can bring so much joy and aliveness into their lives.

Should they feel drawn to serving others with this knowledge, their depth of understanding can greatly enhance and deepen their service.

We could say that all of their research greatly enriches their 'Outer Authority'—their ability to help other people with their knowledge and understanding.

While some people are designed to swim in a sea of details and totally thrive (gotta love those people!), my sense is that they're not in the majority. There aren't many people who are genuinely liberated (or practically helped) by a super deep level of study.

I've witnessed many people who've spent years in study getting caught in the quagmire. Their relationship with the system has become increasingly mental, nit-picky and relationally isolating (to the point where some can only hang out with people who can 'talk tone.')

Another challenge, when we go into these deeper layers of the system, is birth time accuracy. The deeper we go into a design, the more accurate the birth data needs to be in order for the information to be relevant. Because it is difficult to assess the total accuracy of one's birth time, getting super attached to the deeper aspects of one's chart can be risky business.

That said, sometimes my intuition leads me to look more deeply at someone's design, and good comes of it. Especially for those with little Definition, or whose Definitions are mostly 'Red' or unconsciousness, understanding deeper layers can be super helpful.

I've certainly gotten some real value and validation through learning about some of the deeper aspects of my own design, and I know many others who have as well. Usually, however, a relatively simple guideline or keynote is enough to re-align me with my intuitive belly, and to activate my uniquely creative use of the information I receive.

In terms of real usefulness, the simple things (like sensing into and honoring our Authority, and compassionately understanding and tracking the impact of our conditioning) are usually all that we need to transform our life and free up our *Inner Wisdom Keeper*.

Without these basics in place, deeper studies can lead to the fortification of a new, oppressive source of conditioning... making people even more rule-based and heady when decision-making. There are some examples: I can't eat that because it's too light outside. I can't be your partner, because our connection charts have too many Open Centers between them. I'm only here to impact strangers, so I'm not going to share about what I'm doing or my passions with my friends and family. I have to wait for the invitation, so I'm going to resist any impulse I have to engage with the world, hide out in the boondocks, pray for a miracle, and feel very sorry for myself if that miracle never comes.

# THE CHALLENGE OF TEACHING A SYSTEM
# (LIKE HUMAN DESIGN)

Presenting a system like Human Design (or any limited 'typing system' for that matter) in a way that is easy to understand, super accessible, and at the same time, not inadvertently strengthening of a dualistic world view… can be highly challenging.

If swallowed whole, or held on too tightly, **even the most intentionally empowering systems can "get in the way"** and result in a person becoming over-identified, and ultimately, less able to relax, be themselves, open their hearts and surrender to the mystery.

That's the risk we take whenever we work with a system or a map—which, as the transpersonalists say, is never to be confused with the 'territory.'

I've also found that when an approach to learning a system relies too heavily on the mind, people more easily fall prey to external conditioning.

No matter how brilliant or non-dualistic the theory behind a system is, if the main way in is through the mind, and people aren't given sufficient opportunities to experiment, embody or try on the theory to see if it fits, they're more likely to swallow the whole nine yards… and bypass the enormously informative process of living experimentation.

For me, giving people a lot of heart-based permission to experiment with a system *(and when the system is openly acknowledged as limited, or still evolving)* is both important and valuable.

This has been one of my deepest intentions in creating the *Designed to Blossom* Course, and now this Resource Book: to provide people with plenty of opportunities to explore, expand, have fun, challenge, test, take risks, take what fits and leave the rest, and ultimately, to add the unique fruits of their own discoveries to the expanding collective research pool.

## We're all in this together!

Another one of my deepest intentions is to form a bridge between traditional Human Design and some of the beautiful transpersonal work being done by Richard Rudd (through the *Gene Keys*) and Werner and Laura Pitzal (through *Integral Human Design*).

# WHAT IF I WANT SOMETHING JUICIER?
# GENE KEYS, INTEGRAL HUMAN DESIGN & ASTROLOGY

**Richard Rudd**, one of the original Human Design enthusiasts, author of *Circuitry: A Complete Guide to Circuits, Channels and Gates* (a wonderful reference and keynoting guide) and of the *Gene Keys* (more about this later in this *Resource Book)*, infused a great deal of artistry, poetry and wisdom into his Human Design writing. I loved that about him.

Ra Uru Hu was also a talented lyricist and musician with his own unique style of expression, which I also enjoyed. For him, the greatest gift of Human Design was practical, not poetic. His writing reflected that priority, which I genuinely appreciate.

When I crave beauty, richness, nuance, cultural/spiritual/psychological/sociological depth, or poetry in relation to the Human Design experience, I consult the *Gene Keys* (or Integral Human Design, which integrates the language, depth and frequency-based orientation of the *Gene Keys* into the Human Design map). I also have a special appreciation for Astrology (although I am not an astrologer myself), with its symbolic soul language and infinite scope, ranging from the deeply personal to the vastly collective.

Human Design inevitably has more of a mechanical feel to it, because the focus is more on capturing 'alignment' and 'operation' (the most aligned movement of energy), than on 'content' and 'essence' (the energy or 'soul' itself).

We could say that when people operate correctly, the rich, beautiful, poetic, unique content/essence of their beings emerge naturally.

In that sense, the Bodygraph is more like a 'way-of-the-individual-Tao-guide,' than it is a soul descriptor.

Human Design can help the soul live in a way that allows its greatest, most free expression. If you want a juicy description of the soul, I'd encourage you to incorporate the *Gene Keys, Integral Human Design* and astrology into your explorations! (That is over time, as we don't want to overload our minds, when the purpose is to relieve it of too much busy work!)

# BE Yourself: Petal One

In the *Designed to Blossom* Course, Petal One begins with the question, "Why is this Self-Love/Life-Purpose Thing so hard?" Even when we know everything up in our heads, we still feel overwhelmed, confused, stuck, frustrated, unfulfilled or not good enough. One reason for our messed-up condition is that we're not alone up in our heads. Our minds are literally brimming with 'shoulds,' each one reflecting a conditioning message we've received from our parents, teachers, peers, bosses, institutions, cultural leaders, business coaches, flashy celebrities, and global opinion trends. Everyone is simultaneously telling us what to do, and why *not doing it* would be a bad, even dangerous idea. Usually the multitude of 'shoulds' contradict each other, making our task of 'figuring out' what to do even more impossible.

There are few things more essential to the Human Design experiment than a willingness to explore our own conditioning. In Petal One of the *Designed to Blossom* Resource Book, I'll be sharing some of the questions, reflections and contemplations that have arisen over the years, in relation to the de-conditioning process. I hope that you find resonance, comfort, compassion and inspiration in the pages that follow.

## TO LIVE AS YOURSELF IS TO BLOSSOM.
## BLOSSOMING REQUIRES RISK!

Have you ever worried about being too much, or taking up too much space? If so, you're not alone.

One of my all-time favorite quotes is by Anais Nin:

> "And the day came when the risk to remain tight in a bud
> was more painful than the risk it took to BLOSSOM."

On the surface, 'blossoming' sounds like such a sweet and simple word. For most of us humans (especially the sensitive, empathic, creative, not-necessarily-conforming types), it can be one of the most difficult, terrifying, painful and seemingly dangerous things to do.

Blossoming requires risk.

Blossoming doesn't always feel comfortable or natural—even if it's in perfect alignment with our true nature.

Blossoming requires that we become increasingly transparent and generously expressive of our whole being.

So that means we see, embrace and share more of our light, more of our dark, more of our joy, more of our sadness, and more of our gifts.

It also means we share more of the thoughts, fears and internalized messages that hold us back from sharing those gifts.

As shared earlier, it means that we don't wait to be perfect, or to feel whole and complete, before we share.

It means that even if our minds are temporarily gripped by a brutal and potentially paralyzing self/other comparison trip, we share anyway!

In the end, when it comes to what we put out there in the world, it's all about the energy and intention seeded in the expression.

I've certainly been blown away by an obviously gorgeous work of art.

I've also been moved to tears by a stick figure drawing, pulsating with truth.

We are each unique expressions of this beautiful Universe, and everything that comes out of us—if it is real and sincere—will carry its own beauty and wisdom in it.

If you are feeling tempted to hold back (because you're afraid of being too much, or too little), then start by sharing that!

The way to transmute the stuckness of shame is through the sharing of it. (Ask Brené Brown!)

As you move through your Human Design experiment, practice starting from exactly where you are. There is beauty to be found there. There is the potential for richness, love and growth... even in the darkest of shadows, in the most painful moments of self-doubt, in the eye of a shame hurricane.

# BECOMING A SOMEBODY

*"The game is not about becoming somebody, it's about becoming nobody."*

*~ Ram Dass*

So so true…

Sometimes, as I also learned from Ram Dass, we've got to become a somebody first.

As someone who grew up in a family where survival meant relinquishing personal needs and burying feelings for the sake of a more harmonious world, as someone who's spent plenty of time in spiritual communities purely focusing on 'higher frequencies,' (and as a Manifesting Generator who tended to skip essential steps!), I needed to do a little healthy backtracking along my self-development path.

I needed a visceral sense of my own right to exist—as little old Rosy (shadows and all). Not just as some archetypal, all-positive manifestation of the Great Mother (the superhuman being everyone seemingly wanted and needed me to be).

Human Design provided me with a profoundly practical opportunity to get to know, be, and express 'me' (with the little 'm.')

I got to experience in my body what it meant to be healthfully individuated, liberated as a unique and free entity. I learned I didn't necessarily have to compromise my authenticity or abandon my 'self' for the sake of the 'other.' I watched how my most healthy relationships blossomed in ways I'd never have expected, when I stepped out of 'mergy,' co-dependent patterns. Other relationships that were perhaps based on less healthy (unconscious) agreements naturally faded away or withdrew into the background.

Unlike what my mind feared might happen, as I embraced my 'self,' I became much more accepting of others, and generous—in the truest sense of the words.

As it is experienced so often in Human Design circles, when we truly embrace ourselves and appreciate the beauty of diversity, blame and guilt truly do dissolve.

Of course, in the end, concepts like uniqueness, separation and 'differentiation' are all illusions. We're all walking the same sacred path towards nobody-hood. Regardless of your Type, if you're skipping the step of exploring your somebody-hood, I recommend a little back-stepping. Human Design is a fabulous way to approach that process!

# EXPANDING OUR UNDERSTANDING OF CONDITIONING THE POWER OF ANCESTRAL TRAUMA

In Human Design, we are often encouraged to explore our positive as well as painful conditioning. Many of us gain profound insights by examining our childhoods, early relationships as well as personal traumas. These insights help us understand the forces that pull us away from a more authentic existence, and ground us more healthfully in our experiment.

Our identities, behaviors and world view, however, are not only influenced by our parents and early life challenges. They're also influenced by our teachers, peers, politicians, religious leaders, celebrity role models, corporate trendsetters, and the increasingly all-encompassing 'media' to which we're exposed our whole lives. We are social, sexual, ethnic, national, ecological beings, both collectively and culturally conditioned.

Especially when dealing with trauma, it is important to remember that we are also the recipients of generations and generations of internalized messages and fears, stemming from the deeper wounds carried by our early caregivers, their caregivers, and theirs…

Not only our minds (conscious identities and Open Centers), but our **bodies** (the *Design* aspect of our Bodygraphs) are deeply influenced by our ancestors and the experiences they've had over the course of centuries.

I come from a Jewish background. As it is with so many 'peoples,' mine carries a long and painful legacy with its share of repeated trauma. This legacy has at times inspired in me—and other members of the 'tribe'—a great deal of compassion and dedication towards alleviating oppression wherever it surfaces. At other times, it has manifested as a deep-seated, cellular fear with tragic self- and other-destructive consequences.

It can take countless generations for a people to work through a collective trauma, whether the trauma is human-made or nature-made.

There may be some unique and awe-inspiring individuals, such as the holocaust survivor and wise man, Viktor Emil Frankl, who despite the atrocities he experienced firsthand, was able to offer us teachings like:

"When we are no longer able to change a situation, we are challenged to change ourselves."
"Between stimulus and response there is a space. In that space is our power to choose our response.
In our response lies our growth and our freedom."

"Everything can be taken from a man but one thing: the last of the human freedoms—
to choose one's attitude in any given set of circumstances, to choose one's own way."

Unfortunately, people like Viktor Frankl are as unusual as they are inspiring.

The majority of first generation people to experience a collective trauma spend their lives (understandably) focusing on survival, pushing their trauma deep underground.

Typically, their children (the second generation, post-trauma) take on the giant task of 'making a better life' for *their* children—an endeavor that is often more materialistically or security-focused, than spiritually or emotionally focused. From years of counseling experience, I've found that some very deep shadow material gets passed on to this third generation.

A common saying in the "New Age" or human potential movement is "we're never given more than we can handle." Whether or not that's true in every case, it's certainly applicable (and encouraging) to those of us who feel authentically called to do the work of healing transgenerational trauma.

We probably wouldn't even hear this call unless enough of our 'people' managed to collectively achieve sufficient survival and material stabilization.

It takes a great deal of outer safety and inner security to be able to wake up to the deeper patterns that stem from ancestral wounding, and lean into our legacies of addiction, illness, abandonment, betrayal, poverty, violence or abuse.

Though it rarely feels that way, it is actually a privilege and sign of liberation to be able to feel and heal the pain of our ancestors that lives within us.

Given humanity's tendency to deal with trauma by re-traumatizing each other, many of us end up simultaneously being first, second and third generation trauma survivors. (This cultural trauma healing work is not for the faint hearted!)

That said, when we are free enough to work with our inherited pain, without allowing it to drive our decisions and actions (the gift of Human Design and the Gene Keys), we can have a powerful impact on the present... and even on the past. Relationships we thought could never heal or transform, do.

True healing is timeless and boundless.

# IS IT POSSIBLE TO GET RID OF
# SELF-SACRIFICING CONDITIONING?

Most people I've worked with are big-hearted and service-oriented. Some understandably wonder whether it's even possible to get rid of self-sacrificing conditioning. I've wondered the same thing.

As you probably already know, the de-conditioning process is a life long journey, not an overnight fix. Many of us need to be reminded, over and over again, that we can't support anyone with sad empty cups; that it's not only OK, but important to honor ourselves.

In relation to working with my own self-sacrificing conditioning, it's been essential for me to uncover the layers of anger, pain, shame and grief that I believed had to be repressed or overridden in order to avoid hurting the people I loved, or feeling the depths of my own hurt. Only when I became aware of these primal feelings could I begin to accept, honor and harvest the wisdom within them.

From a Human Design perspective, it was only through a deep acceptance of the more 'shadowy' aspects of my inner life that I became able to trust and follow my Authority's guidance, thus 'live as myself.' As long as I was in denial of, or fighting, these more 'childlike' (or forbidden) feelings within me, I couldn't hear, much less trust my Sacral Center's responses. Even when I felt my belly saying 'no,' I didn't dare act on it.

Similarly, if I felt too guilty about my shadowy feelings or defensive of my 'goodness,' I couldn't follow my belly's 'yeses,' or trust that my Open Solar Plexus could handle uncomfortable yet potentially healthy confrontations and transformative interactions.

I needed to make peace with my 'id,' or inner child, in order to change entrenched self-sabotaging patterns, soften into true compassion, and honestly live out my design.

My wise mother always said, "We all come by who we are honestly."

We've all received our share of conditioning. Most of the time, the people who conditioned us were passing along that which was handed down to them (usually, with 'the best of intentions').

These days, I don't have the goal of getting rid of conditioning, not for myself, or the people I work with.

Instead, I focus on cultivating a more compassionate and loving attitude towards the whole humbling human shebang.

I recognize those "Be good," "You should…" pressuring voices when they show up.

I don't push them away. I don't cling too tightly either.

I just try to hold them as lightly and lovingly as possible, while acknowledging that there's another part of me, a younger part, who understandably doesn't appreciate being pushed around! A part that needs to know it's worthy of love, regardless of whether it's capable or willing to fulfill all of those expectations.

I do my best to make sure that I don't act on these 'be good' pressures (unless my own Authority, or *Inner Wisdom Keeper*, gives me the green light).

In my opinion, Human Design is not really about stopping the conditioning, or getting rid of anything, or wishing that we weren't as open, receptive or sensitive as we are.

It's more about learning how to embrace our sensitivity, without letting the messages we take in through our sensitivity drive everything we do.

You get to keep your open, loving heart.

You get to be a sensitive, empathic and generous person.

You don't have to make your decisions because you're afraid that if you don't sacrifice yourself, you'll be bad, abandoned and worthless.

# WAITING FOR THE 'CORRECT' VS. WAITING FOR THE 'PERFECT'

As a Sacral Being primed to respond to life through creativity, I've needed to learn to trust my innate impulses to participate in this world, even when it's felt scary.

Even before I encountered Human Design, one of my greatest life lessons was learning to feel safe sharing an idea, insight, experience, creation or project BEFORE it passed through the *Perfection Inspection*.

Like many people, I was deeply sensitive to the opinions of others and painfully aware of the 'external gaze.' Receiving feedback felt so vulnerable, and I had trouble trusting people's ability to receive my complexity with compassion. I feared their positive projections as much as I did negative criticism.

Whenever I sensed someone might judge, misunderstand, idealize or box me in, I either headed for the hills (or into a cave), or exhausted myself trying to cover all the bases, to avoid being perceived as shallow, limited or imperfect.

This was Vanity, of course; a fear-based, approval-addicted form of self-consciousness that made it hard to honor and follow my innate Sacral responses, and where they led me.

Perhaps you can relate.

Regardless of the specifics of your design, you may fall into a similar trap of expecting yourself to birth fully formed ideas and perfected creations.

Whatever your design, pay attention to whether and when you're holding yourself back.

Learn to discern between the art of healthy waiting, and the habit of self-sabotage and second-guessing.

Human Design teaches so many of us that waiting is an essential practice.

- Generators wait for their Sacral response.
- Emotionally Defined beings wait for their clarity, or their 'right timing.'
- Projectors wait for the invitation.
- Reflectors wait out the moon cycle.
- Manifestors wait for a deep knowing about what they're here to initiate, who they're destined to impact, and when they actually have the energy to 'go for it.'

Let's just make sure that we're not waiting until we know for sure what we're doing, how it's all going to turn out, or for whole, complete and perfect expressions.

Living our design is ultimately about surrendering to and participating in a divine dialogue with the Universe.

It's about embracing the creative potential of the uncomfortable.

It's about letting go of mental control.

It's about learning to see seeming mistakes or incomplete expressions as our way of participating in collective creative-collaborations and communal course-corrections.

I invite you to let yourself be a messy-yet-sincere participant in the mix, and to shape-shift as you go.

Give yourself a big dose of breathing room as you enter or deepen your Human Design experiment.

And see what happens.

# CAN HUMAN DESIGN HELP PEOPLE WITH SERIOUS PSYCHOLOGICAL CHALLENGES?

## (Or who are dealing with Trauma, PTSD and Attachment Issues?)

Over the years, I've given a lot of thought to the role Human Design can play when dealing with more serious issues—like trauma, addiction, depression and attachment issues.

I've traveled between various populations and approaches to working with people over the years, so to be a responsible professional, I've needed to consider both the gifts and limitations of each approach, modality and orientation.

I've often asked myself, "What is within the 'scope' of Human Design, when it comes to the healing (not just thriving) process? Especially when we're dealing with deeply entrenched psychological and physiological wounds?"

Of course, this is too big a topic for a short article. However, your question is too important to not address. So, I'll take a stab at it, knowing that this is just the beginning of this essential inquiry.

My first thought is that Human Design may not be able to solve, treat or 'cure' some of the deeper problems that people suffer from. However, if people can access and honor their designs, they can much more easily find and choose those resources and service professionals that are best able to address their deeper, core issues, and the environments that will be the most conducive for their healing process.

For example, people who suffer from what we might call an 'attachment disorder' could use their Human Design practice to find a therapist or counselor with whom they can engage in an extremely healing long-term therapy process, where the relationship itself becomes the healing vessel.

Those suffering from an addiction could use their Human Design practice to find the right 12 step group, hypnotherapist, shaman, or spiritual addiction center able to help them break the self-destructive pattern.

Those suffering from depression could use their Human Design practice to find just the right combination of counselor, psychiatrist, nutritionist, homeopath, naturopath, movement practice, meditation approach, support group or intentional community to help them emerge from their depression.

Those suffering from a serious case of PTSD could use their Human Design practice to find a trauma-specializing therapist, or someone who works with a modality like EFT or EMDR, or a shaman who does soul retrieval, or…

In other words, Human Design isn't necessarily the 'healing destination' for everyone, but it can certainly play an empowering role in getting to that destination. It can help people become increasingly aligned with a healing process that truly works for them.

That said, there are some forms of suffering or wounding, or mental/behavioral tendencies (disorders), that I believe make it very difficult for people to make use of a practice like Human Design.

Just as an example:

When gripped with powerful anxiety, a serious addiction, or when under the influence of certain powerful psychotropic medicines, it can be difficult, if not impossible, for people to even hear their inner Authority, much less follow it.

Deeper psychological problems that are more relational in nature can sabotage a potentially helpful or healing relationship (even with a Human Design specialist!).

Hormonal challenges can add a dimension of complexity to the Human Design experiment too—making it quite difficult to discern between a genuine truth and a hormonal disturbance.

Keep in mind: Human Design has many layers and sub-schools within it. There is a more psychologically oriented school that helps people align with the correct 'inner motivation.'

There is a health-oriented school (Primary Health System) that can support people in choosing the right foods, eating behaviors and environments that can improve their health and digestion, thus perspective on life. There are some great teachers within the Human Design community that have specializations, including addiction.

There are likely Human Design analysts who would say that this system, if understood and practiced radically and properly, could solve all problems. They may be right.

Personally, I've come to hold Human Design with a degree of humility… and to see it as one of the most empowering potential 'healing collaborators' I know.

I also have such gratitude for all the ways that Human Design has helped me in my life, and for the unbelievably supportive role it has played in the empowerment and development of countless people I've cared about—people who have been drawn to and have been blessed with the ability to benefit from this system and practice.

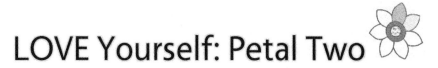

# LOVE Yourself: Petal Two

*Your Unique Kind of Flower*

In Petal Two of the *Designed to Blossom* Course, the four Human Design Types are introduced as Flower Families in our great human garden. Just as it is with flowers in nature, some of us tend to thrive with certain kinds of food, climate and environment, while others of us do better with other kinds. Each Flower Family has a healthy growth path, or Strategy—one that leads us to the proper nutrients, people, environments, opportunities and experiences we need to thrive. When we follow our Flower Family Strategy, we learn how to make good decisions, how to recognize when we're on the right and unique path, and how to surrender to the flow of our lives.

I'd like to dedicate Petal Two of the *Designed to Blossom* Resource Book to a deeper and wider exploration of Type and Strategy. I'll be drawing from questions, explorations and conversations I've had over the years, sharing alternative perspectives, and even a controversy or two!

## THE TWISTS AND TURNS OF TYPE-CASTING

There's been plenty of controversy within the Human Design community about Type (and Strategy). Steve Rhodes, for example, (the founder of Bhan Tugh, a 'break-away' or revolutionary approach to Human Design), believes that there is no place for Type at all. Over the course of many years of studies and experimentation, he's come to see Type, Strategy and Authority as disempowering mental prisons—blinders that have kept many students trapped by unnecessary and oppressive rules. In his books and teachings, he throws out many of these rules, and brings his focus to aspects of the Human Design transmission that he believes are essentially more liberating. (His cutting-edge work is certainly worth checking out.)

From an Integral Human Design perspective, Type and Strategy (as well as Authority) are also seen as limited over-simplifications. A person's essence can't be captured by a Human Design chart or blueprint, just as their Strategy can't be gleaned from a general Type description.

Though for years Ra stressed the importance of Strategy and Authority above all else, he was also aware of the limitations of this simplified focus. In his sincere attempts to make Human Design (an otherwise complex system reflecting a deep and wide transmission) easier for people to understand and put into practice, he may have dumbed it down, or 'nut-shelled' us, a bit too much.

The bulk of Human Design teachers and enthusiasts, however, feel that an exploration of Type is highly worthwhile.

Ironically, that still doesn't mean they agree on everything. Even Human Design folk that totally embrace Type have their own points of contention.

Some feel, for example, that Manifesting Generators and Pure Generators should be considered their own Types, because they are so different from each other.

Others feel the same about Mental Projectors. (It's often said that there are more kinds of Projectors than any other Type, because of the incredible diversity of that group.)

One thing to keep in mind is that in Human Design, Type and Authority are addressing two different aspects of our lives.

Type, from a typical Human Design perspective, is here to help us understand our very basic Strategy for life.

For example, it doesn't matter whether you're a Pure or Manifesting Generator. Either way, your life will tend to be more flowing if you allow life to come to and enliven you. Continually trying to 'push the river,' based on some mental agenda that might not even be yours, isn't likely to be too satisfying.

While Type is about basic Strategy, Authority is about the particular truth compass we're designed to rely upon when making decisions, e.g. Do we engage our will? Our intuition? Our feelings? Our gut? Our happiness-compass? Our relationships? Our own voice? Our ability to feel into an environment?

An Emotionally Defined Generator and an Emotionally Defined Projector might both need to tune into their feeling state when making decisions and cultivate patience. Their Strategies are essentially different.

Emotional Generators have a better chance at finding out if something is worth their energetic investment when they 'respond to what life brings them **over time**.' Emotional Projectors are more likely to determine whether an invitation is worthy of their acceptance when they give themselves plenty of time to 'feel out invitations for the big things in life.'

Personally, I find the word "Type" confusing, because we could easily create all kinds of types within this system (or any system). "Type" is just an umbrella term for any group with shared traits.

All people with Emotional Authority could be considered a type. All people with only Tribal Circuitry could be considered a type. All people with Defined Egos could be considered a type. All people with Triple-Split Definitions could be considered a type.

We could say all people with certain combinations (Emotional Projectors with the 2/4 Profile on a certain Incarnation Cross, with all Right Variables, etc.) could be considered their own type.

In Human Design, the word 'Type' has been specifically associated with one thing—Strategy, and so we make do.

I still see the usefulness in exploring Type and Strategy, but also wary of pitfalls that show up in any Typing system.

While it may be true that Pure Generators share something basic in common, they are all deeply, magically, wonderfully unique beings.

Perhaps even more importantly, we all have the opportunity to experience and express our Nature through differing levels of maturity, wisdom and love.

We can also relate to our Openness or sensitivities with differing levels of awareness and graciousness. At any moment, we can respond to what and who we encounter from a place of reactivity, repression, or grounded wisdom.

Aside from the fact that no two people can receive identical conditioning, this is another reason why we can meet two people with identical designs, and completely different personalities.

This is where Richard Rudd's *Gene Keys* come in, with its *Spectrum of Consciousness*, which is beautifully woven into the *Integral Human Design* Bodygraph and matrix, through *shadow*, *potential* and *essence* (or Shadow, Gift and Siddhi). These works offer us a multi-dimensional prism through which we can deepen our understanding, experiments, and ultimately, our full-hearted expressions of our unique designs.

According to Integral Human Design, Strategy isn't to be followed like an operating manual; it's to be seen, intuited and understood like an improvisatory dance. To dance with grace, the context of the dance must be taken into account; it must include the entirety of the Bodygraph, the person's multi-faceted, forever-changing, living experience, as well as their level of awareness and maturity. Because of this, each design imprint (such as Strategy) offers an entire spectrum of possibilities, not just one.

When we are genuinely connected to our own life code, we don't need know our Type or follow a Strategy. We simply are who we are. We let life move through us. We become life itself. There is no separation. When we are connected to our essence in this way, it's not even possible to be any other 'type' of human being than the one we are, not even if we tried.

When we are *not* genuinely connected to and through life, all we can do is 'try' to be true to our Type. We can *try* to live out our Strategy. The problem is that as soon as we're 'trying,' we're separating ourselves from our own life code. We are perceiving ourselves as a 'subject' and our body/life source as an object to be directed, manipulated or willed into shape. When caught in this world- and self-view, no generic set of Strategy instructions could possibly guide us or tell us how to live our lives. Trying only serves to separate us even further from our True Self.

While some Human Design teachers strongly believe that we cannot awaken or become fully liberated from our Not-Self, without an awareness of our Human Design, not everyone agrees. It seems unlikely to me that awakening would be solely reserved for people who have access to their birth data! During one of his contemplative deep dives, and a sustained practice of working with his Human Design, Richard Rudd received one of his greatest revelations. He referred to it as the Automatic Activation of Type. As we raise the frequency of our DNA beyond our shadow (or fear-based) patterns, we naturally bring ourselves into a higher harmony with all of Creation. When we are in harmony with our inner potential and outer environment, we can't help but live out our Human Design. We don't need to intellectually understand a thing about it. We simply become healthy cells in a larger cosmic body. Living our design is a natural byproduct of raising our frequency.

In the end, we are all so much more wonderful and mysterious than any typing system could ever describe.

At some point, even Human Design must fall away…as an even more expansive map for understanding ourselves and those around us arises.

…until we need no map at all.

While I am a Virgo, with an Open Mind, and a love for the mental discernment and refinement process, I try to remind myself, my students and clients, to hold it all lightly, whenever I can.

# ALIGNMENT IS EVERYTHING FOR EVERYONE

If Human Design is about anything, it's about the power and beauty of interpersonal chemistry.

You don't have to be a Projector to benefit from right relational alignment. We're all here to find our right connections and to enjoy synergistic collaborations.

We're all here to learn the art of being healthfully selective—whether we're a Projector receiving (or rejecting) an invitation, a Generator responding (or not responding) to something with our precious energy, a Reflector choosing (or not choosing) to place ourselves at the center of any given community or enterprise, or a Manifestor making choices about where, with whom and how to make our impact.

Most humans have been conditioned, expected or pressured at some point in their lives **not** to be selective enough. We've been encouraged, in other words, to make relational choices that are not necessarily healthy for us.

Although Manifestors, for example, don't need invitations like Projectors do, they do need to be energetically 'matched' (received, met, wanted, recognized, etc.) by those they're meant to impact. If that right fit isn't there, it can be very painful for them.

Manifestors tend to be more instinctively afraid of being controlled, and Projectors tend to be more afraid of being alone, so Manifestors and Projectors can tend to favor certain kinds of compromises. I've found that Manifestors are more likely to compromise relationship in service of self/freedom-preservation, whereas Projectors are more likely to compromise 'self' in service of relationship.

That said, as Manifestors and Projectors move through their de-conditioning process, things start to look very different. Manifestors start taking risks in order to move towards and benefit from 'relationship'—even though it can be scary. They're here to learn that intimacy and freedom can co-exist. Projectors start to experiment with more aloneness—which can be equally scary. They learn that they can survive—even thrive—when they're not bending over backwards to maintain their relationships, at any cost.

That's just an example. I encourage you to make your own observations, and contemplate your own experiences with right relational alignment, and what helped you learn how to be more healthfully selective in your life.

# NOT ALL TYPES ARE ALL ALIKE!

When I began learning about Human Design, years ago, I went absolutely nuts running charts for everyone I knew, making all sorts of exciting connections.

So many things clicked into place as I came to understand people so much better, noticing patterns, tendencies and characteristics in them that reflected particular Types, Authorities, Profiles, etc.

One thing I found helpful was a simple, essential approach to viewing the Types. I came to see Manifestors as essentially proactive, Generators as essentially responsive, Projectors as essentially interactive, and Reflectors as essentially digestive.

I also found value in using simple Integral Human Design guideposts for understanding the positive and negative chemistry themes of each of the Types. For example, it can be helpful for Manifestors to know that they're heading into shadow territory when they're being more provocative than empowering. When expressing their negative chemistry themes, Manifesting Generators can be more obstinate than dynamic,

Pure Generators more frustrated than in rhythmic communion with their bodies and surroundings, Projectors more as interfering than integrative, and Reflectors more dissipating, than embracing and being embraced.

A more Integral approach showed me how helpful it can be for people with different Types to consciously cultivate certain attitudes. Manifestors can feel more free and unimpeded when they embrace an attitude of courtesy. Manifesting Generators can experience more satisfaction when cultivating an attitude of patience. Similarly, Pure Generators can benefit from an attitude of resilience, Projectors from an attitude of faith, and Reflectors from an attitude of trust.

The deeper I went into Human Design, however, the more complex the picture became, and the harder it was to make broad generalizations about anyone.

One thing I realized was just how differently people within the same Type could express themselves. Take Pure Generators, for example. They may all be designed to respond to life creatively as it comes to them, but that's where the commonality ends.

What each Generator is designed to respond to, and when, is infinitely unique. Two Generators with the exact same Definition (Gates, Channels, etc.) will respond differently to any given situation.

While two Generators both have the Gate of 'saying yes,' of taking adventurous leaps, one might respond to leaping onto a plane to Spain so that they can walk El Camino, and another might respond to leaping into a car on the way to couple's counseling! They'll both be perfectly aligned with their design.

Another thing I noticed after a while, despite some intuitive successes, was that it got very difficult to guess peoples' designs.

When not activated by their passions, creative, energetic Generators can look a lot like unplugged Projectors.

Projectors—running on and amplifying the energy in their environment—can look a lot like Generators.

Manifestors can spend their lives mistakenly waiting to be initiated by others.

Reflectors, at the mercy of whatever environment they happen to be in, can end up acting out the dysfunction all around them and be completely unrecognizable to their true selves.

The more I know, the more I approach this knowledge with a degree of humility.

Even though the basics of Human Design are pretty simple to understand intellectually, the art of living in accordance with our true nature is far from easy. No matter who you are, or what system or practice you're applying to your life, living an authentic life requires courage, awareness, compassion, patience, and often, a lot of support.

One last thing I discovered, as I delved deeper into the study of Human Design, was that each Bodygraph is a profoundly intricate synthesis…a beautifully unique work of art.

I no longer see design elements on their own; I see them as threads in an intricate web, the Bodygraph delicately woven together with the person's actual life experience, cultural influences, and psycho-spiritual maturity. This is why over the years I stopped giving Readings, and chose to focus more on integrating Human Design into in-depth counseling.

With my Open Head and Ajna, I've let go of working so hard to figure it all out. Instead, I've learned to enjoy the mystery…remembering that in the end, we're all One anyway, and all maps (even the coolest ones) were designed for temporary use.

# DIFFERENT TECHNIQUES FOR DIFFERENT TYPES

Most people drawn to Human Design have already been exposed to all sorts of 'alternative' environments, teachings, trainings, educations, practices, modalities and techniques.

As you embrace your Human Design experiment, this kind of exposure will likely continue. A plethora of opportunities to make choices awaits you. Each opportunity will offer you a wonderful opportunity to practice being true to yourself, as you decide which techniques to try out, and which ones to pass up.

If you're a Generator, and a new technique pops up on your screen, your job is to check in with (and trust!) your beautiful belly—your experimental, intelligent and highly creative gut-brain. You may find your belly lighting up, even though at first glance, to your mind, the technique seems strange, unbelievable or irrelevant to your current life. (Lord knows when I first encountered Human Design, my mind was very confused by my strong positive response.) Or, your belly might not light up, even though to your mind, the technique seems perfect for you and your life.

If you have Emotional Authority, you might need to sleep on it, or revisit the sales page a few times, or try the technique out a few times, or with different practitioners, to finally get a clear sense of whether this technique is right for you.

If you've got Sacral-Splenic Authority, you might get an instant hit on whether this is an 'uh huh' or 'uhn uhn.' Remember, just because you get a 'no' right now doesn't mean you won't get a 'yes' tomorrow (or 20 minutes from now)!

If you're a Projector, remember that you can always move towards whatever you love, or whatever brings forth love and passion in you. When it comes to a new technique, you don't even need something to 'pop up' in your field in order to do it. If you feel (intuitively, or emotionally, or heart-fully) drawn to a technique, you're free to go for it.

That said, when you do go for it, pay special attention to the relationship you have with the practitioner or teacher using the modality. The relational chemistry you experience with any practitioner or teacher is likely going to be as, if not more, important to you than the technique itself.

If you hear about a technique through someone else, and it kind of feels like an invitation, take a little time to assess just how 'meant for you' the invitation is. Often suggestions are made lightly, or in forums where general recommendations are made. These might feel like invitations (like someone tags you and a bunch of people on FB), but they aren't necessarily. For you, we want invitations to be as personal and specific as possible, and to be coming from the right people.

When someone knows you well or you feel 'gotten' by them, you may find yourself saying 'yes' to an invitation that your mind has plenty of doubts about. That's totally OK. Open to the adventure and see what happens (remembering to honor your Authority as you go).

Regardless of your specific design, if you come across a technique (teaching, training, modality, practice, etc.) and you're feeling resistance, I encourage you to explore the nature of your resistance. Where might that resistance be coming from?

- Is it your genuine Authority at work?
- Is your intuition just saying 'no'? (Spleen)
- Does it simply not feel right? (Solar Plexus)
- Do you not have sufficient will-power or a strong enough desire to give it a try? (Ego/Heart)
- Does contemplating the technique not make you all that happy? (Self-Projected/G-Identity)
- Does this technique and the environment in which it's offered not feel particularly appealing? When you speak about it with trusted people, does your excitement build? Once those people leave, does your excitement remain? (Outer Authority)

Could it be that outdated conditioning voices (now showing up as stubborn beliefs, opinions and assumptions) are influencing the resistance you're feeling, thus the decision you're tempted to make?

Are you thinking, "Nothing can work that quickly," or, "That kind of thing would never work on me."

It's always a good idea to do a conditioning or Openness check-up when resistance is present, just to make sure that any arising doubts or judgments you're having aren't masking your true Authority, your *Inner Wisdom Keeper*.

# I'M NOT A PROJECTOR, BUT I FEEL LIKE ONE!

If you've ever had this thought, you're not alone.

Just because you're not an official Projector, it doesn't mean you can't relate to aspects of the Projector's path.

The deep need to be seen and recognized for who you are, to feel welcome and energetically received, to be surrounded by kindred spirits, and to learn how to trust and live a surrendered life, free of mental agendas…are universal human needs.

Interestingly, from a Human Design Perspective, many non-Projectors still have what we call "Projected Channels"—aspects of our beings that call for the Projector Strategy of 'waiting for the invitation.'

Wherever you have one of these Channels in your chart, or areas of specialization, these are good places to invite in patience, and to remember that you'll benefit from waiting until you're recognized by others, who can invite out your beautiful Projector qualities.

Even Manifestors can have Projected Channels. Although Manifestors are here to initiate people, they may still need aspects of themselves to be recognized and invited out before they have the courage, capacity and right timing to start a fabulous ball rolling… or even to get a good sense of who they're meant to initiate!

By the way, Generators can also have "Manifesting" Channels, which carry with them themes and directives we normally associate with Manifestors.

As it is with many deep systems, things can get quite nuanced. Which is a good thing!

**A special invitation to everyone:** Even if you are not a Projector, you may relate to and benefit from much of what's shared in the following section, where I answer many questions that have been asked by Projectors. Trust your intuition (or your *Inner Wisdom Keeper*) as you sift through the articles, and enjoy those that apply to your life.

# PROJECTORS

## *THE ART, AGONY AND ECSTASY OF WAITING*

It takes courage to put our designs to the test, especially because our Human Design experiments encourage us to do exactly what we learned NOT to do in order to feel safe and connected to others.

Manifestors who've been waiting to be initiated their whole lives are suddenly asked to step up and do the initiating. Reflectors who've been in a hurry to figure it all out and take action are asked to slow down, a lot! Generators who've been moving towards the Universe head-first, initiating one activity after another, are asked to wait for the Universe to come to them.

Projectors who've been constantly extending invitations and working harder than anyone else are asked to slow down, chill out, and trust that others will notice, recognize and invite them in. After spending much of their lives carrying the bulk of the work load, they're asked to trust that others will step up and relieve them of their superhuman sense of responsibility, not to mention their exhaustion.

It's no small thing to stop doing what we're used to doing. We do what we usually do for a good reason. The reason usually involves some sort of a deep, unconscious survival fear—whether it be emotional, relational or physical in nature.

For Projectors, the instruction to 'wait for the invitation' can be especially scary. Sometimes in their attempts to 'get it right,' conscientious Projectors mistakenly think they're supposed to wait for the invitation to do *anything*, even go to the bathroom! Some end up feeling paralyzingly isolated, quite a painful state for such relational beings.

If you're a Projector, remember that first and foremost, when it comes to waiting, we're really only talking about the four big things in life: your most fulfilling romances, vocations, living environments, and relationships (of the more significant kind).

These major life arenas are more likely to blossom effortlessly when they come through direct, personal invitations from people who truly see you for the magnificent being you are.

For the rest of your life decisions, tune into your unique Authority, whether it's Splenic, Emotional, Egoic or 'Outer.'

Since your waiting process is intended for the big things in life, you're probably going to wonder…

- What do I do while I'm waiting?
- What does waiting even mean?

Good questions!

There's the painfully passive kind of waiting, where you basically sit alone, in a room, out in the boondocks, picking your nose and praying that someone, someday, will miraculously show up at your door, holding a golden envelope, inviting you into your perfect life. (I'm not saying there aren't gems to be gleaned from such a radical approach to waiting. There definitely are. More on that later, but that's certainly not the only kind of waiting that exists.)

There's a more active kind of waiting as well, one that's still aligned with your Projector nature, and one that allows your potent aura to do its magnetic work for you.

This kind says, "While you're waiting for the big invitations in life, you don't have to wait to do what you love! Just go ahead. Enjoy!"

If you love to paint, study, hang out with people, take a yoga class, do research, dream, create gorgeous vision-boards, whatever it is you love to do… you're always free to do it. No need to wait for permission, or an invitation from anyone.

You'll soon discover that when you're genuinely immersed in a passion, your right people are much more likely to recognize your depth and beauty, and extend wonderful invitations your way.

## But what about my personal sharing?

Do I have to wait for people to ask me what my thoughts, visions and dreams are before I even get to talk about it, much less move towards it?

When you're in a nourishing environment with people you trust and who are genuinely interested in you, I encourage you to share your feelings, thoughts, intentions, dreams, passions, longings and visions with them.

All sorts of miraculous things can happen when you share who you are and what you love with the people in your life, especially those who understand, appreciate and celebrate you.

Personal sharing works especially well when you're not attached to a specific outcome.

Remember, for you, in any interaction, there are few things more important (and challenging!) than letting go of your personal agendas.

Many Projectors, because they carry such a deep need and longing to be seen and recognized (often because this essential human need wasn't met early on), have a hard time discerning between a non-attached personal sharing, and the kind that carries an underlying (often unconscious) wish. They can have difficulty trusting others to just naturally see and appreciate them.

They may think, "Oh, I'm just sharing who I am," or "I'm just sharing what I want to do."

But really, they're really secretly hoping that the person they're speaking to will see their potential and invite it out of them in a deeply fulfilling way. They can also be afraid that if they don't work really hard to make that happen, it won't.

If or when it doesn't happen, they can feel quite disappointed, and even more invisible…and bitter.

If you're a Projector, one of the things I invite you to do—while you're waiting for the 4 Biggies and contemplating how to put yourself out there in the world—is to embrace an open inquiry into your deeper motivations.

Whenever you feel a strong impulse to share something (and you haven't been directly invited to speak), ask yourself:

- Where am I coming from?
- Do I have a secret wish or expectation here? What might that be?
- Do I have a strong need to feel seen and recognized by this person, in this situation?
- If I'm honest with myself, do I feel invited to speak right now (if not directly, then energetically)?
- Am I actually having to exert some force in order to be seen and heard?

Be honest with yourself, even if it's hard.

So many Projectors with so much to offer end up sabotaging themselves because of a lack of awareness of their own hidden motives. When they have a hidden wish, they can transmit an energetic neediness that others pick up on, and then resist… which is the last thing on earth Projectors want or deserve.

One great way to discover possible hidden motives is to explore your areas of Openness. (This kind of exploration can be useful to anyone, actually, regardless of Type.)

Let's say you're with someone, and you feel a strong impulse to share about your desire to become a radio host one day and to make a good living from it. You feel pulled to let them know how qualified you'd be for this kind of work.

Before you go ahead and share your dream, ask yourself:

**If you have an Open Spleen:**

- Am I secretly hoping this person will be a good networking connection for me?

- Am I afraid that I won't be able to make a living without this person's support or funding?
- Am I afraid they won't like me if they don't know that I have a meaningful or exciting ambition?

**Or if you have an Open Ego/Heart:**

- Do I feel like I have to prove myself to them, or impress them in some way?
- Am I afraid they might respect me less if they see me as flaky and unreliable?

Another helpful inquiry for Projectors who are contemplating initiating a personal share with someone, is to honestly assess their personal connections. When you're not operating out of a place of urgency or hidden agenda, you become much freer to use your Projector gift of reading energy, of sensing just how energetically 'invited' you are in a given interaction.

- Is this truly one of my people?
- Does this person actually have the capacity to understand me?
- Do they seem to be interested in my dream?
- Do they want to hear what I know?
- Are they resisting me in any way, even if their words say otherwise?

Most Projectors know the pain of not being seen, recognized, met or welcomed. It's awful, for most humans. Projectors instinctively understand that they need the magic of *relationship* in order to fully share their light with the world. For them, this form of pain and discomfort is especially hard to tolerate.

That said, **so much good** can come to Projectors who make 'waiting to be seen' and 'tolerating the discomfort of feeling unseen' their spiritual practice.

- They hone their non-attachment muscles.
- Their magnetic aura grows.
- They learn to be healthfully selective.
- They draw better people to them.
- They feel increasingly aware of the value of their unique talents, gifts and wisdom.
- They stop working so hard, all of the time, with everyone.
- They become more relaxed, patient.
- They experience more synchronicity and ease.
- They find that the people around them truly appreciate them, and want to support and join them.
- They feed fewer 'pearls to the pigs.'
- They experience less exhaustion and burnout.
- They feel more connected to Spirit.
- They have more time to be, learn and grow.
- They liberate themselves from an over-reliance on external validation.
- They begin to taste what it truly means, and feels like, to trust in Life itself.

# *RICHARD RUDD'S TWO KINDS OF PROJECTOR BREATH*

Years ago, Richard Rudd wrote *Living Your Design: A New Manual for Awakening*. In it he shared an absolutely beautiful guided meditation, inviting Projectors to explore two kinds of Breath: the *waiting breath*, and the *breath of recognition*. Many Projectors have found this distinction to be profoundly helpful. I will share an excerpt from this piece of writing here, along with the encouragement that you find the rest of it online, if it touches you.

> *"Projector, you are the only Type that has two breath patterns in your life…you have the waiting breath and you have the breath of recognition.*
>
> *Come now into your first breath pattern—the waiting breath. This breath pattern is the backdrop to your life. It is how you breathe as you move about the world. It is tied uniquely to whatever is undefined in your design. Picture now your own Definition… Allow the colors to fall into the background for a moment and look into the white in your design. Look into your undefined world.*
>
> *This is where the waiting breath lies. Although it is not who you are, this white area in your design is where you reflect the breathing of anyone in your life, all the time. It is here that you measure the people around you—it is here that the great gift of your design lies—your incredible ability to know who is right for you and who is not—to know who belongs in your aura and who clearly does not. Feel the quality of this waiting breath. Feel its coolness, its patience, its openness— feel how your waiting breath adapts to all beings, humans, animals, plants and places. This breath, this waiting breath is in fact your anchor in the world…*
>
> *Projectors, you have another breath—the recognition breath. This breath is unmistakable for you. It is far more than just a physical breath—it is a frequency that only engages within you at specific times in your life, and it can only be activated by specific auras of certain other people…Feel into your Definition…feel how specific and refined it is. Try to understand that only a few people in the world can ever truly resonate with this frequency… See if anyone you know resonates totally to the frequency of your definition…*
>
> *As you recall this someone who totally meets you, who sees you utterly for who you truly are, know that you are now experiencing your recognition breath. Notice how different it is from your waiting breath. See how it spreads throughout your body—how it literally fills you from head to toe… Whenever you feel this you know that something wonderful is about to happen in your life…*
>
> *These two breaths live together within you—the waiting breath and the recognition breath—one an anchor, the other only to be sparked by the presence of another specific aura… See how surrendered you must be in the waiting breath— powerless to hurry life along—relax now into your waiting breath and smile inwardly to yourself knowing that everything comes to you in its own time."*

# A COMPROMISE CHECK-LIST

If you're a Projector, what are the things you find yourself doing, or not doing, to avoid the pain of not being seen and recognized? What kind of compromises do you find yourself making? How might you be stepping outside of your integrity, or your most natural way of being in the world, in order to forge a connection?

For example:

- Do you often reach out to people who don't respond, or don't seem capable of receiving you?
- Do you find yourself overwhelming people unintentionally, in conversation, or through your written sharings?
- Do you find it almost painful not to give unasked for advice?
- Do you often find yourself sharing your opinions with people who either don't get it, or feel criticized and defensive?
- Do you keep pursuing or nurturing relationships that are neglectful, unhealthy or abusive at their core?
- Do you adjust the way you dress, speak and behave in a way that doesn't feel fully authentic?
- Do you laugh at jokes you don't find funny?
- Do you attend parties and events you don't really enjoy?
- Do you find yourself hiding away, or withdrawing into a corner, hoping someone will discover you or notice that you're missing?
- Do you find yourself complaining or criticizing more than you really want to, because that seems to be the only way you can attract attention, or get anyone to listen to what you have to say?
- Do you find yourself martyring yourself, even when you don't want to?
- Do you end up giving yourself an unfair amount of negative attention?
- …

**Now it's time to honor your gems!**

To reward yourself for being so courageously honest, I'd like to invite you to make a list of (at least 5!) things that you appreciate and love most about yourself, regardless of what anyone else sees.

_____

_____

_____

_____

# I'VE GOT SO MUCH WISDOM. WHY CAN'T I SHARE IT?

The art of **NOT giving advice unless it's truly asked for** is such a central part of the experiment for Projectors. (Personally, I feel it's an essential lesson for all beings, no matter the Type, though the potential benefits to Projectors who learn this art can be especially wonderful.)

If you're a Projector, not immediately acting on the impulse to share what you see and know can be so hard. There are few things more potentially freeing for you.

Keep in mind that this piece of 'strategic advice' is an invitation for you to experiment, as opposed to a rule to obey. There's so much for you to learn, no matter what you do.

Each of your experiences will inform the next, so please don't be afraid of 'making mistakes.'

There will be times, for example, when you give un-asked for advice, and it'll feel super uncomfortable. As you learn to be in the world as your wise, service-oriented, yet sensitive self, having the chance to feel the resistance coming towards you from someone who isn't ready for your wisdom or penetrating gaze, and to feel how profoundly that resistance/rejection impacts you, can be so revealing, and helpful to you in the long run.

There will be other times, however, when your un-asked for advice will be surprisingly well-received. My guess is that in these situations, you've been energetically invited in, and you're intuitively sensing that. These make wonderful opportunities to hone your *energetic* invitation-detecting skills.

Learning to sense whether an invitation is *energetically* genuine or not, will always come in handy. Sometimes people say they want your advice, but they actually don't. Things aren't always as they appear on the surface.

The opposite can also be true. Sometimes no one is saying anything, but a genuine invitation is being sent your way.

Your job is to get better and better at reading energy (which is something you were born to be good at!).

In the end, your calling is to sense invitations from the Universe Herself!

That said…

There may be other times when your growth edge isn't to practice restraint, but to practice 'agenda-free' self-expression.

In these situations, you may choose to take a risk, and to consciously share what's on your mind—just because you feel like it, or want to see what'll happen, or know that you can survive whatever happens, or because you're not in the mood to hold anything back, sit on your energy or protect someone from your power or insight.

If/when you try this, remember that all-important Projector lesson of non-attachment. Take a deep breath and then exhale your need to be liked, loved and received by everyone.

There will be times when the most fruitful thing for you to do is to simply witness the person or people in front of you. To sit in stillness, hold space, and wait for an invitation to speak—one that may come, or may not come.

This last one is a particularly good experiment for Projectors who are at the beginning of their experiment, for it often brings up the understandable fear that if you don't speak up, you'll never be seen, heard, recognized or received.

This fear is so important for you to be able to hold, feel and move through. Your freedom depends on your ability to not only tolerate but embrace this feeling… and to make it to the other side, where you realize that you don't just survive, but you actually thrive when you're not working so hard to be seen and understood.

It's so important that you learn to watch what arises in you when an invitation to share your insights doesn't come. By witnessing instead of acting, you give yourself the opportunity to notice whether the person you're with is someone you want to continue holding space for, or whether it's time to let go of the relationship, or perhaps adjust the amount of time you spend in that person's presence. Perhaps it's time for them to start paying you for your time and energy!

Again, in my opinion, this kind of an experimentation is relevant to all human beings… The importance of listening (empathically, carefully and respectfully) before speaking can be argued for any Type (for different reasons), and for anyone who's interested in helping humanity along in the healthy relationship department!

# I CAN'T RELATE TO THIS WHOLE "BITTERNESS" CONCEPT

One thing I've learned from my wonderful Projector clients and students is that we're all unique, even if we share a Type.

While one Projector might experience *Bitterness* as a form of resentment, another might experience it as a form of 'burn-out,' or an arising sense of guilt quickly followed by self-defensiveness, or a critical mind, or a feeling of being misused, disrespected, or simply feeling 'unseen and uninvited.'

For some, I've found, it's more like a feeling of hopelessness—a deep giving up on people, on intimacy, on career, on the possibility of ever finding a place in this world that is thoroughly theirs. A giving up on ever feeling deeply valued by the people and culture around them.

Though all Projectors experience *Bitterness* differently, many of my Projector clients have expressed something like this:

"No matter how hard I try, no matter how loving, capable, wise, generous, creative or helpful I am, no one seems to get what I'm about. No one seems to know how to see, hold or love me for the one that I am. I don't even dare hope that I'll ever find someone who is capable of truly meeting, matching, receiving and supporting me. I don't even know if it's worth trying to find a place for me in this world that is truly mine. I might as well give up, or just be who they want me to be, or…"

Another thing I've noticed over the years is how *Bitterness* can surface as an amplified inner critic, or an overly-active judging mind. Many loving, compassionate, service-oriented Projectors tend to turn that critic in against themselves. They can be very hard on themselves.

When the climate within them becomes too harsh and self-abusive, they can find themselves judging the people and the world around them in ways that make them feel so guilty they turn the critic towards themselves.

In this way, they get caught in a critical loop or cycle, where they go back and forth between being hard on themselves, and hard on others, and then hard on themselves for being hard on others, etc.

If you are a Projector and you're getting lost in this kind of a loop, this is a really good time for you to unplug and be exceedingly gentle and compassionate with yourself.

Ask yourself:

- How am I not feeling seen or received?
- How might I be feeling lonely?
- What am I grieving the loss of?
- What is my deepest longing right now?

What matters here is that you allow yourself to dive beneath the bitter angry critic, and find the sadness and vulnerability.

Sometimes, to get to the sadness, you may actually need to make even more room for the anger.

Part of your repetitive loop may be caused by your repressing or not giving yourself full permission to feel angry.

If this is what you sense is happening, ask yourself (on your own, or with someone you feel very safe with):

- What do I feel most powerless about?
- Where don't I feel respected?
- Who isn't treating me the way I deserve to be treated?
- If I weren't worried about being a bad person, what would I dare to think, feel or do?

Usually, once your anger is felt and expressed fully, safely and without judgment, your tears can easily flow.

Sometimes your sadness is easiest to access and sits on top of some anger. In this case, you've got to feel the sadness in order to get to the anger and self-respect instinct beneath! It's a dance!

Beneath all of the layers of emotions, very likely, is Love.

When Ra Uru Hu, the founder of Human Design, talked about Projectors and *Bitterness*, he often shared that there is an aspect to the Projector's *Bitterness* that is actually healthy, understandable and appropriate.

Our world, in its current state, is a real mess. Human beings do horrible things to each other, based on a seemingly bottomless ignorance. There are countless good reasons to momentarily question and lose faith in humanity as a whole.

Occasional experiences of this kind of *Bitterness* can lead to raised awareness, healthy emotional release, empathy, compassion, humor, healing, acceptance, and a growing desire to connect more deeply with others and to make this world a better—less embittered—place.

What we don't want for you, if you're a Projector, is the kind of *Bitterness* that imprisons you—the kind that eats away at you, and isolates you, and doesn't allow for or inspire movement and growth.

Here are some discerning Projector contemplations:

- Is this moment (or phase) of *Bitterness* that I'm feeling isolating me?
- Am I stuck in it?
- Can I feel some movement, even if it's subtle?
- Can I allow myself to feel whatever it is that I'm feeling more fully?
- Am I open to the possibility that this present pain can help me connect more deeply to myself, and ultimately to someone else?
- If I were to connect to someone and share this pain I'm feeling, who might that be?

Nothing melts *Bitterness* away like true intimacy.

# WHY IS LETTING GO SO HARD?
# (AS A PROJECTOR, AS A HUMAN BEING...)

Many of us (regardless of Type) end up in situations, working for people, living in places, being involved in relationships, that aren't the best fits for us. Yet, we have trouble letting go.

We can get stuck for so many reasons.

We can be afraid for our financial or emotional survival.

We can worry about what others will think of us, or how they'll feel about us, if we say 'goodbye.'

We can be terrified that no new or better door will open for us, if we close a door.

As we get older, the stakes of 'letting go' climb ever higher—which on the one hand, makes risk-taking that much scarier. On the other hand, it makes the time we've got left feel that much more precious, which can tempt us to let go and leap before we're ready, or from a place of panic instead of trust.

Because Projectors' ultimate fulfillment relies especially heavily on their relating to (working for, collaborating with, etc.) people who they resonate with at a very deep and authentic level, the question of 'right fit' adds an additional and essential dimension to this inquiry.

I often tell Projectors that it's so much more about *who they're with* than *what they're actually doing*. If you're a Projector, you could have the most amazing job, where you're expected to use all of your genuine passions and impressive skills. If you're working for or with people who don't appreciate, get, recognize or resonate with you, you're still going to be miserable.

The opposite is also true. You could be doing something that you don't (or think you shouldn't) feel particularly passionate about (e.g. sweeping floors). If you're surrounded by colleagues who you totally love, people who bring out your natural brilliance, and you're in an environment that makes you come alive, you can be ecstatic.

Projectors can clean a toilet stall with a best friend, and be in BLISS. (Not to say all Projectors should be cleaning toilet stalls for a living, but you get the idea!)

If you're a Projector, I invite you to start thinking more and more about the WHO, and less and less about the WHAT. When the WHO is right, the WHAT tends to fall into place.

Because Projectors need right relational alignment to find and live out a fulfilling purpose, they can also become particularly vulnerable to compromise. They can feel, for example, like they have to stay somewhere, or be with people they don't truly resonate with, just because they were invited in, or seem to be wanted or liked.

Projectors can understandably fear that if they let go of a place, job or relationship, they'll end up with no support, or without the relational energy that enlivens them and gives them a sense of purpose and momentum.

If you are a Projector, the more you learn about your gifts and challenges as a Projector, the better you'll get at not letting those kinds of fears run your life. You'll get better at knowing when it's time to let go, as well as who and what's right for you once you've taken your leap.

That said, letting go is not always easy. Please be patient, kind and compassionate with yourself.

If you're not a Projector, you likely have aspects of your design that are Projector-like. I invite you to receive this sharing as well, wherever you feel it connects with your own experience.

# *WHEN A GOOD INVITATION TURNS BAD*

If you've ever received an invitation that felt so right in the beginning, but in the end, left you feeling disappointed and understandably bewildered, you're not alone. This is an experience shared by many Projectors.

It takes time to learn how to trust your *Inner Wisdom Keeper*, or Authority, and to learn the art of invitation discernment. It also takes courage to allow yourself to say 'no,' or 'not quite yet,' to offers and invitations that seem great on the outside, but are either not what they seem, or coming at the wrong time.

If you have Splenic intuition, keep in mind that you may get a 'no' one moment to an invitation, and then a 'yes' the next. Similarly, if you have Emotional Definition, you may arrive at a clear 'no' during one time of your life, but at another time, the same invitation may be just wonderful for you.

Regardless of which type of Authority you have, remember that your Authority isn't only here to help you discern who and what is right for you. It's here to help you discern **when** something or someone is right for you. The quality, feel, and potential of an invitation can change tremendously—in a matter of moments for a Splenic Projector, and in a matter of days, weeks, even years for other kinds of Projectors.

Even if you override an inner 'no' and accept an invitation that isn't ideal, not all is lost. You will still be giving yourself the opportunity to learn what happens when you don't listen to your *Inner Wisdom Keeper*.

More importantly, you'll learn something all of us need to learn, regardless of Type: how to keep opening our hearts to life, even when life doesn't always open up to us in the ways we wanted or hoped for, even when we feel deep disappointment.

Some invitations can be especially painful and disappointing, especially when they're in the realm of intimacy.

Someone might approach you, expressing a strong desire to be intimate, or to renew a relationship that had become estranged. It can feel like a dream come true. When push comes to shove, the person just isn't able (or willing) to show up in a way that feels real, consistent, safe, or nourishing.

Such experiences aren't only disappointing. They're confusing.

> Why would someone reach out to me in the first place if they don't actually want to form or deepen the connection?

> Why would someone pursue me, if they never had the intention of participating in the relationship?

They can also be disillusioning.

Some Projectors have had enough of these kinds of experiences that they've consciously chosen a 'wait and see' approach. At the beginning of relationships (whether new or about to be renewed), they try to remain neutral for a while before jumping in.

Sometimes their neutrality comes from a healthy place of openness, non-attachment and grounded realism. They bring a curious mind and a soft heart to each new situation. A beginner's mind. An innocence.

Other times, their neutrality masks a deeper need to guard against hurt—a low-level pessimism that's always there beneath the surface, ready to be disappointed at any turn. When the world has let us down more than once, it's very tempting to dim, lose or tuck away our innocent heart in an attempt at self-protection.

A beginner's heart is a vulnerable, transparent and impressionable thing. It is also beautiful and strong, as it pulsates with tenderness and optimism. It takes courage to keep opening up to life, no matter what it brings us. I can think of very few practices worthier of embracing.

A little discernment can go a long way. If you ever find yourself in a situation, where a high stakes relational invitation has come your way, here are a few questions to support your process:

- Do I feel open, relaxed and present? Can I truly be in the moment with this person, this invitation?
- Do I feel empowered to be keenly observant, agenda-free and healthfully selective?
- Can I sense an undercurrent of hopelessness, bitterness or guardedness?

● Is this situation in any way reminding me of an earlier, painful experience that shook my faith in humanity? Might that memory be preventing me from opening up and being fully present to what and who is right in front of me now?

Even if you've been burned on way too many occasions, see if you can remain simultaneously true to yourself and courageously optimistic, with each new invitation that comes your way.

If someone reaches out, but leaves the ball in your court indefinitely, or doesn't engage with you in a way that feels real, mutual, and fulfilling, then just graciously let them go. Stop pursuing. Don't even worry about not getting back to them. They'll get back to you if they're truly interested, in the way that you were hoping they'd be, and the way you deserve.

If you sense enough genuine care and connection with the person, you might want to take the risk of sharing what you need from the relationship in order to continue feeling motivated to nourish it with your presence and attention. Do so with a tender heart, towards yourself and the other.

In the end, we want you to become great at 'yes' to wonderful invitations, 'no, thanks' to the less wonderful, AND, to become increasingly resilient, so that you can meet new invitations with Beginner's Mind and Heart.

# *LONERS OR SOLITUDE LOVERS?*

Projectors can experience a tremendous amount of magic on their own. Learning, reading, writing, being creative, communing with nature, relaxing, listening to or playing music, enjoying vitality in their bodies, etc. are all ways that the Projectors I know tap into the delicious beauty of life.

*At the same time, there is a particular kind of magic that makes Projectors thrive… and that kind is deeply relational.*

There are few things that light up a Projector more than a beautiful, authentic, inspiring relationship that just 'clicks.' It may be with an intimate partner, a dear friend, a professional collaborator, a creative buddy, or a client who hires you to do some work for them. Sometimes it's enough to have someone on the other side of the planet who totally believes in you, knows what you're capable of, and is cheering you on.

What matters is that you have someone in your life (or more than one person) with whom you are genuinely, at your very core, gotten. This kind of a connection can actually give you the kind of energy and trust you need to transform lonely times into times of delicious solitude, or to engage fully and actively in the world, in ways that you find deeply fulfilling.

One thing I've noticed is that when Projectors really begin to practice their strategies, they begin to prefer solitude over being with people who don't truly get them.

That said, if they make sure to carve out regular time to be on their own, so that they can fill their cup and unplug from the craziness of the world, they tend to prefer being, working and playing with kindred spirits over most other things.

That doesn't take away the magnificence of the magic you've experienced in your own glorious company.

One of our most essential relationships is the one we have with ourselves.

And then, of course, the ultimate relationship is the one we have with 'Spirit.' We can easily enjoy that without anyone around.

## ISOLATION, BY SANDRA ROJO, A MENTAL PROJECTOR

Thank you for your beautiful contribution, Sandra!
(You can learn more about Sandra at: j-tal.com)

Humanistic and Existential theorists such as Rollo May, Fromm, and Maslow sustained that long-term isolation could drive an individual insane. Isolation is not to be confused by temporary loneliness, boredom, or occasional alone time; these are just byproducts. Instead, when isolation is endured long-term and unwillingly, it can be a painful, wicked experience. This is where my journey begins.

In early 2007, I was enthusiastic by the fresh air and new beginning that Colorado Springs seemed to provide. Not long after settling in the new city, I found it difficult to connect with people, something that was unfamiliar to me. Though I enrolled in a creative class and engaged in volunteer work, this particular city seemed uninclined to welcome me. I would meet new people, invite them to my home, and then not long after that, they'd drop off the radar.

I continued to participate and network with a variety of groups, both professionally and personally, but my experiences with people grew stranger over the years. I blamed myself for not trying hard enough, or for not persisting more. The more I initiated, the more frustrated and disappointed I became. I even used Law of Attraction techniques to shake whatever obstacle I thought I was manifesting.

As time went by, I felt increasingly unseen and unmet. My sense of isolation turned into a painful experience of alienation. I felt like an apparition, floating around observing, but never being observed. I felt my life sinking into a deeper and narrower hole.

Though I was not fully conscious of this fact, nor aware of how important 'right environment' was for me, I was not living in the right place. How could I thrive personally and professionally if my soul wasn't recognized? The people around me joined the New Age conditioning voices I had already internalized, reinforcing the beliefs that I needed to "make the best of it," that "it was just karma," that "I should be able to be content anywhere." I felt trapped, hurt and misunderstood.

As a Mental Projector, when you are isolated, and don't have a deeply empathic person to turn to (who can provide a different perspective, or be a sounding board for you), you can feel so lost, like you're on the periphery of your own life. This was my experience.

I have always relished my alone time, even as a child. To this today, I enjoy and require time by myself, where I can replenish my energy, and then come out of my cave refreshed, focused and ready for the world. The experience of isolation I'm describing here was different than that. It was more like a mental and psycho-social prison sentence. I was trapped between two worlds: the inside and the outside. I felt emotionally unsafe, rejected, bombarded by doubts and negative self-talk. Isolation crept up on me like a disease, eating away at my life force.

When I discovered Human Design, my temporary disenchantment with New Age platitudes had already taken me deep within myself. My identity was already slowly "disassembling." Many times, I thought I was going to die, literally. My body ached, my mind was disoriented and my life purpose was annihilated. Long-term isolation brought me to my knees. I had short periods of weeping spells, followed by intense awakenings, then deep cynicism. My existential crisis was both painful and blissful. I knew that if I were to come out alive, I'd be changed forever.

Though I had experienced transformative experiences in the past, and I was never one to shy away from deep emotional processing or looking honestly at my shadows, I see that period of my life as the true beginning of my de-conditioning process. My essential choice was to allow my life force to slowly wither away, or to fight for it. I chose to fight (I intentionally use the word fight because it felt like a battle). I found it especially helpful when Rosy reminded me that everything I had ever studied, practiced and prepared for had come down to this moment. I had to cross this daunting bridge to move to the next level of growth, and to experience a more purposeful life.

Eventually, I realized that the deepest source of my suffering was a lack of intimacy in my relationships. Intimacy requires vulnerability, authenticity and transparency. I had plenty of it to give, but in this environment, I was continually encountering people who chose distance, aloofness and superficiality over closeness and authentic connection (the kind I had experienced with my family and friends growing up).

As defined by Abraham Maslow's hierarchy of needs, we all need a sense of belongingness and love. Through Human Design, I learned that while my needs were healthy, chasing after them like a hungry child wasn't. I learned from Rosy that the more I trusted in life and surrendering to its flow, I would be guided to the right environments, and "my people" would begin showing up, among other delicious miracles.

I began to put into practice my Strategy, Authority and Motivation (HD terms). I received the gift of stillness. I learned that I am a very sensitive person, open to the world. I learned that although I require time alone, I also thrive with my correct people who recognize me as a guide and intimate companion. I learned that when invited to share by the right people, I become a fountain of wisdom. Although self-trust is a daily practice, I no longer blame myself or am hard on myself as I used to be. I experience a more spacious way of being, a new understanding of who I am.

Things I used to think were important no longer matter to me. The ones that do matter are not important for me to share, unless I'm genuinely asked, because I know my wisdom or depth are not for everyone. My career is evolving into a richer experience because I am less afraid to shine. Some of my more challenging relationships have strengthened and healed. I have let go of many of the relationships that were not correct for me, without guilt. I now trust that when I am recognized for the soul I am, my true friends and loved ones stand by me.

Long-term isolation gave me an embodied understanding of what it means to wait, to surrender, and to resist the impulse to rush to respond or act. I enjoy a deeper understanding of life, her flow and the cycle in which she moves.

I feel blessed to have found the correct person to guide me back to myself. Having a supportive relationship where I felt safe to shed tears, face shadows, address feelings of failure and acknowledge my gifts was essential. If you are a Mental Projector, or you are moving through a painfully isolating time in your life, I encourage you find someone who can hold space for you, with gentleness, grace and patience. Since we are each unique, I also invite you to imagine what an experience of long-term isolation might offer you, what gifts and wondrous transformations it might bring.

# CAN BUSINESS-MINDED PROJECTORS BE SOLOPRENEURS?

There are so many variables at play when it comes to starting one's own business, many of which have absolutely nothing to do with one's design or Type.

For one thing, most of us are on techno-communication overload. Even the most wonderful products and gorgeously marketed services easily go unnoticed.

Our American-influenced obsession with 'fast food,' quick fixes and sound bites exacerbates the dilemma of anyone wanting to offer something of depth that requires a degree of focus, readiness and commitment.

If you're like me, and happen to be living in a big progressive area (like the Bay Area), where you can't take a step without bumping into a self-help guru, creativity workshop, inspirational speaker, alternative business training or networking event, the challenge of promoting your solo-business can get even bigger.

A while back, a dear friend and colleague of mine (a Projector, actually) went with me to a spiritual networking event in order to promote one of our art immersion workshops. I'll never forget it. We looked around and started laughing. We were surrounded by a flock of wonderful, talented, dedicated, creative women, all of them there to make a unique, life-transformative offer. There were so many of them; it was dizzying, bordering on absurd!

If we plucked out any one of these fabulous women, and dropped her down in the middle of a smaller town (or country), she'd be a spiritual rock star! Here in the Bay Area, she was a piece of chopped liver wrapped up in a rainbow Goddess scarf.

No wonder my Sacral belly didn't respond to sharing anything about our offer that evening, or about what I did in the world. Not even when asked!

I'm not even scratching the surface when it comes to the challenges of starting up a business, *for anyone.*

Like, for example... Being an entrepreneur can take time, a LOT of time.
A *LOT* OF TIME!

First, it takes **time to find clarity**—to hone in on that magical intersection between our personal passions, capacities, and the world's actual needs. Whether you call it niche, target audience, an eye towards essentialism, or simply an inner sense of 'right-enoughness,' clarity about what we're here to offer can take years to find. Once we find it, this clarity usually evolves, requiring constant fine-tuning.

Second, it takes **time to do the *inner work***—to get out of our own way so that our business seeds can sprout and thrive. We have to learn how to make room in our lives, release self-doubts, trust in our unique message, feel worthy of 'success,' set healthy limits, lick our wounds when we receive difficult feedback, and bounce back with resilience. We need to literally **become the person** who is capable of doing our life's work in a balanced, authentic and self-honoring way.

Third, it takes **time to do all of the OUTER work** business-building requires—the 'putting it out there' even when it's scary, the constant refining, the making peace with these 'hyper-teched' times and feeling into which aspects of the business-building process resonate with others at a deeper level.

It doesn't only take time. It takes courage to keep showing up, and showing up, and showing up. For ourselves, and for others... regardless of the immediate results.

All of this would be true, even if you weren't a Projector. It can be a highly challenging for all Types (even Manifestors) to find a genuinely authentic, balanced way to grow a healthy business these days.

You *are* a Projector, living in a Generator world run amuck. You get to give yourself some extra compassion.

Unless you're someone who genuinely LOVES engaging in social media madness and easily slips into the popular business-building/marketing templates like a pair of warm slippers, you might feel a little more than overwhelmed by the task of Solopreneurship.

## OK, all that said...

There is no doubt in my mind that a Projector can be an extremely fulfilled entrepreneur.

A Projector can even be an outwardly successful Solopreneur.

It's the "SOLO" part that I worry about for most Projectors (even though some have more consistent access to energy in their designs through their Solar Plexus, Root and Emotional Centers).

In my experience, Projectors are happiest and most fulfilled when they aren't working on their own. It doesn't mean they can't be running their own business. If they don't have anyone to spar with, receive support from, collaborate with, it can be a lonely and extremely exhausting affair.

Even those who've been genuinely invited into a field, profession or calling… who are Manifesting, Generating, Reflecting within it… successfully… can end up really tired when they've got to do all of the work on their own.

Despite my distaste for generalizing, I've found that Projectors do best (not by 'flyering,' cold calling, advertisement blasting, or going down endless marketing to-do lists) when they allow their relationships to work for them.

Word of mouth, relational referrals, 'joint ventures' (I'm not fond of that term, it sounds so business-y, but you know what I mean), magical encounters, contagious conversations, serendipitous meetings, energy-bringing collaborations (that aren't even necessarily money-driven)… These are all the things I've seen work best for the Projectors that I know and love.

If you're a Projector and you want to write, for example, I'd suggest a writing coach, writing group, or buddy—someone to keep you connected to your inner fire, someone to hold you accountable to your true voice, someone who shares your passion for the written word.

If you're a Projector who wants to run your own business, I highly suggest that you gather together a group of supporters. One might be a friend; one might be a coach; one might be someone who takes care of some of the busy work (if that's not your thing); one might be a colleague. I'd also seriously consider joining forces with someone (ideally a Generator with lots of energy, and one who appreciates and values what you contribute, even if it's different than they do!).

Not everyone is genuinely drawn to writing a newsletter, or a blog, or making a video, or running a teleseminar, or a FB campaign, or creating a super sophisticated website, or… but you may be one of those Projectors who actually loves doing these kinds of things. Just make sure you're doing them under the most free, genuine, fun, creative and authentic conditions possible.

## Here's a success story for you

I had a wonderful client who had a full and thriving counseling and teaching practice in one city. He felt 'invited' to move to a new city, and was terrified of how he was going to build an entirely new practice. He had all kinds of thoughts about what would be required of him. In his mind, he could only imagine pushing, pushing and pushing.

Together, we decided to let this move be an opportunity to experiment with Trust. He was to trust in his relationships, above all else (his old, current and about-to-be relationships).

Whenever he visited the new city before the big move, instead of trying to market himself, he focused on two things: 'right relationship' and doing what he loved.

He had to be very brave. There were times when he met people that his mind thought would be good professional contacts for him. If the fit didn't feel right, he let the relationship go, and kept following and trusting that yummy relational thread.

It took some time, and there were moments when he panicked and considered pushing himself back into over-exertion mode. Eventually, he found himself (just naturally, organically) finding his people, his colleagues, his friends, his organizations, his groups, his self-care supporters, who all eventually became his best referral sources.

Now his practice is full. Not just full of clients, but the kinds of clients he actually loves to work with.

Though he did all of the work himself, I do believe that our connection throughout that time, and the faith and support I was able to give him, did play an important role in his staying on a more relaxed and relational track.

If you're considering going the Solopreneur route, make sure that you have GOOD support from at least one ally, someone who knows you, who believes in you, and believes that there's a way for you to succeed without having to sell your soul, or have your adrenals go poof.

# GENERATORS

## *PASSIONATE RESPONSE OR ADDICTIVE DISTRACTION?*

Whenever we're engaged in an activity, *where we come from* is so much more important than *what we're actually doing.*

For example, you can be playing a game on your smart phone out of pure pleasure and passion, and have your body's (Sacral Center's) total blessing.

You can also be playing the game to avoid feeling something painful, being confronted with emptiness, or doing something that would actually be healthy and empowering.

One moment, your game might be just what your Sacral Center needs. Another moment, the very same game might be an attempt to avoid a genuine Sacral Center impulse, or an example of your giving into an external pressure or conditioning source.

It's really not about the game.

Though some of us struggle more profoundly with addiction than others, we all experience addiction on some level. A personal experience of addiction, if we add our compassionate awareness to it, can lead us down a profound self-development journey, where we learn the subtle art of Response vs. Addiction Discernment.

Such a journey takes time, life experience, and courage. It usually takes some loving, trusting relationships as well.

The Human Design experiment provides us with a wonderful forum to learn what it actually feels like to have our body's blessing. It helps us learn to recognize those moments when we're engaging in activities that truly enliven, restore, relax and inspire us in the moment.

If we allow it to, our experiment can also increase our capacity to wake up to our tendencies to 'check out,' numb out, shut down and cut off. We can see when we're using empty, busy and junk food-like activities to mask over deeper feelings of isolation, loneliness, dislocation and hopelessness.

The deeper we understand the nature and patterns of our own addictions and habitual conditioning, the better we get at discerning between genuine self-loving and subtle self-numbing acts. Our growing self-awareness ultimately opens our hearts to others who are still in the grips of painful, unconstructive coping patterns.

Whether you choose to 'play the video game' or not, see if you can stay curious and open.

Even our seemingly unhealthy impulses, addictive distractions and past indulgences can end up informing and positively feeding our lives, relationships and work in the world.

If you find yourself uncontrollably binge-watching a TV series, remind yourself that your experience can also—*ultimately*—serve you and the people in your life…as long as you are able to sprinkle into the experience some witnessing, creativity and tenderness.

I can't tell you how many times I've found myself sitting with a client, and suddenly feeling inspired to share a scene from a TV series or movie that I wasn't particularly proud of watching—only to find that the scene opened us up to a surprisingly deep and healing conversation.

The Universe is eternally forgiving, always providing us with new chances to be fully present, authentic, flexible and creative.

While you're working on freeing yourself from conditioning, honoring your unique 'Authority' and making the healthiest decisions for yourself, remember not to box yourself in.

Just as following a genuine Sacral response can land us in the right place, with the right people, and with the best opportunities, so can less than perfectly clean Sacral responses… *if* you stay awake to what the next moment offers you.

Even bad choices can lead to great ones. It's never (or rarely) too late for you to course-correct. No matter what happens as a result of your choices, you can always choose to learn and grow from the experience.

One last little thing about babies and bathwater:

Even if you realize you're doing something out of an addictive/evasive impulse, see if you can assume that there's something healthy in there. See if there's something worthy that you're drawn to—a feeling, an experience, a perspective, a need for self-soothing, an attempt at emotional regulation, a longing for connection with others, a deep desire for Spirit, etc. Assume that there is a beautiful little pearl hiding in the oyster of your activities.

Offer your 'coping mechanisms' some loving attention and genuine curiosity, before rejecting them hook, line and sinker.

# WHAT'S THE DIFFERENCE BETWEEN MANIFESTING AND PURE GENERATORS?

In response to the suggestion that Generators be divided into two official Types, Ra Uru Hu expressed the concern that Manifesting Generators would inadvertently use their new separated status to avoid the basic truth of their Strategy… which is to respond. They'd toss out the more receptive aspects of their nature in favor of the more yang-driven and culturally sanctioned aspects, and end up bulldozing their way through life as if they were true Manifestors.

Ra, and many of the Human Design teachers out there today, stress that for ALL Generators, response is everything.

What happens for Manifesting and Pure Generators **after** they've responded, (i.e. how quickly they move into action, how efficient or thorough they are, how consistent they are, how many steps they take—or skip—along the way, whether they experience plateaus followed by breakthroughs, or leaps followed by back-tracks, or fantastic shortcuts, etc.) can be very different, and reflective of their 'sub-Type.'

# THE 'MANIFESTING' PART OF THE MANIFESTING GENERATOR

One of the most important things for Manifesting Generators to acknowledge is that they've got the word "Generator" in their Type title.

In other words, if you're a Manifesting Generator, you're not just a productivity warrior. You've also got this beautiful Buddha being in you, with a deeply receptive presence. This means that you're essentially a responsive being, here to wait for life to come your way and turn you on.

Once your creative engine has kicked in, then you can manifest. Woah, can you manifest!

Also, once you've gotten your belly's blessing and have entered into manifesting mode, many of the qualities and strategic advice we often give to Manifestors are likely to apply to you too.

Let's say you stumble upon an ad in the paper about a giant office space. Your whole body lights up, as you become flooded with inspiration. Your body-mind is now activated by a strong desire to transform this space into an art school for kids.

Like a Manifestor, you're probably going to need to experience a degree of autonomy and freedom to move forward. In other words, you don't have to spend all of your time asking anyone for permission in order to honor your genuine response.

At the same time, also like a Manifestor, it would do you well to spend time gathering information about the space, the population you desire to serve, as well as informing the people who are likely to be impacted personally, financially and creatively by your dream-in-the-works.

Before plunging ahead, do some real listening. With each bit of concrete and practical information you glean about the project, and with each relevant 'relational pulse' you take, you will be gifting your Sacral Center more opportunities to respond. Each of your steps will help your manifestation path become more grounded, aligned and refined.

An understanding of Type is here to offer us some operational guidance, not an identity to cling to with rigidity. Everybody has a Manifestor in them, just as everyone has a Generator, Projector and Reflector in them.

If your Type is a Manifesting Generator, and you're experimenting with this knowledge, you might find yourself benefiting a great deal from the practice of being a *Buddha first*, and *Warrior second*.

Here's another important distinction between Pure and Manifesting Generators that I share more deeply about in the *Designed to Blossom* workbook.

If you're a Manifesting Generator, it's not enough to simply feel a positive gut response to something that appears in your life.

To find out if something is truly right for you, you need to actually engage your body. Move toward a 'possible yes' with your actions. Take a step in the direction. Try it out. See how it feels.

Even if you're designed to make highly intuitive and spontaneous decisions (Splenic-Sacral Authority), you may still have a two-layered process towards getting clear on whether something is right for you. You probably won't need as much time as an Emotionally Defined Manifesting Generator would need, but you'll still benefit from first recognizing that inner 'uh huh,' and moving towards and into the experience, to see if that "uh huh" sticks.

If your body continues to feel that 'yes,' and to have the energy to keep going, then you know you're on the right track. You're entering into the flow.

# MANIFESTORS

## *DO MANIFESTORS HAVE TO BE THE LEADER IN A GROUP?*

Everyone can have leadership abilities, not just Manifestors. Some Manifestors aren't at all what you'd typically think of as 'born leaders,' while plenty of Generators, Reflectors and Projectors are!

There are all kinds of leaders. Those that lead like kings and queens, those that lead like shamanic warriors, those that lead like generals, and those that lead from behind the scenes. There are those that are leaders in their field, those that lead like elected officials, those that lead through skilled facilitation or teaching, those that lead through innovative thinking, and those that lead through personal example, through their mere presence.

When you think of Manifestors, think "initiators" more than leaders. They're designed to inspire, to get the ball rolling, to spark ideas, enthusiasm or action in others. They can do this from the front of the room or sidelines. They may decide to stick around to support the building of an empire. They may work their initiating magic, and then happily slip away. (They don't tend to thrive in too much maintenance work.)

What matters most is that they are not waiting for life to come to them and light them up. They are waiting to feel lit up from the inside, and then allowing that inner light to shine out and have its impact, setting the course for themselves and ideally the 'right' others.

(Ironically, similar to Projectors, I've found that many Manifestors feel very unfulfilled in misaligned relationships. There are few things more frustrating—or angering, or hurtful—than trying to initiate people who don't appreciate or understand the value of what they have to offer and want to give.)

There are different kinds of Manifestors.

Emotionally Defined Manifestors might wait years to get clear on what they're here to initiate, while a more Splenically-oriented Manifestor may be extremely spontaneous in her/his initiations.

No Manifestor is here to initiate things based on ideas alone.

Just like the rest of us, Manifestors aren't here to make mental decisions, which I think surprises a lot of people... including Manifestors, who would LOVE to be able to just manifest their ideas.

An Ego Manifestor—blessed with a very strong will—may look a little more like what we tend to think of when we think of Manifestors.

Two people with the same exact design can be living that design out in very different ways, depending on their conditioning, level of self-awareness and emotional maturity. An Ego-Manifestor operating from fear can do a great deal of damage; another Ego-Manifestor operating from love can make an enormous, loving contribution to the world.

# OBLIGATION ALLERGIES
# "IF I HAVE TO DO IT, I DON'T WANT TO DO IT."

Many Manifestors love to help people and be of service. As soon as their sense of obligation surpasses their desire to do the task, they don't want to do it anymore. Even if they're judged for being lazy and uncommitted.

What may seem like an Obligation Allergy may actually be a fantastic Freedom Honing Device. There are few things as important for Manifestors as the experience of Freedom. They need to feel 'at choice' in their lives, not chronically acting out of a sense of obligation or guilt. The freer they feel—no matter what they're doing or who they're doing it with, the more powerful, inspiring and positive their impact will be.

Interestingly, Freedom is a state of being that Manifestors can slip in or out of, depending on how they're holding what they're doing, and what's happening in their awareness. It's all about learning how to assess, at any given moment, whether they're 'in the freedom zone,' or not. When they're in the freedom zone, they're on track.

If you are a Manifestor, give yourself freedom-alignment check-ups by asking these simple questions:

- Do I feel like I *have* to do this?
- Do I actually want to do this?

Remind yourself, "I don't have to do anything that doesn't feel right to me."

(Of course, this doesn't apply in all cases. If you've manifested a family and your child needs you, you may *have* to step up!)

Reclaiming your personal autonomy feels good.

Ironically, it can actually pave the way for you to return to your original activity with renewed empowered passion.

Think of this like a chiropractic adjustment. Same body. Same spine. Same limbs. Just better aligned when motivated by choice and freedom.

In the end, where you're coming from when you do something matters more than what you're doing. Am I coming from a place of expansion, freedom and passion, or am I coming from a place of contraction, guilt, and enslavement?

# HOW DO I MANIFEST MY PURPOSE?

We're so used to thinking about Purpose as something we're meant to do in this world, what we're meant to 'manifest.'

The more I contemplate Purpose, the more I realize how little it has to do with what I'm actually doing. It has so much more to do with who—and how—I'm **being**.

One could say that the true Purpose of the Manifestor is to **be and embody freedom**—to truly understand, claim and emanate what it means to be a free human being, to soar on the wings of pure consciousness.

There are the actions, projects, or 'things' that the Manifestor gives shape to in the material world., but these are just vessels through which the deeper Purpose of Freedom moves. They're not the Purpose itself.

I prefer to look at all of the elements of Human Design as archetypal invitations for all of us to play with.

You may not be a Manifestor, but there is a Manifestor in you.

We are all here to experience freedom in our lives, to feel genuinely 'at choice,' empowered and surrendered.

Perhaps our 'Strategies' or 'Authorities' are different, or the way our paths unfold are unique, but in the end, we're all learning how to get 'in the flow'—in the flow of our True Nature, in the flow of the natural world, in the flow of the cosmos.

When we're 'in the flow' or aligned with ourselves, we naturally enjoy what we're doing—even if requires effort. We experience ourselves as unique cells in the planetary body, being fed and nourished while we're feeding and nourishing others. In such a state of fluid grace, there is no such thing as self-sacrifice, obligation or compromise.

The question "Do I really HAVE to do this?", or "Would I still be doing this even if I didn't have to do it?" are good questions for all of us.

*Just a bit of Type tweaking:*

- A Projector might ask, "Even if I think I HAVE to do this, do I have to do this with this particular person?"

- A Generator might ask, "Even if I think I HAVE to do this, do I have the energy to do it right now?"

- A Reflector might ask, "Even if I HAVE to do this, is this the environment or community I need to be doing this in?"

# AM I AS A MANIFESTOR DESTINED TO BE REPELLING?

No, you're not.

Just because you're a Manifestor, and your aura is built to protect your freedom and autonomy, doesn't mean that you're destined to be a cold, intimidating person who's incapable of healthy relational attachment!

I speak from personal experience here, since I've been married to a Manifestor for almost 25 years, and he's one of the most warm, delightful and intimacy-loving people I know.

As it is with any Type, you're going to find all kinds of Manifestors.

There are certainly some Manifestors that have aspects to their designs that can enhance their capacity to exude warmth or coolness.

When it comes to Definition or Nature, for example, Emotionally Defined Manifestors can sometimes radiate a certain juiciness, which can make them feel more approachable. Others with the Channel of Sensitivity can bring an element of care and connectedness to their auras and relations. Manifestors with the Channel of Openness can bring a degree of graciousness and a capacity for deep listening, just as Manifestors with the Channel of the Prodigal (or a prominent Gate 13, the Gate of the listener) can feel more directly and easily accessible to others.

My husband is an Emotional Manifestor with three Defined Emotional Channels. As I shared earlier, he's a very warm man. (Not that he hasn't—or that we haven't—also benefited a great deal from his learning how to inform! Believe me; that's been a big support in our marriage.)

The amount of Openness in a design can also make Manifestors feel more accessible and their auras feel more inviting. Open Solar Plexus can certainly enhance a capacity for empathy, compassion and relatedness. It is their relationship to their Openness (as it is with all of us) that determines the quality of their presence and ability to embody connectivity. Their conditioning backgrounds can make a very big difference when it comes to how Manifestors experience their designs, and their expression of them.

The extent to which Manifestors are supported as children can play a big role in determining the amount of trust they develop in themselves and in others.

Was the Manifestor child encouraged to feel and be free and independent? Was the child allowed to do their own thing, left in peace when that was what was needed? Was the Manifestor child listened to and respected? Or controlled and manipulated? Did the child learn how important, interesting, impactful and beautifully powerful they were, or how unimportant, uninteresting, too impactful and overpowering? Was the Manifestor taught how to communicate in a loving, respectful way, or not?

All of these factors influence the Manifestor's relationships and aura later on in life.

What matters here is this: the greater the trust a Manifestor has learned to have in themselves and others, the less 'edgy,' charged or defended the boundary or aura needs to be. Their healthy boundaries can allow them an enormous sense of personal freedom, without pushing people away.

When it comes to self-development, what matters even more than the raw material of our Human Design blueprint, or how we were treated growing up, is how we've learned to be with and express our true Nature over time, as we've entered into adulthood and taken responsibility for our lives.

- Have we taken the time it requires to get to know our true Nature and to work through some of the more painful aspects of our conditioning?
- Have we been brave enough to receive feedback from the people we love?
- Have we learned that it's safe to be honest with ourselves?
- Have we taken risks and learned to leave our comfort zone, in honor of our soul's growth?
- Have we learned to be with our strong feelings, without repressing or reacting to them?
- Have we learned how to communicate lovingly yet clearly about what we want, need and how we feel?

## WHEN IS INFORMING ESSENTIAL?

When it comes to the Strategy of informing, a few key questions for the Manifestor to ask are:

- Who will be impacted by what I want to do?
- How will they be impacted?
- *How much* will they be impacted?

The greater the potential impact, the more important it is for the Manifestor to give a heads-up, or to practice the information-gathering and listening aspects of their strategy.

The impact of a Manifestor's action isn't only determined by the 'bigness' of the Manifestor's decision. It's also determined by the sensitivity of the person being impacted, the degree of intimacy that exists inside the relationship, and the amount of interdependency that's happening in that moment.

I remember times when our daughter was a baby, when my husband would simply leave the room without letting me know where he was going, or for how long he was going, and I felt very frustrated (especially during those moments when I'd been holding a baby in my arms and hadn't been to the bathroom in 6 hours!).

You see what I'm saying? The objective situation doesn't always have to be a big deal to *feel* like a big deal.

There were plenty of other times when he went ahead and did something really big, without saying a word to me, and I was totally cool with it. Because the impact of what he was doing to me and my life was minimal.

Something I've noticed in some of the Manifestors from my counseling practice is that they either:

- don't believe people will be interested in what they want to do
- believe people will try to change or control what they want to do, or…
- don't realize how much they actually matter to the people in their lives, or what a big difference their presence—or lack of presence—makes.

From what I've witnessed over the years, the process of awakening for many Manifestors seems to involve an opening up to intimacy, a profound realization that they matter to others, and a growing capacity not just to 'inform' about projects, but to engage in intimate communication, where they both share and listen, with increasing amounts of vulnerability and transparency.

Over time, Manifestors on a self-development journey learn that people can be trusted so much more than they ever imagined, if they dare open up their ears, their hearts and their communicative mouths!

The happiest Manifestors I know are those whose 'informing experiment' has led them to realize that they can be free, respected and deeply connected all at the same time.

This process may come more easily to some Manifestors than others, depending on their Definition (the raw material they're dealing with), and their conditioning (the help or harm they've received along the way). Ultimately, everyone has the potential to embrace an attitude of self-love and a path of self-development. The more we embrace who we are, and learn to free our true natures in a way that honors our relationships, the more our auras will shine, and our relationships will benefit.

# MANIFESTORS AND INVITATIONS

Many Human Design students experience momentary bouts of Other Type Envy. It's only natural to think the grass might be greener somewhere else.

Even my husband, the Manifestor, has envied Projectors, wishing just once, someone who really 'got him' would come along and extend him a fantastic invitation!

When I asked Kim why he felt so envious of the Projector Strategy, he thought a bit, smiled wide, then said that the part that *really* appealed to him about the invitation piece, at least theoretically, was the fact that he wouldn't have to work so hard going out and 'selling himself' and what he wanted to manifest in the world.

He loved the idea of someone coming along, inviting him into a fabulous situation, handing over the funds and whatever tools he needed, so that he could go and say, do and create whatever he wanted…in peace.

Interestingly, soon after that conversation, a lovely woman from my *Designed to Blossom* Course asked him a question about his experience of being a Manifestor, and **invited** him to share his answer on video.

Almost immediately, he said, with the blunt assertiveness stereotypically associated with Manifestors, "I'm happy to answer the question, but I'm not going to do it on video."

There it was, as we witnessed his invitation-related dilemma playing itself out in real time.

The truth is he loved the question. He welcomed the invitation to share about his experience as a Manifestor. He just didn't want to do it on video.

More importantly, he didn't want to do it (anything) on someone else's terms. **That** experience felt very familiar, to the both of us.

Countless times, something—an opportunity—would come towards him. He'd feel happy and excited about it at first. He'd then learn a bit more about the opportunity, and suddenly, it would start to lose its spark. He'd start to feel subtly controlled, constricted or entrapped. He'd feel the weight of others' expectations and hopes. He'd sense strings attached. His whole body (and aura) would recoil.

This mini-experience opened up a very interesting and revealing conversation between us. Here's the gist of what Kim said:

> *"You see, even if I like an invitation, it's hard for me to embrace everything that comes with it. I feel afraid that the invitation is going to come with too many strings attached. I'm going to end up beholden to someone else's agenda, or their ideas for me, or their needs.*

*I get squeezed into a box that I know I won't be able to live in for too long. The whole invitation thing doesn't feel worth it in the end, even though a part of me wishes I got more invitations, and fantasizes about how much easier my life would be if they came. The truth is, they make me nervous. I wouldn't want a job where someone else felt like they could tell me what to do, or give me too much unasked-for input."*

We started thinking back to the times Kim was an employee.

In the States, he's mostly been self-employed. In Denmark, he worked with children within institutional settings. We realized, as we talked, that his favorite jobs were always those where he was given his own domain within the institution. Within that domain (whether it was the art therapy room, or a video project, or the creation of the institution's website), he was in charge. He was able to do what he wanted to do.

He loved having colleagues. He loved being part of a team. He loved the energy, creativity and inspiration he received from the people around him.

He didn't even mind having bosses.

As long as his domain remained his own.

In the most ideal scenario, he was the only one within the institution who knew what he knew, who had that particular skill set. He was therefore the recipient of a great degree of trust and freedom.

Just a bit of food for Manifestor thought.

# A CUSTOM-DESIGNED MANIFESTOR MANIFESTO
# I CREATED FOR MY HUSBAND

*(Feel free to use as inspiration for your own Manifesto. Yours will look different.)*

## MOST IMPORTANT TO YOUR HAPPINESS:

- You need to feel free.
- You need to feel in charge of what you do.
- You need to be able to follow your creative inspiration to the end (and then you can open up to feedback).
- You need to be willing to take bold action, even when you're scared.

- You need to feel capable. And you can only feel capable if you feel empowered, creative, and in charge of what you're doing.
- Money may help you to feel more free, but freedom is what determines your happiness. And you can experience that with or without money.

## RED FLAGS:

- If you're losing enthusiasm for a project that you were once excited about
- If you feel stuck and depressed
- If you feel dependent on someone else to move forward
- If you're being hard on yourself, judging yourself as not good enough or incapable
- If you find yourself waiting for someone to get back to you
- If you won't move ahead, because you're waiting for someone else's opinion
- If you're avoiding a conversation because you expect someone to disapprove of what you do, or what you want to do
- If you're not trusting your instincts, because you're afraid someone won't want to pay you
- If you're waiting for someone else to be ready
- If you're waiting for someone to get clear about what they want
- If you're fantasizing about getting a stable job
- If you're not reaching out to someone, because you don't want to seem desperate
- If you're not reaching out to someone, because you feel hurt, disrespected, or undervalued
- If you're not reaching out to someone, because you expect that they'll want more control over the project than you want to give them
- If you're avoiding contacting someone, because you expect to be taken advantage of
- If you're afraid that doing things your own way will mean skipping steps
- If you're afraid of disappointing someone

## For each current project:

1. Look for the red flags that are present.
2. Then ask yourself:

- Where do I feel most stuck?
- If I were totally free to do what I wanted here, what would I do?
- Who am I afraid of upsetting? What can I tell them that'll help me feel more free?
- What bold action can I take, even if I feel scared? How can I reclaim my self-respect in this situation?

# REFLECTORS

## *BEFRIENDING THE MOON*

As a Reflector, you are a Moon being. In your very essence, you are connected to the Moon, the collective, and the Soul of the world.

Some Reflectors find it very helpful to track the transits and their specific impact on their unique Human Design charts. Some don't. Regardless of where you fall on the 'design-tracking' continuum, finding concrete ways to commune with the Moon energetically, simply understanding the Moon's cycles, can be a profound and worthy exploration for you.

When you befriend the Moon, do it from a variety of perspectives—from the astronomical, to the astrological, to the archetypal, to the ceremonial. Such a whole-hearted and multi-dimensional exploration is likely to deepen your Human Design experiment in surprising ways.

An astrologer, author and spiritual teacher, Barbara Hand Clow, has written beautifully about the Moon. In her book, *The Pleiadian Agenda*, she gives voice to the Moon herself:

> *"I am the moon.*
> *I mirror the consciousness of earth back to you.*
> *Moons are reflectors of what you're feeling.*
> *To reflect your emotions is our primary function.*
> *Like all moons, I am a reflector of planetary feelings.*
> *As the moon, I feel energy through silvery ray vibrations.*
> *The closest thing you know of this kind of perception, is the silvery gossamer light, shimmering on the surface of water as the full moon rises.*
> *My light is opalescent and translucent…*
> *I have canyons and craters on my surface, which is almost devoid of electro-magnetic energy.*
> *My vibrations are so ethereal that there's almost no charge in me.*
> *I'm completely balanced.*
> *Humans, animals and various other life forms literally magnetize or draw consciousness from me.*
> *These are extremely subtle vibrations which differ from the polarized interactions that exist on the surface of your planet.*
> *These are feelings that mirror back memories related to experiences you have, which then modulate your responses to everything.*
> *I hold memories of your soul experiences, life after life. And the only way you can explore this is to examine your subconscious mind while you are in a body.*
> *I enjoy reflecting back to you your own deep understandings of yourself."*

These words act as a profound invitation to Reflectors to dive deep into their own subconscious minds, while trusting that their minds are intrinsically connected to the Cosmic Mind itself. Given our interconnectedness, your inner explorations will undoubtedly benefit all of us.

If you are a Reflector, your unique *Inner Wisdom Keeper* works through a process of crystallization, where clarity is found over time, as visible and invisible threads of thought, memory, emotion, sensation and intuition weave themselves together into a beautiful tapestry.

Barbara Hand Clow writes that the Moon holds our subconscious memory banks. Some of those memories are traumatic. They are what exist in our minds as repetitive and negative belief systems, telling us all that we can't do, all that we're not worthy of.

It is these belief systems, stored in your subconscious and based on old traumatic memories, that ultimately limit your expressive potential.

Similarly, it is the positive conclusions that you have been able to draw from happy memories that form the basis of your free actions.

When you consciously work through and release early life (or even past life) traumatic memories, in whichever way feels most authentic and right to you, your body begins to feel more harmonious and safe. Your creativity is unleashed.

You can also resource yourself by remembering and reclaiming happy memories that got pushed underground. These beautiful memories are always available to you, if you make yourself available to them.

> *Through attunement to the spiritual emanation of 13, triggered by my journey through your nights, you will always feel more subtle vibrations. That is my gift to you. I'm always there for you. Just as the sun rises every day, Lunar or feminine essence is what enables you to let go of thinking for a while and just become responsive.*
>
> *~ Barbara Hand Clow*

Whenever you can, I encourage you to spend some time in meditation, in silence, in solitude. Listen to music that moves you. Make art or write poetry in a way that connects you to your deeper, more hidden feelings. If you don't already have a journal, start one. Consider making it an art journal, so it's not just everyday words that you're expressing, but a collage of poetry, images, colors and texture. Let it all just flow out of you, uncensored and unintellectual.

For you, having regular times during the day, week and month to 'get out of your head' is especially important. It's about dropping in, going deep, staying open, and communing with all that swims beneath the surface.

Your subconscious mind is perfectly designed to bring towards you everything and everyone you need to feel, look at, or move towards.

Allow the Moon to provide you with a supportive structure for your deep dives. Set your intentions, launch dreams, and say 'goodbye' in accordance with her rhythms. Allow the Moon to guide and pace your crystallization journey, and see what happens!

*You are attuned to me and feel my surface when you work with ritual consciousness in relationship to my subtle light. When you do Moon ceremonies and Eclipse meditations, you are accessing direct lines into my subtle, emotional vibrations. These ceremonies are some of the most potent ones available to you on earth. Whether you tune into me or not, I shower you with subtle sensations.*

*During my cycle of 13 Moons, observe the reflected Solar light increasing to the Full Moon, and intensifying those feelings. Then let go of all feelings and become empty within it, as it wanes.*

*Become an empty vessel for the New Moon. You can wash away your ego every month, from the Full Moon to the next New Moon. You can be reborn with the New Moon 13 times a year. If you do this, a practice that was very advanced on your planet a long time ago, and still exists in Bali, you will feel less driven by Solar forces and planetary agendas.*

*~ Barbara Hand Clow*

# WE NEED MOON BEINGS NOW MORE THAN EVER

## The Moon Speaks

*These days I'm very concerned about your polarized emotional bodies. You've become dualized because you emphasize your masculine side over your feminine. This can block my soft lunar screen and overexpose your planetary vibrations, such as control and manipulation. I am mirroring the cosmic data bank to you, month by month. Remember I am a screen for the planetary solar and stellar forces, and a new cosmology is forming.*

*~ Barbara Hand Clow*

These are intense times, all over the world. As stated above, our world is more polarized than ever. Wherever we look, light is being shined upon the darkest, most wounded places inside of and all around us.

Whether or not you believe you've signed up for this, if you're alive on the planet, you're participating in a massive transformation. We're all individually and collectively moving through a giant, shattering, alchemical and collective portal. We're being invited, in each cell of our bodies, to understand our profound interconnectedness—with each other and with the entire cosmos. Our lives depend on it.

As a Moon Being, you are innately primed to 'get' this collective journey we're all on. We need your keen vision. We are actually counting on you to spot, celebrate and liberate those of us who dare to say 'yes' to Love, no matter how big the Fear. We need you to help us all navigate this shift into a kinder, gentler, feminine-celebrating, stillness-embracing, and earth-honoring phase of our human existence.

As a Reflector, your ability to keep your eyes and heart open (to yourself and those around you) will help to determine just how this epic human story unfolds.

The fact that you were born to feel and reflect collective energies, and that this is one of your great gifts and services to the world, can feel overwhelming, especially during times like these.

It's especially important that you find safe, contained, nourishing, supportive and loving ways to hold yourself, and be held by others.

As you move through your days, please don't be in such a hurry to have answers. You don't have to know exactly where you belong at any given moment, or exactly what you're supposed to be doing.

Be large with yourself whenever you can. Be patient. Let your feelings flow, even your disappointment.

Allow yourself time to experiment, to be drawn to places, people and environments that you resonate with at a deep level.

Trust your guidance. Trust your deep connectedness to Spirit, the Moon, your blood, the ocean's waters.

Give yourself regular opportunities to retreat, to be silent, to get your bare toes in the grass or the sand.

You'll find that your clarity will 'fly together' in mysterious, surprising ways.

# Observe Your Energy Flow: Petal Three

*Take a gander at your magnificent Blossoming Body!*

In Petal Three of the *Designed to Blossom* Course, the Blossoming Bodygraph is thoroughly explored from a variety of perspectives, both conventional and Integral. We look at all that it can tell us about ourselves—from Personality and Design, to the Magnetic Monopole, to the Nine Centers.

Here, in Part Three of the *Designed to Blossom* Resource Book, I'll also be offering up some of the fascinating questions, percolations and paradoxes that have surfaced over the years, in relation to aspects of the Bodygraph. We'll explore how (and whether) our Centers are related to the physical body and where our energy actually comes from. I'll share additional (Integral-friendly) information on Circuitry and the Emotional Wave that I wasn't able to include in the *Designed to Blossom* Course because of space limitations. We'll also touch on the fascinating topics of environment, voices, serendipity and twins! I hope these explorations serve to broaden your perspective and keep your experiment fresh and alive.

## THE 'BLACK AND RED' ISN'T SO 'BLACK AND WHITE'

As described in the *Designed to Blossom* Course, in order to arrive at a complete Blossoming Bodygraph, two calculations are necessary. One is traditionally called the Personality calculation. Represented by all of the black lines in your Bodygraph, the Personality is derived by your actual time of birth, and reflects aspects of your being that you're likely to find in a traditional astrology chart.

The other calculation, which is unique to Human Design, is called the Design Calculation. Represented by all of the red lines in your Bodygraph, this is a prenatal calculation, made exactly 88 days or degrees of the sun, before the day of birth. Some say this is when the soul fully enters the body before we are born.

The Black in your Bodygraph is said to represent **what you already know about yourself**, what you find most easy to relate to. This conscious part of you reflects who and what you think you are.

The Red in your Bodygraph is said to be what you *don't* know about yourself, what you don't have access to. In Human Design, the Red is termed 'unconscious.' Unlike the Freudian or Jungian 'unconscious,' the unconscious in Human Design is more akin to your body's mind, your genetic hardwiring, or your innocence—the inherited aspects of you that can show up suddenly, and as a surprise.

I'd like to add a couple of Integral Human Design perspectives on this subject.

One is that the Bodygraph cannot ever really show a person's level of consciousness. Consciousness is not an intrinsic part of the Human Design imprint; it is what can be developed out of the imprint. We all have the opportunity to come to know and recognize both Red and Black aspects of our Human Design—as a result of our life's journey and our ability to process the feedback we receive from our evolving relationships and environment.

Another is that in the end, Consciousness is all that exists. We all live in a sea of awareness; we are nothing but drops in a boundless ocean of love. On one plane of existence, where individuality and duality exist, we are designed to experience an 'I,' and to live in and through a highly-personalized vessel. On another Plane, we are Consciousness itself. All of us, regardless of how the Red or Black shows up in our Bodygraph, have the potential to connect with this ocean of awareness, our true home.

The last is that the Bodygraph, when combined with sustained contemplation, can actually be used as a frequency-raising tool.

## HOW ARE THE CENTERS RELATED TO THE PHYSICAL BODY?

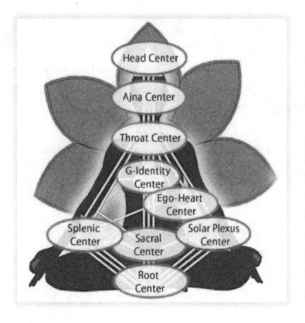

According to official Human Design, each Center (whether Defined or Open, whether currently in a state of blossoming or wilting) is said to correspond to a specific body part, biological system and/or set of organs.

- **HEAD**: Pineal Gland
- **AJNA**: Anterior and Posterior Pituitary Glands
- **THROAT**: Thyroid/ Parathyroid Glands, Metabolism
- **G/IDENTITY**: Liver & Blood
- **EGO**: Stomach, Heart, Gall Bladder & Thymus Gland
- **SACRAL**: Ovaries & Testes
- **SPLENIC**: Lymphatic System, Spleen and T-Cells
- **SOLAR PLEXUS**: Kidneys, Prostate, Pancreas, Nervous System, Lungs

**ROOT**: Adrenal Glands

Some Human Design teachers believe it's misleading to directly tie the Bodygraph's Centers to bodily parts or physical organs, since the Centers don't actually exist in the physical body in the way we might imagine. Steve Rhodes, for example, recommends that we think of a given Center as something more abstract, more akin to an energetic field or set of conditions that can exert influence over certain kinds of activities.

From this perspective, the Throat Center is not an actual throat with vocal chords and parathyroid glands. It doesn't even have exclusive rights to the acts of self-expression or manifestation. It is more like an energetic permission-giver for activities we normally associate with the Throat Center, such as speaking, expressing, metabolizing or manifesting.

Whichever perspective you resonate with most, a basic understanding of a Center's physiological associations can still be useful.

Doing a *life scan* with the Bodygraph in mind can illuminate which parts of your body might be in need of your attention. Let's say you identify an area in your life which is 'wilting' (as described in the *Designed to Blossom* Course), one that carries themes commonly related to the Solar Plexus Center. Perhaps you feel emotionally overstimulated much of the time, or you find yourself unintentionally provoking people, getting into one unproductive conflict after another. Along with doing your de-conditioning work and grounding yourself in your unique Authority, you might want to take a look at the state of your kidneys, prostate, pancreas, nervous system and/or lungs. Your life struggles could be a reflection of or connected to your body's cries for help.

Similarly, doing a *body scan* with the Bodygraph in mind might lead you to a deeper exploration of a life arena or Center theme. If you are experiencing a physical challenge, such as adrenal fatigue, you might benefit from looking more deeply into your relationship with your Root Center. Whether your Root is Open or Defined, its themes (e.g. stress) and related conditioning pressures may be calling out for your loving attention.

Ultimately, it's more important that we rely on our particular truth-detecting systems than our intellects when it comes to deciding what to do for our bodies, and when to do it.

If you're a Generator and you can see that you're struggling with themes usually associated with the Splenic Center, this doesn't mean that you should make a mental decision to do a spleen cleanse, or follow someone's advice about how to heal your lymphatic system. It's better to hold the intention of caring for your spleen, and then allow your Sacral Center to do the decision-making for you. See what comes towards you (via articles, conversations, etc.) and notice what lights you and your body up. Do what you genuinely have energy for, not what your mind has convinced you that you should do. (Be open to responding to something that has absolutely no association whatsoever with the spleen. You know you're honoring your design when you are open to surprise!)

Some people find an understanding of their Primary Health System (PHS) to be a tremendous support for their physical body and all around health. The PHS is an advanced level of Human Design knowledge that focuses primarily on the body and digestion. It recognizes that each body is unique, requiring a particular approach to self-nourishment. According to PHS, the more we honor our body's unique digestive needs, the healthier our bodies will be, and the more we'll thrive as whole beings. Some approaches emphasize *what* gets eaten and how; others emphasize the environment or external conditions under which eating and digestion take place.

Again, being grounded in our actual practice trumps any knowledge we might accumulate about our PHS, no matter how fascinating or seemingly relevant that knowledge may be. PHS addresses only one aspect of what makes a healthy diet. There are many additional ways we can nourish and care for our bodies.

Human Design is ultimately about releasing ourselves from mental decision-making and surrendering to our *Inner Wisdom Keeper*.

**Note:** If your inner Truth Compass genuinely leads you to exploring your PHS, remember that for this information to be useful to you, your birth data needs to be quite accurate. Sometimes just a few minutes can make a big difference. If you don't have super accurate birth data, no need to worry. This knowledge is not necessary to live an authentic, healthy life.

# WHERE DOES OUR ENERGY COME FROM? (THE 'MOTOR' CONTROVERSY)

Typically, Human Design considers four of the nine Centers to be energy Centers, or 'motors': the Sacral Center, the Root Center, the Ego/Heart Center, and the Solar Plexus/Emotional Center (which is on its way to becoming an Awareness Center, like the Ajna and Spleen). Each of these Centers represents a particular kind of energy.

The energy of the Sacral Center is associated with the kind of availability and putt-putt power necessary to respond to the world's needs through service, to maintain sexual fertility, and to sustain creative work. The energy of the Root Center is associated with the fuel we need for life itself, the energy required to initiate, desire, need, move, change, restrain, begin new experiences, etc. The energy associated with the Ego/Heart Center is associated with will power, courage, competition, loyalty and the energy necessary to make meaningful contributions and keep our commitments. Finally, the energy of the Solar Plexus is associated with emotional energy and its various waves.

People who do not have any of these four Centers Defined are often referred to as 'non-energy beings.' They are encouraged to see and accept the fact that they don't have consistent access to energy.

Some people, when they receive this information, become deeply relieved. The 'non-energy' label doesn't bother them at all. In fact, it feels like having a giant weight, or sense of pressure, lifted off their shoulders. Finally, they can allow themselves to relax more and push less, and stop trying to be the exhausting energizer bunnies that they're not.

Others have the opposite response. They feel unseen, diminished and doomed by the non-energy label. Suddenly what they've always experienced as genuine life energy is in question, tossed into a pile of Not-Self rubble.

As you might imagine, there's an energy or motor controversy in the field of Human Design. Some believe that the entire concept of a 'non-energy being' is absurd. Steve Rhodes and others like him don't think Human Design has any way of telling us how much energy we actually have. One person may have all four of their Motors Defined and another none, but they may actually have the same amount of energy.

From this perspective, the only thing our Definition can tell us is what kinds of activities, or under which set of conditions, we're 'allowed' to use our energy, however much energy we happen to have. Instead of seeing the Sacral, Root, Ego/Heart and Solar Plexus as exclusive energy hoarders, these Human Design enthusiasts look to all of the nine Centers as possible (yet conditional) hubs for energy to be used and expressed.

They believe that energy can be used for anything—for inspiring (Head), for analyzing (Ajna), for presenting (Throat), for loving (G-/Identity), for desiring (Ego/Heart), for having fun (Solar Plexus), for surviving (Spleen), for offering a service (Sacral), or for driving something into existence (Root). Centers aren't limited to certain experiences or activities. The Emotional Center isn't the only place where we can experience emotional material. Similarly, we can do anything using any Center, as long as we're honoring the conditions set by whatever happens to be Defined (Gate, Channel, etc.) in that Center.

A Mental Projector may, for example, only have one Channel that connects their Throat Center to their Ajna Center. As long as they're presenting some sort of analysis, or analyzing a presentation, they're going to naturally have all the energy they need for that activity, without needing the energy from any of the four 'Motors.' If the Projector tries to use their energy to do something else, (like serve someone by helping them to survive), they may lose steam. That's all.

This is an alternative perspective that you're free to explore. As Human Design continues to evolve, more interesting, potentially empowering (and paradoxical) perspectives will likely emerge. I can't keep up with it all myself.

Your job isn't to spend all of your precious energy (whether you believe that energy is sourced in your Energy Centers or not) trying to form rigid opinions about what's the ultimate truth in Human Design, or to force those opinions on others. Your job isn't to start making decisions based on your formulated opinions either.

If you find yourself thinking too much about anything in Human Design, you're probably losing the thread of its usefulness.

Stay open, and notice how whatever you're learning impacts you. Chances are you're on the right track if what you're learning:

- frees you up
- increases your self-trust
- makes it easier to be you
- makes you more courageous (when it comes to withstanding pressures to be who you aren't, or to hide who you are)
- opens your heart to yourself and others
- enlivens you
- increases your willingness to experiment, play and explore

# *CIRCUITRY*

When we speak of Circuitry in Human Design, we're referring to pathways that make their way through the Centers and Channels of the Bodygraph. Though not the same thing, these pathways are reminiscent of what we've seen in ancient mystical and health traditions (e.g. the Kabbalah's' tree of life, the meridian network connecting acupuncture points in the body, etc.), and similar to what we see in modern biochemistry and neurology, where neural and hormonal pathways and circuits in the body are acknowledged and studied.

Human Design takes the concept of pathways in the body to an entirely new level. An understanding of Circuitry can shed light on our conditioning and relationships. It can help us see how society as a whole is structured, and how each of us fits into the bigger human picture. From an Integral Human Design perspective, when we deeply contemplate our Circuitry and come to understand the essence of our design, a portal of awakening is opened to us as individuals, and as part of an evolving gene pool. Our Circuitry has the potential to become an intricate vessel for currents of light, triggering the release of our DNA's highest potential, the expansion of our auric field, and the liberation of body-strengthening hormones.

Back to the Human Design Bodygraph. Channels are made up of two Gates. When joined together, these Gates connect two Centers, activating communication between them and creating what we call Definition. They also represent a quantum leap, a move beyond duality and the holding of paradox.

There are three main types of Circuits: Individual, Tribal and Collective. Each main Circuit is composed of sub-circuits.

Essentially, Circuit groups divide all human interaction into fundamental principles. If you're into anthropology, you might recognize some of the language and categorizations used when describing the groups.

I'd like to do a little Circuitry review here. While an understanding of our Circuitry is not essential to our Human Design experiment, it certainly adds a deeper dimension to our experience. Since our Channels often reflect different and competing aspects of our nature, this knowledge can also heighten our sense of compassion for ourselves and each other.

In this section, I will be focusing on how each type of Circuitry can be experienced and expressed when it is Defined in a chart. If you have a whole lot of one type of Circuitry, and very little of another, this can illuminate something profound about your nature, as well as the areas of your life where you're particularly open to being nurtured, or influenced.

Keep in mind, however, that while our Defined Circuitry can shed light on who we are, the streams and pathways represented by the Circuits and Channels reflect archetypal aspects of the human experience.

In the end, it all belongs to all of us. Whether you have full Channels or hanging Gates in a given Circuitry group; whether you are designed to specialize in one Circuitry group through your Definition, or you are attracted to exploring and interacting with a variety of Circuitry themes through your Openness—consider all of it deeply relevant to your life.

Though a bit of what I share will be inspired by Integral Human Design (brought into the world by Richard Rudd, author of the *Gene Keys*, and Werner and Laura Pitzal), it won't reflect the vastness and richness of that body of work. Should your *Inner Wisdom Keeper* feel drawn to going deeper into a *Gene Keys*/Human Design synthesis, I highly recommend an exploration of Integral Human Design.

If you're still just getting started with your experiment, you might want to wait until you feel nice and grounded in your practice. We want any additional explorations you do to support your experiment, not overload your mind with more information than you can handle (fascinating though it may be).

*Integral Human Design: THE STREAM OF LOVE*
*Essence: Love*
*Potential: Creativity*
*Shadow: Chaos*
*Purpose: Impact/Empowerment*

If you have Individual Circuitry in your Bodygraph, you are designed to experience and express your individuality in a specialized and unique way. You are here to do more than maintain the customs and traditions of the culture around you. You are here to be deeply interested in yourself, and through your self-discovery process, to bring something entirely new to the people around you and the world.

You offer your gifts to the world by honoring your uniquely creative impulses, but even more importantly, by simply being yourself. You are what we call a *mutative force*—a living agent of evolution itself. You don't only bring change; you *are* a living, breathing source of change for people. You are responsible for our direction as a species. You are one of a kind. One of your soul's central tasks is to empower others by becoming empowered yourself.

You may not always appreciate being told what to do, or influenced too much by others. There may be times when you're actually 'deaf' to external influences. This deafness can be a saving grace, because your knowing must come from within.

Because of your Individual Circuitry, you will not always feel like you belong. Even if you are a deeply social being, there may always be a part of you that feels like an outsider, or a stranger—a part of you that doesn't easily fit into society. Fitting in is simply not what you're here for.

Sometimes the people around you understand and appreciate the new energy that you're bringing. Sometimes they don't. During the times that they don't, you may feel lonely, misunderstood or depressed. These feelings are perfectly OK, as long as you don't make the mistake of thinking that something is inherently wrong with you.

In fact, one of your biggest gifts to our world is your capacity to bring outsiders into the fold, to make strangers feel welcome and at home. You wouldn't be able to do this if you weren't such a strong Individual. Because you know what it feels like to be an outsider, you can empathize with alienated, vulnerable or marginalized people and help to embrace them.

Having Individual Circuitry can bring with it a tendency towards moodiness and melancholy. Your life can feel unpredictable, marked by alternating experiences of ups and downs, order and chaos, times when you *know*, and times when you're absolutely clueless. Such human tendencies are not only OK, but the very essence, root and source of your genius. They feed the highly fertile soil (or compost!) of your creativity.

You are also a deeply acoustic being. You are deeply nourished when you have something moving to listen to, and when you are listened to by those around you. When you are feeling melancholic, your creative potential comes alive. I invite you to milk your melancholy with resonant music, poetic expressions and artistic explorations. Surrender to your moods by creatively matching and feeding them, instead of trying to snap yourself out of them. As you cultivate the ability to love your lows as much as your highs, you will naturally uncover the gifts hidden in the shadows.

When you resist, rationalize or judge your melancholy, or spend too much of your precious time blaming yourself or everyone around you for the way that you feel, your deeply creative potential is more likely to manifest as a deeply paralyzing depression. In the end, self-acceptance is the deepest medicine for you.

## IF YOU HAVE CENTERING CIRCUITRY...

*Integral Human Design: THE STREAM OF SPIRIT*
*Essence: SPIRIT*
*Potential: CENTEREDNESS*
*Shadow: SELFISHNESS*

If you have Centering Circuitry in your design, you have a specialized gift for conditioning or influencing people. You can get them to behave differently than they normally would. When at your best, your radical love of life and self-embrace are not only thrilling to you, but contagious for others. Just by being who you are, you empower people to love themselves, follow their unique paths, and embrace life with gusto.

To be centered is to respond to life. To live out your Centering destiny, you must be willing to surrender to a future that cannot be known or planned. Self-love doesn't even require self-awareness. Just a deep-belly trust in who you are.

Ultimately, what your soul longs for most is to positively impact others, to empower them to love and celebrate themselves. When this longing isn't met, a deep melancholy and loneliness can arise in you. During these times, remind yourself that you're naturally built for the self- and other-love business. Stay connected to your *Inner Wisdom Keeper*, and it'll all happen naturally, just when it's meant to.

## IF YOU HAVE INTEGRATION CIRCUITRY...

*Integral Human Design: STREAM OF DIGNITY*
*Essence: Dignity*
*Potential: Self-Expression*
*Shadow: Survival*

If you have Integration activations in your Bodygraph, you were blessed with a specialized way of embodying self-empowerment. No matter what else you've got in your chart, there is a big part of you that is here to live in the now! Being (what you might have been trained to think is) selfish is actually quite healthy for you.

I give you full permission to learn and embrace the art of self-love. One of your greatest life lessons is to learn to put yourself first, to be self-absorbed and self-centered.

You are here to become a self-sufficient and empowered person. To fully unleash your gifts, you must first individuate. This means following your own path, embracing your animal nature, your deep and primal impulse to survive and thrive. All of the wonderful contributions you are destined to make must arise out of a deep well of self-love.

## IF YOU HAVE TRIBAL CIRCUITRY...

*Integral Human Design: STREAM OF SYNARCHY*
*Essence: Synarchy*
*Potential: Cooperation*
*Shadow: Fragmentation*

If you have Tribal Circuitry in your Bodygraph, you have a specialized way of engaging with family and your immediate community—whether it be personal, professional or spiritual. You are deeply tactile. You need to be touched.

The Tribal Circuit represents the archetypes of the family, tribe and community. The tribe is the bedrock of human society; it's the foundation upon which we structure and maintain our social codes, our laws and our way of life.

Tribal Circuitry lives and breathes in the material world; it engages us in the aspects of life that we tend to dismiss or diminish as mundane—though if we look carefully enough, we're likely to find a whole lot of magic there! Tribal Circuitry insists that we make our contribution to the whole, so that the whole can thrive. It's all about giving and receiving support.

The tribe has two roles. One is to transform individual ambition into successful teamwork, so that the community is protected, people are supported, and everyone is blessed with a perfectly designed role in the community, one that makes the most of their unique gifts. The other is all about maintaining the well-being, growth and health of the community.

The Tribal heart is communal by nature. It's not individual. That's why in Human Design, we talk about the Tribe as being sticky. It keeps people together, sometimes like glue! Being a Tribal member always requires some sort of individual sacrifice. It's all about the bargain. "I'll scratch your back if you scratch mine." "I'll go shopping if you pick up the kids." "I'll make the money if you make the beds." You get the idea.

If you've got a lot of Tribal Circuitry in your design, you're likely a salt-of-the-earth person, with a deep need for grounded relationships and physical affection. Having 'enough' is important to you, whether it's enough affection, money or food in the fridge. Although you may still be longing for heart's true tribe, and you may be drawn to unconventional groups, having a sense of family and community is important to you.

You have the potential to truly enjoy your work, especially when you feel genuinely valued for your contribution. Learning how to value yourself and what you offer is essential to your self-development journey, even if it hard sometimes. One of your life's biggest lessons is finding that just-right balance between work and rest.

Your Tribal Circuitry can give you a strong sense of touch and smell. If you want to work with someone, meet them in person first if at all possible. See how it feels to shake their hand. Put that sensitive nose of yours to work. It can literally smell the people who belong to your tribe! For people like you, we say, "Don't trust anything (or anyone) unless you can smell it!"

## IF YOU HAVE DEFENSE CIRCUITRY...

*Integral Human Design: STREAM OF HARMONY*
*Essence: Harmony*
*Potential: Relationship*
*Shadow: Isolation*

If you have what is traditionally called Ego or Defense Circuitry, please don't worry. It doesn't mean that you're meant to walk around like a defensive ego maniac! These two Circuit groups are actually about sensuality, sexuality and nurturing. They're all about the ways we humans pass on our love, intelligence and genetic potential to our offspring, so that they can survive and thrive. If you're blessed with this kind of Circuitry, you've got a specialized way of pulling people into the heart of a community, even the most stubborn or fearful outsiders.

Having this type of Circuitry can have a particularly strong influence on your entire Bodygraph. This stream of Channels colors everything. It can even add a Tribal touch to your most individualistic leanings. Even if you *love* to do your own thing, these suckers are going to pull you back into the group, the family, the community…because you've got something important to offer there. Your support is needed.

Keep in mind that community life, in its truest, healthiest form, is always *mutually* supportive. This is why it's so important that you honor your *Inner Wisdom Keeper's* guidance. By trusting your unique way of accessing truth, you increase your chances of ending up supporting the groups, families and communities that can support you too!

## IF YOU HAVE COLLECTIVE CIRCUITRY…

Collective streams govern entire gene pools. If you have Collective Circuitry in your Bodygraph, you are designed to enjoy a deep and specialized interest in humanity. You've also got a special flair for the visual. Because so much of your joy arises out of an experience of life sharing, it's essential that you learn to acknowledge and embrace your essentially social nature.

*There are two types of Collective Circuitry: the Logical and the Abstract (Sensing).*

## IF YOU HAVE LOGICAL CIRCUITRY…

*Integral Human Design: STREAM OF TRUTH*
*Essence: Truth*
*Potential: Service*
*Shadow: Dissatisfaction*

The Logical Circuit is by nature visionary, truth seeking and forward-looking. Your special knack for logic equips you for understanding certain patterns that arise in life. It projects these patterns into the future in order to solve problems and lead humanity down a new-and-improved evolutionary path.

The Collective Circuit is the foundation for scientific thought. You could say that you're a born scientist. Certain subjects are likely to ignite your capacity for focused concentration. You can have an insatiable need for answers—even though the answers you come up with aren't likely to satisfy you enough to keep you from asking more questions!

When gripped by a potent inquiry, you (and others) may find yourself to be skeptical, doubtful and/or detail-oriented. You've got what it takes to enjoy a healthy debate. At times, you may be quite serious and have strong opinions.

Logic is based on repetition and mastery. In relation to some life arenas, you are here to repeat something over and over again until you master it. Your commitment to improving this world of ours can also lead you to become extremely talented in any field that your *Inner Wisdom Keeper* is drawn to.

One of your deepest needs is for your life to reflect a natural sense of rhythm. Without a deep connection to rhythm, you may feel insecure. You have the potential to be very cool-headed at times, and to have a specialized and sophisticated taste.

Deep down, there are few things that matter more to you than being of service. Because the Logical Circuitry isn't directly hooked up to a motor, you may occasionally find yourself looking for energy from others (often in the form of funding!) in order to share your talents with the world, and to find your right collaborators.

In the end, your gift for reading patterns, anticipating trends, and seeing things objectively makes you one of society's specialized and natural leaders.

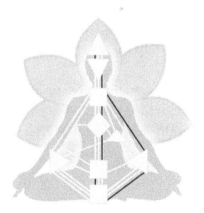

### IF YOU HAVE ABSTRACT (SENSING) CIRCUITRY...

*Integral Human Design: STREAM OF FULFILLMENT*
*Essence: Ecstasy*
*Potential: Fulfillment*
*Shadow: Desire*

The entire Sensing or Abstract Circuit is a magnificent reflection of what Ra Uru Hu called, 'the human experiential way.' It's about achieving the deepest fulfillment through life experience itself. Instead of figuring things logically out ahead of time, you're meant to dive deep into life and swim around. Then, when your experience comes to a natural close, you can get out of the water and reflect upon what your experience has taught you about what it means to be human.

The Stream of Fulfillment represents the spiral of life. It celebrates the cyclical nature of our human experience—each cycle with its beginning, middle and ending. When you're true to yourself and your *Inner*

*Wisdom Keeper*, even the greatest crises can bring about positive change. One of your most essential life lessons is to understand that there is no such thing as success or failure, only discovery.

Since the Abstract or Sensing Circuits are part of the larger Collective Circuit (which is inherently social), your life is also about sharing. Whatever you're especially designed to share—whether it's your feelings, experiences, emotions or reflections—it's for the benefit of the collective, for humanity as a whole. You are here to learn from your own past and from our shared past, for the sake of all of us. We actually *need* you to learn from the past!

Think of yourself as genetically programmed to become a growing repository of wisdom and life experience. A deep desire for change drives you, whether you know it or not. You may feel restless or bored when things don't seem to be changing, or when something you expected to bring a change, doesn't.

When it comes to the part of you that hungers for a particular change or destination, your job is to continually remind yourself that it's all about the journey. What matters is the experience itself. There is no goal worthier in life than to be fully present for an experience, and if you're lucky, to learn something valuable from that experience that you can one day share with others.

That's your Hokey Pokey. That's what it's all about.

This can be hard for you to get, because you're very human, and humans tend to carry hopes and expectations into their life experiences. We think, "If I do this, then I'll get that!" This very normal way of thinking, especially for you, can be a big set up for disappointment. (Because, as you've probably already learned by now, things rarely turn out the way we expect them to.)

Remember, the key for you is to learn to see all of your experiences as opportunities for discovery. All discoveries have value—even the discovery that you're sure as heck never gonna do *that* again!

Another key is to release the expectation that you should be able to make sense out of your life as it's happening. One of your greatest lessons in life is patience. If you are Emotionally Defined, then you better find a way to fall in love with patience. While you're at it, throw in a healthy dose of humor! That'll go a long way.

# OBSERVING OUR EMOTIONS

In Human Design, as in life, there are countless ways to understand and work with our emotions. Here are just a few.

## The Solar Plexus

An entire book can be written about the Solar Plexus and its importance, both from a traditional and Integral Human Design perspective. I share about the Solar Plexus extensively in the *Designed to Blossom* Course, so I won't repeat myself here.

What I do want to stress is that the Solar Plexus is one of the most powerful Centers we've got (whether it's Defined or Open in our Bodygraph), and that the well-being of our whole planet and our evolution as a species depends on our capacity to relate to this Center's inherent themes and energies with awareness, restraint and compassion.

Before I share a few ways we can learn about our emotional lives through Human Design, I'd like to share a taste of the Integral perspective here, based on Werner and Laura Pitzal's and Richard Rudd's work, to whet your appetite should you want to dive deeper into this vast world.

Aside from the brain, the Solar Plexus has the greatest concentration of nervous ganglia in the body. According to esoteric teachings, it's also known as the home of the Astral or Desire body. The themes of the 7 Gates in the Solar Plexus, as described through the *Gene Keys* and their *shadow-potential-essence* keynoting language, shed light on some of the greatest challenges, and possibilities, we face as human beings.

Richard Rudd shows how the 7 shadow states of the Solar Plexus Gates join together to form a gestalt of sorts, one that depicts 'hell on earth.' As illustrated in many ancient teachings and art forms, the 'core hell gates' of the Solar Plexus connect us with the archetypes of Conflict (6), Desire (30), Victimization (55), Reaction (49), Weakness (37), Dishonor (22) and Crisis (36). Yup, that pretty much sums up the state of our world, when we look at it from a shadow perspective!

When we look at our world from the perspective of potential and essence, however, the picture is quite different. It is also the Solar Plexus that provides us with 7 portals through which we can collectively walk into our most wondrous future.

Whenever we engage in the emotional realm with greater self-awareness, (in other words, when we learn not to repress or react out of our shadow experiences, but instead see them clearly, hold them tenderly, and allow them to reveal underlying fears, so that we can increase our compassion for ourselves and others), we are actually increasing our potential to experience and transmit Diplomacy and Peace (6), Lightness and Rapture (30), Empowerment and Freedom (55), Revolution and Rebirth (49), Equality and Tenderness (37), Graciousness and Grace (22), and Compassion and Humanity (36).

So, think of it. Any time you are able to hold any shadow, of your own or someone else's, with awareness, equanimity and care, you are providing the conditions that will allow the highest or (deepest) potential of that very Gate or *Gene Key* to unfold. Since our DNA operates within a holographic field within the body, every Gate is connected to every other Gate, and Channel and Center. It's all interconnected.

I could go on and on here, but mostly, I want to plant these seeds of possibility inside of you, so that they can gestate and grow over time, and you can fall in love with your Solar Plexus (whether it is Open or Defined), and be less afraid of its occasional intensity.

I also invite you to keep all I've just shared in mind as we move through this Petal and explore topics like the Emotional Wave, Openness, melancholy and hormones. We don't have to be victimized by any aspect of our Human Design. In the end, it is our perception of and attitude towards our Human Design that determines our experience of it and its expression.

## The Emotional Wave

People whose Authorities are centered in the Solar Plexus have what we call an 'emotional wave.' The emotional wave reflects a specialized internal chemistry or emotional climate inside of a person. Its particular feel, movement and nature exists independently of where the person is, or who they're with.

If you have one or more emotional waves, know that you have the capacity to learn how to surf them with a combination of awareness, skill, relaxation and excitement. You don't need to continuously get sucked in and tossed around by them.

If you are Emotionally Defined, this also doesn't mean that you're so jam-packed with your own emotional material that you're completely incapable of being sensitive to what's happening around you or the feelings of others. It just means that there is a distinct, deep and rich quality and movement to your emotional life, and, perhaps even more importantly, a tendency to metabolize truth and find clarity over time.

An emotional wave's ebb and flow can be experienced quite differently, depending on who you are and how you're designed. One person's wave might carry them back and forth between states of hope and pain, experiences of mini-deaths and rebirths, or simply between times of high energy and low energy.

There are several kinds of waves for Emotionally Defined people—Tribal, Individual and Collective. Each wave reflects the Circuitry or Stream it's a part of, with its own trajectory and rhythm.

Without going into too much detail, a Tribal wave usually involves some kind of a build-up (or ratcheting up) of energy, a slow but steady movement towards a peak of hope, optimism, energy and power, followed by a sudden crash. The crash may seem to be catalyzed by something external, like an insensitive remark or an angry look, but the emotional system is usually already sensitized and primed for a dip. Depending on a person's level of self-awareness, emotional maturity and capacity to feel fully without reactivity or over-analysis, a dip or crash may bring about a wonderfully healthy release, or lead to a destructively reactive explosion.

While the pain of the Tribal wave comes like a crash, the pain of the Individual wave moves like a pulse. People with this kind of wave can putter along for quite some time, not necessarily feeling emotional, or even identifying as emotional beings. Then, all of a sudden, their emotional state can shoot straight up like a rocket, or plunge way down. When they're up, life is fantastic and all is aglow. When they're down, it can feel like getting hit by a tidal wave of melancholy. They can easily lose perspective and have trouble believing that they'll ever feel good again. Understanding that they're only experiencing a wave, and that hope will always return to them if they relax and trust (and get creative!) is key to their awakening process.

The pain of the Collective wave is said to be cyclical. Unlike the sudden rises and crashes of the previous waves, Collective waves are more reliable, in that they constantly move up and down like a never-ending landscape of hills (or like a roller coaster!). For people with this type of wave, it's about learning to enjoy the ride, and to know that there may be times in their life when they feel a deep sense of belonging, and other times when they don't. That's perfectly normal. Everything changes, and it's all OK.

Some people have only one kind of wave, lending a certain predictability to the pattern of their inner emotional life. Others have two or three kinds, all intertwining in a dynamic (and not so easily trackable) dance. Some people have Emotional Definition that is conscious and accessible, while the emotional life of others lives largely beneath the surface of their awareness. Many people have some combination of the two.

If we've got an emotional wave—or we're emotionally overwhelmed for whatever reason—it can be tempting to blame how we feel on someone else or the situation we're in, or if we tend to internalize, on ourselves.

Whether we're experiencing a crash, dip, spike, pulse, explosion or downward pull, (or we've got an Open Solar Plexus and are amplifying what we're picking up from an emotionally charged environment), avoiding the temptation to lash out—or over-analyze—is key. When we can be with our emotions without immediately reacting, crashes become grounding cleanses, dips turn into creative dives, and conflicts become portals to intimacy.

While Human Design offers useful descriptions of the various emotional waves, you may or may not relate to them. If you are Emotionally Defined, I encourage you to explore the unique experience of your own wave/s. Here are a few questions to get you started:

- If you were to describe the internal movements of your emotional life to someone, what would you say?
- How quickly would you say your wave/s move through you?
- Would you say your wave is steady and predictable? Sudden and unexpected?
- What have you found to be most helpful when working with emotional material?

## The Open Solar Plexus

The emotional lives of people with an Open Solar Plexus can be greatly influenced by the emotional climate around them...not just influenced, but amplified. So much of what I just described about emotional waves is likely experienced by people with Open Emotional Centers, times one hundred!

In fact, if anyone is likely to feel emotionally flooded or identify as super emotional, it's those of us with an Open Solar Plexus. We must learn to work with all of the same temptations that Emotionally Defined people do: the temptation to over-react, over-analyze, blame others, blame ourselves. Because our nervous systems aren't quite as well-equipped to deal with emotionally stormy weather, we run an even higher risk of trying to 'get lost,' losing ourselves, or losing it completely.

When we are Open Emotionally, it doesn't mean we don't have our own emotional life. It just means that our emotional lives are deeply impacted by, interacting with, and amplified by the emotional field around us. Our process requires a little extra discernment. In the end, it doesn't matter where our feelings come from. If we're feeling them, they're our responsibility. Whether we become emotionally wise and constructive communicators, or reactive blaming nutcases, is up to us.

If you have an Open Solar Plexus, I encourage you to explore your own emotional life. Here are a few questions to get you started:

- What helps you discern between feelings that are 'yours' (sourced from within) and feelings that seem to be coming through your interactions with (and reactions to) others in your environment? How can you tell the difference?

- Think of a time when your ability to make such a discernment was helpful to you, and/or a relationship.

- How do you experience your emotional life when you're alone?

- When you're with others?

- With certain others?

- How have you learned to work with your own reactivity? What has helped you learn to witness and embrace whatever you're feeling, without letting the feelings take over?

- Can you tell the difference between conflicts that are worth having, even if they feel uncomfortable, and conflicts that are best walked away from? If so, how? Think of an example of each.

- What tools have helped you turn potentially unconstructive conflicts into intimacy-building conversations?

## Creative Melancholy

As shared earlier in the Circuitry section, many of us have what we call Individual Circuitry. We don't have to have a full Individual Circuitry Channel in order to be full participants in the Stream of Love and Creativity. The emotional theme of melancholy in relation to the creative process may play more of an obvious role for some of us than others, but we are all artists of life. We are all creative beings.

Melancholy is an essential part of the creative process. It's the primordial soup out of which form arises; it's the darkness of Winter which gives birth to the Spring. As essential as it is, it can be hard to be with and surrender to. Many of us judge our melancholy, seeing it as bad or a meaningless form of stuckness.

When we strongly resist the dark, or desperately cling to the light, we not only risk falling into a real depression, but missing out on so much of our creative potential.

Regardless of how much Individual Circuitry you've got in your Bodygraph, I encourage you to explore your own relationship to sadness, darkness, stuckness and the experience of melancholy.

- Are these states ones you can relate to? If so, how? When are you most likely to experience them?

- Have you learned how to be with and allow for dark nights of the soul in your life? If so, what and who helped you cultivate this kind of courage?

- Can you think of a time that you surrendered to your melancholy, and something beautiful came out of the experience? An inner realization? A closer relationship? A creative project?

- Can you think of a time when you resisted feeling low, and things got even worse?

- How can you acknowledge the creative being in you even more?

## The Role of Hormones

One can't underestimate the role of hormones in our emotional lives. I encourage you to explore the role hormones have played in your own emotional journey.

- Have you noticed over the years, for example, that your relationship to your feelings have changed—in ways that seem more biologically or hormonally related than anything else?

You're likely to find that your unique relationship to the emotional realm is a mysterious weave of all of the above, and more!

# CAN EMOTIONAL BEINGS EXPERIENCE MAGIC AND SERENDIPITY?

Although people with Emotional Definition are often (wisely) encouraged to take their time before leaping into new relationships and experiences, this doesn't mean that they never get to experience magic or spontaneity. When we're true to ourselves, no matter our design, synergistic and divinely orchestrated experiences are our birthrights. Things tend to move more easily, effortlessly and seemingly quickly when we surrender to the natural current of our genius.

Even when it comes to the realm of decision-making, I have witnessed quick, serendipitous manifestations occur in the lives of Emotionally Defined people, whether they are Manifestors, Generators or Projectors. From the outside (even inside!), the decision-making experience looked and felt quite spontaneous. There was no waiting, no 'playing hard to get'—just instant, joyful opportunity turning into action.

One aspect of the Emotional metabolizing process that we tend to overlook is the fact that it's actually happening all of the time, often beneath the surface. Emotionally Defined beings don't always know when an emotional process of clarity-finding has actually been initiated.

An Emotional Manifestor may have planted a deep longing or creative inspiration years ago. For years, their emotional system may have been mulling it over, digesting and crystallizing it at a deep subconscious level. An Emotional Projector may have received an invitation into a vocation long ago that for whatever reason went underground, until it suddenly reappears. An Emotional Generator may have attracted an opportunity, relationship or inspiration that they forgot all about, until it bubbles back into their memory.

When this happens, Emotional beings can have unusual experiences that feel a lot like successful and spontaneous decision-making. Though on the surface it looks like they're leaping without waiting out their wave, the truth is that their wave has been at work behind the scenes, and an underground clarity seed's sprouting time has come, without their having had to endlessly monitor their inner process, much less remember that it was happening!

Few things feel more wonderful than when things instantly fall into place, when a percolating inspiration is ripened within the Manifestor, an old invitation becomes relevant to a Projector, or a forgotten opportunity comes to life for a Generator.

If you're Emotionally Defined, take heart. You get to have some magic and synchronicity in your life…even in the realm of decision-making. There will be times when a well-digested growth process will be ready to harvest, and it will feel like a sudden gift from the Goddesses and Gods. I encourage you to enjoy those seemingly miraculous experiences when they come.

Knowing that this is possible can give you the incentive to let go, relax and take your time around decision-making most of the time. So much is happening beneath the surface. You're constantly pregnant with something wonderful. Keep befriending your depth-full ways and falling in love with patience. Slow and steady (most of the time) wins the race. Every once in a while, you get to win a race you didn't even realize you were running!

# WHERE DO OUR VOICES COME FROM?

There are several ways to look at the voice when it comes to Human Design (aside from the bizarre fact that Ra Uru Hu, the founder of Human Design itself, received the entire download of this system through an entity he called *The Voice!*).

## The Voices of the Throat Center

The Throat Center is commonly associated with the voice—in the verbal sense. (The Sacral Center has a voice of its own, but it's not verbal.) The Throat is where the words come out.

(Whether those words are actually speaking our truth, or speaking on behalf of our conditioning is an entirely different story! I won't address that here, since I share so much about it in the *Designed to Blossom* Course.)

There are 11 Gates—or *Gene Keys*—coming out of the Throat. Each of them is said to correspond to a particular kind of verbal expression. If you happen to have one or more of these Gates 'colored in' or Defined, you are more likely to verbally express yourself in the way that corresponds with the specific Gate/s.

Qualifiers: If your Throat Center is Open (white or transparent in the Bodygraph), your verbal expression may be quite impacted by where you are and who you're with. Certain people or environments might bring out certain voices in you. Some of these voices (in cases where you have 'colored in' or hanging Gates in your Throat Center) will be connected to your own innate Nature, waking up dormant aspects of your voice. Some of the voices might be more reflective of the people around you. You may sometimes find yourself speaking in ways that feel a bit foreign or unusual.

If your Throat Center is Defined, certain ways of verbally expressing yourself will be more stable and consistent. If a particular Gate in your Throat Center is red, you may not necessarily recognize or feel like you have conscious control over the associated verbal tendency. If a Gate is black, you're more likely to have awareness and conscious access to it.

**Here's a list of the verbal expression styles or orientations that are associated with the 11 Gates of the Throat Center:**

(To see which of these may be playing a role in your expressive life, take a look at your Bodygraph. Notice if any of the following Gates have red, black or striped lines coming out of them.)

- Gate 23:  "I know or not."
- Gate 8:  "I know I can make a contribution or not."
- Gate 20:  "I am now or not."
- Gate 16:  "I experiment (identify) or not."
- Gate 35:  "I experience (I feel) or not."
- Gate 45:  "I have or not."
- Gate 12:  "I know I can try or not."
- Gate 62:  "I think or not."
- Gate 56:  "I believe or not."
- Gate 31:  "I lead or not."
- Gate 33:  "I remember or not."

Nothing is written in stone here. These simple statements are pointing at tendencies to focus one's expression in a given direction, and our Centers aren't the same thing as our actual biological organs or functions. (See "How are the Centers Related to the Physical Body.")

Also, if your Throat is completely Open (white), it just means that you have limitless potential to express yourself in lots of ways, depending on your circumstance.

## The Voice of our Centers

Each Center represents an aspect of life. For example, the Solar Plexus represents our emotional life and nervous system. It follows that when we're expressing feelings, or something that relates to the emotional realm, we may be speaking on behalf of something that's going on in our Solar Plexus. This doesn't guarantee that whatever comes out of our mouth will always express or reflect a clear, pure, emotional truth. That will depend on so many aspects of our design, conditioning, life experience, and our overall maturity level.

It also doesn't mean that our Solar Plexus has exclusive rights to all emotional energies and experiences. (See the section below.)

Similarly, since the Spleen is the seat of our intuition, immune system, and our experience of fear, our Splenic Center may be activated when we find its related themes showing up in our speech (i.e. "I have a hunch…", "That doesn't feel healthy for me…", "I'm terrified of…", etc.).

This doesn't mean that what we're saying is the ultimate truth, or something we need to listen to when making decisions. It just means that when we speak about certain things that are associated with the various Centers (which in a way are archetypes), chances are those Centers are being lit up in some way.

The Voice of our Circuitry

As I shared earlier, each main Circuitry or Stream in the Human Design Bodygraph relates to one or more of our senses…all of which can impact our voice, how we express ourselves, and what we speak about. For example:

- Collective Circuitry has to do with sight and taste. ("I like the look of that!" "I didn't like the taste of that conversation.")
- Tribal Circuitry has to do with touch and smell. ("She gives me the goosebumps." "Something stinks about this deal.")
- Individual Circuitry has to do with hearing. ("I hear bologna.")

As you become increasingly aware of your voice, see if the Streams are speaking through you!

# WHAT DOES THE BODYGRAPH HAVE TO SAY ABOUT ENVIRONMENT?

Anyone who catches the Human Design bug soon discovers that this system goes very deep. Not only does the *location* of each Gate in the Bodygraph mean something, but each Gate in the Bodygraph is encoded with layers of information. Beneath each of the 64 Gates, you'll find 6 Lines; beneath the Lines, you'll find 6 Colors; beneath the Colors, you'll find 6 Tones, and more. Each location, layer and number means something.

When we want to learn which kind of *Environment* we're most likely to thrive in, we look to the Colors and Tones beneath the Gates that are associated with the Nodes on the Design (the red/unconscious) side of your Bodygraph. Whew! That was an eyeful! (Keep in mind that the deeper you go into your chart, the more precise your birth time needs to be in order for the information to be accurate, thus helpful.)

According to Human Design, when you're in the right Environment, you're more likely to draw the right people and experiences into your life. You're also more likely to have the right perspective or view of the world. Keep in mind that you don't need to live full-time in a given environment in order to thrive. You just need to have a sufficient amount of access to it, whatever works for you.

In my experience, you really don't need to know your design at this level. If you genuinely experiment with the basics of your design (as presented in the *Designed to Blossom* Foundational Course and Creative Workbook), your *Inner Wisdom Keeper* will naturally guide you to your right environment/s.

Here's a taste more of this world if you are genuinely drawn to going deeper.

There are 6 different Environments (at the Color level):

**The Cave**

People with this Color tend to do well—if and when they need to reground themselves—in a relatively enclosed, safe space, where there aren't too many windows or openings, and not too much going on. Some of them, depending on other aspects of their design, do well with just one other person at a time. Others can have more activity going on around them, as long as they're safely in the background and have some control over who enters the space and how long they stay.

**The Market**

These people tend to do well out in the 'market place'—where there's lots of hustle and bustle. Some of them do best when they're going out for a very specific purpose. Others do best when they're simply putting their bodies in an urban, lively or busy environment and observing. For them it's about being in the mix, engaging in inspiring and practical exchanges with other people who are also in the mix.

**The Kitchen**

These people really thrive, literally, in the kitchen...a gathering place where alchemy of all sorts happens. Some tend to thrive in 'wet' or humid environments—whether they're kitchens or laboratories. Others prefer dry, desert, hot or temperature-controlled kitchens/settings. What matters for these people is that their environments fuel some kind of transformation. It can be physical, emotional or spiritual. Whatever (or whoever) goes into the kitchen must come out...changed!

**The Mountain**

These people do best when they're up high, looking out at the world. Even a little oxygen deprivation can do them good. When they're at a high altitude, they tend to think clearly. Though being on an actual mountain top is sheer bliss for some, others are just as happy in city apartments that are above ground floor, or in an office situated at the highest point of a little town. What matters most is that they feel they've got room to breathe, think and gain that bigger perspective. Others need no more than a simple perch to sit upon, where they can observe and witness what's going on around them.

**The Valley**

These people need a certain kind of acoustic environment to thrive. They do well when it feels like they're down in the valley floor. Some really need to have sounds coming directly at them, like through headphones or one-on-one conversations. Others do best when they can take in noises 'from the side,' in a more diffused way. It's all about being where civilization is, where people and things are coming through, moving from one place to another, and stopping along the way for a nice chat or meaningful exchange.

**The Shore**

These people tend to thrive in areas that are transitory, places that are 'at the edge.' Some do best by a coast, a river, or some kind of natural shore. For others, it's not about being by an actual body of water. It's about being between two different kinds of places, between two different kinds of energies. They may be right at the transition between the big city and the suburbs, or between the suburbs and the countryside. What matters is that they have the opportunity to look out at a different world, with a different rhythm and feel. They may move back and forth between the worlds, or simply enjoy knowing that another world is just around the corner.

Remember an environment is correct for us if it inspires our 'right perspective.' It's not necessarily about getting us to do or be anything in particular.

Once you're sufficiently grounded in your Human Design experiment, you may want to find a Human Design professional who can help you go much deeper into this subject. I'm just scratching the surface here.

In the meantime, there's so much you can learn from simply paying attention to how various environments make you feel, what they bring out in you, how they impact your worldview, your feelings, your sense of safety, belonging and groundedness. If you've got an Open G-/Identity Center, you're likely to be engaged in this exploration already.

These are suggestions if it feels fun and relevant and empowering. Otherwise, I wouldn't get my environmental panties in a bunch!

# WHAT IF TWO PEOPLE HAVE THE EXACT SAME BODYGRAPH?

Many Human Design enthusiasts want to know how this system applies to twins, or people who are born with the exact same Bodygraph.

When twins are born extremely close together, the detectable differences between their Bodygraphs typically show up beneath the surface, in the deeper layers I mentioned earlier (e.g. Lines, Colors, Tones, Bases, etc.). When the birth time for each twin is extremely accurate, an exploration of these differences can be fascinating (though not necessary).

One of the things I really love about **Human Design** is how it emphasizes the intersection between Nature and Nurture. We've all got our unique Definition, or genetic blueprint or potential, and we've got our Openness, or particular way of taking in and interacting with the world around us.

None of us are static beings operating in a linear vacuum. We're continually responding to our inner and outer environments, making sense of and finding ways to relate to the ever-changing contexts in which we find ourselves. Cutting-edge thinkers like Bruce Lipton—the cellular biologist who helped us understand the intelligence of the cellular membrane and challenged the whole notion of the 'selfish gene'—illuminate how the 'environment' we create through our feelings, beliefs and attitudes (often arising out of our life experiences) can actually directly impact our DNA. In other words, everything impacts everything. We have far more control over our body and internal chemistry than we ever imagined.

Most people with siblings understand the influential power of seemingly simple 'Nurture' distinctions like birth order. My sister and I grew up in the same house, and while we certainly share many of the same perspectives and sense of humor, we have completely different relationships to our parents and memories from our past.

So many factors can serve to separate siblings' experience of themselves and/or their shared reality. Even siblings with identical designs and the same parents can feel like strangers growing up on different planets. One might have been adopted and the other not. One may have experienced more physical or emotional hardship than the other, for seemingly random reasons. One parent may simply have reacted to them differently than the other.

It's certainly easy to see how two people born with identical Bodygraphs, but on opposite sides of the planet, could evolve in completely different ways.

When it comes to genetically identical twins, born minutes apart, living in the same household, and in the same socio-cultural context, it gets a little more interesting.

Here's a fascinating phenomenon that I've witnessed in an identical twin pair.

Especially during their younger years, before they had the chance to individuate from their parents or each other, they expressed a beautiful, dynamic wholeness between them. They each naturally gravitated towards expressing a pole of a given 'theme continuum.' One led, the other followed; one pushed, the other gave in; one protected, the other expressed vulnerability. It was as if they held *shadows* and *gifts* for each other.

Just when their parents thought they had each of their children's personalities all figured out, they'd pull a switcheroo!

In many ways, it felt like they were one being, emanating a multi-faceted essence together as they organically took turns embodying polar aspects of certain character qualities, strengths and struggles. Deep down, we all felt that they were dancing the same dance, that they were made of the same substance.

Life then happened, as it happens for all of us. Their lives unfolded, bringing limitless opportunities for their essentially same Nature to interact with an increasingly diversified Nurturing environment. Some of their experiences were chosen (e.g. they each chose their friends, played their own instruments, and felt drawn to their own extra-curricular activities). Some of their experiences weren't so chosen. One, for example, got a great teacher; the other a bad one. One experienced a heartbreak; the other a breakthrough. One won a soccer game; the other got hit with a health curve ball. One had a streak of bad luck; the other a lucky streak.

As life unfolded for the twins, their differences amplified—not just their life experiences, but their attitudes towards those experiences. They felt less and less like one essence expressing itself differently, and more like different people reflecting different essences.

Even though a Human Design enthusiast might offer similar guidance to these two beings today, in relation to their decision-making process, the opportunities that would come to them, their perception of those opportunities, and their way of engaging with them would be infinitely different. I wouldn't be surprised if one might be very receptive to something like Human Design at this point, and the other not at all.

So it is with all of us. Our combined positive and painful experiences, and our responses to them, have every bit as much impact on our DNA blueprint as our blueprint has on our approach to life. Each micro-decision we make—whether we're consciously choosing an experience or a response to an experience we didn't choose—serves to launch our magnificently unique, forever-evolving and differentiated path.

This is why all of us can use genuinely nurturing support throughout our life. The best kind of support is that which respects the core of who we are, and empowers us to meet whatever happens with grace, authenticity and self-respect, and encourages us to dance with life, as opposed to controlling it.

(P.S. Don't forget karma!)

# Synthesize Your Parts: Petal Four

*Enjoy the best of both worlds:*
*your innate gifts and your beautiful receptivity!*

In Petal Four of the *Designed to Blossom* Course, we take a deep dive into the world of 'Nature and Nurture.' We look at the intricate relationship between Definition and Openness in the Human Design System, and take time to explore the beauty and challenges of Openness. Holding the understanding that all Centers have their strengths and vulnerabilities, regardless of their state of Definition, we then take ourselves through a nine-Centered check-up, asking ourselves, "How are my Centers are doing? Are they blooming or wilting?"

Here in the *Designed to Blossom* Resource Book, we'll be reflecting on the fascinating subject of Openness from a variety of perspectives. After entertaining an alternative view on Openness, we'll take a stroll through the common pulls of each Open Center. We'll learn about other people's experiences with receptivity, and tackle themes such as shame and aloneness. We'll even examine whether our angry thoughts can be felt long-distance.

## WE ARE ALL OH-SO-OPEN!

Before we take a look at the pull of the nine Open Centers through a more traditional Human Design prism, I'd like to offer an alternative view which puts our Definition and Openness into perspective. In Human Design, we tend to put a whole lot of emphasis on Definition, on the Red and Black aspects of our Bodygraphs. We are taught to believe that our highly unique essence can be captured and True Nature described by what is colored in. While so much is determined by our Definition (Type, Strategy, Authority, etc.), it can be helpful to remember that we are all approximately 99.9% Open. ***All of us*** are, regardless of how many of our Centers are Defined. Our Human Design imprint is very important, but it only describes a tiny percentage of our humanness.

In Human Design circles, we also learn that conditioning only happens through our Openness. If we have a lot of Open Centers, we think of ourselves as particularly vulnerable to conditioning. If we see someone with very few or no Open Centers, we tend to think of them as impenetrable, or protected from conditioning.

Though an exploration of our Open Centers can be extremely revealing and helpful, let's remember that in the end, we are all conditioned, just in different ways. Whether Open or Defined, *all* Centers (and aspects of our designs) can be impacted by our relationships and surroundings. Similarly, we all have the potential to give into, or withstand, the influence of negative conditioning. Our levels of awareness, maturity, mindfulness and overall resiliency will ultimately determine this potential. With this in mind, I'd like to take a walk through the nine Open Centers with you.

## *The Pull of Your Open Head Center*

Whether Defined or Open, the Head Center represents the very seat—and pressure—of Consciousness itself. It is always exerting pressure on the Ajna Center (our processing minds), giving it constant food for thought. The Head Center is here to make sure that we keep seeking answers to life's big questions, that we better understand our past so that we can plan for a better future, that we keep evolving as beings capable of boundless awareness. It's all about inspiration.

If you have an Open Head Center, you are designed to be deeply receptive to new insights and to love mental sparks. You genuinely enjoy being filled up with inspiration. You can even enjoy a certain amount of mental pressure, as long as you can resist the urge to become overwhelmed or over-identified with all of the inspiring thoughts, questions and information flowing into that Open Head of yours.

As fun as being mentally inspired can be, it can also be a burden. It can bring up a lot of mental anxiety. The Head Center is usually focused on figuring out those things that are very hard to figure out, or even grasp.

If you have an Open Head Center, and you're around someone with a Defined one, you may not only feel 'inspired,' you may feel under a lot of pressure to think, and to think in the particular way that *they* tend to think.

If you don't understand how your Open Head is designed to work, you can suffer from an overdose of mental pressure. Wherever you are Open, you are not only receiving pressures and energies, but amplifying them (and if you're not careful, identifying with them).

You can absorb other peoples' worries, questions and mental conundrums like nobody's business. You can end up spending WAY too much of your precious time and energy being plagued by doubt and confusion, wracking your brain to understand things you actually don't need to understand, and trying to answer questions that aren't even relevant to your life, just because someone else in the near vicinity happens to spout out some thought.

Let's say someone strolls into your life, gets you to think about a dilemma, and insists that it needs to be resolved right now. If you're not sufficiently practiced at trusting that *Inner Wisdom Keeper* of yours, you're likely to feel a strong sense of urgency and responsibility to resolve this dilemma mentally.

The truth is, if it's not *your* dilemma (which it rarely is), it actually isn't your responsibility to take on the burden of figuring it all out.

Your life doesn't depend on your figuring anything out mentally, although you may need to remind yourself of this on occasion! Think of your Open Head like an open window. Inspiration is meant to come in, and it is meant to go out. Just like the breath. Inhale. Exhale. Ahhhhh…

Mental inspiration is here for your enjoyment. It's not to be clung to or wrung out to a point of exasperation.

As an Open Head being, the process by which you conceptualize is supposed to be influenced, thus conditioned, from the outside. You're not supposed to have a very specialized or patterned style of thinking.

If your Ajna Center is connected to your Throat Center, you might have a specialized way of expressing what's on your mind, but *what's on your mind* will greatly reflect what's on the minds of the people around you.

Ideally, as you learn to hold your own and everyone else's thinking lightly, you have the potential to become incredibly wise about Inspiration itself. You can get really good at recognizing genuinely inspiring people, and at avoiding getting taken in by people who may seem certain about what they're talking about, but actually have no clue. (We certainly have a bunch of those walking around the planet these days!)

From now on, I invite you to pay attention to the mental problems, doubts, challenges and questions that you find your mind wrestling with. Ask yourself:

- Is this question really mine?
- Is it actually relevant to my own life?
- Even if it might be relevant one day, is it relevant at this moment?

If you get a 'no,' see if you can let it go. Practice those deep mental exhales!

Ahhhhh…

If you find yourself trying to answer other people's questions, and feeling increasingly anxious, at the very least, give yourself a little break. Release the urgency. Instead of going crazy trying to solve and figure out, instead of rushing to some kind of action in order to release the mental pressure you're feeling, just listen, reflect, wonder with them.

One of your gifts is mental patience. You have the potential to emanate a deep trust in the natural unfoldment of understanding. You can help those whose brains hurt from thinking too much to take a deep breath, and to trust that life generally has a way of working itself out, even when the mind hasn't figured it all out.

When your mental body is feeling overly charged, you might want to withdraw into a calm space. Let yourself zone out a bit. Practice a form of meditation that isn't too mentally taxing. Try walking or movement meditation. Or knitting. Or doodling.

If your Open Head can't let the thinking go, see if you can simply hold the contents of your mind as lightly as possible. Consider finding something else to fill up your mind for a while. Listen to some good music, or a fascinating podcast. Read a book. You get the idea.

## THE PULL OF YOUR OPEN AJNA

People with a Defined Ajna Center have wonderfully strong minds, with specialized ways of thinking and processing information.

If you have an Open Ajna Center, you've got a wonderful mind too, one that is both literally and figuratively 'open'! Your mind is built to process information in all sorts of ways. Freud, Jung, Einstein all had Open Ajna Centers. Your mind, like theirs, is not designed to be consistent, or certain. It's designed to be receptive, playful, fluid, adaptable, creative, versatile, dynamic and forever-synthesizing. If you leave it be, it might even bless you with blissful moments of pure awareness and boundless emptiness.

Your kind of intelligence is supposed to be ever-changing. Your mind is built to soak up new ideas and concepts like a sponge. It can store huge amounts of information as memory. Though you can't always access what you've remembered at will (which can be frustrating at times), certain people can ignite that memory of yours, and unleash all sorts of inspiring information from you. Your mind is here to surprise and delight you, as well as the people around you.

Because you can adapt to the way others think, you also carry the potential to successfully converse with just about anyone. Your mind's limitless potential and ability to weave together various strands of thinking and understanding can make it quite helpful to others. It makes a great Outer Authority.

All minds have what Human Design calls Outer Authority—the capacity to be 'authoritative' (mentally helpful) for others. Minds, whether Open or Defined, are here to help us to do our research. They help us communicate about everything we learn and have come to understand. Ultimately, they help us share the essence of what it is to be human—with their multi-dimensional prisms. They can look back in time and out towards the future. They can even contemplate life's deepest philosophical and spiritual questions, 'effing' the ineffable.

No minds have Inner Authority, and our minds are particularly helpless as an inner Authority.

It doesn't matter how brilliant your mind is. It's not built for figuring out what the heck you're supposed to do with your life.

The mind is essentially dualistic in the way it processes information. It can only show you the advantages and disadvantages of any decision you're about to make. The mind can do an incredible job of researching a decision, of setting up a perspective, but it doesn't have the ability to actually judge one side over the other.

It also doesn't have direct access to energy.

The Ajna Center is an Awareness Center, not a motor. Only Centers that are associated with motors have the capacity to do, express, will or manifest.

Interestingly, the Ajna Center is the only Awareness Center that is completely locked away from the body's energy systems. It not only isn't a motor; it has no direct access to a motor.

This is actually a good thing! If we could immediately act on every thought that whips through our Monkey Minds, we'd all be in trouble. As it is, we give our minds much more power than they deserve. Much of the time, they take that power and act like petty, fickle dictators.

Can you remember a time when you were trying to make up your mind about something, and you made a list of pro's and con's? If you're like most people, you probably ended up with lists on both sides of relatively equal length, leaving you even more confused than when you started.

Either that, or you actually ended up with a clear winner. Despite your ability to see the obvious choice, you couldn't bring yourself to make it.

These kinds of experiences point to the fact that there's something else inside of us, an *Inner Wisdom Keeper*, a way of knowing that transcends logic. It takes courage to resist doing the 'reasonable' thing, just as it takes courage to trust and act upon your true guidance system. No wonder why many people end up either lost and paralyzed with indecision, or pushing themselves to take the logically-approved path, only to deal with an aftermath of mental doubt and second-guessing. "Did I do the right thing? The wrong thing? What might have happened if I did something else?"

It's no surprise that all of our anxiety Gates sit up in the Ajna Center.

As an Open Ajna being, the quality or intensity of your thought process is going to be dependent on who you're with. Whether you are thinking logically, abstractly or mystically can actually depend a great deal on the Definition of the mind sitting next to you.

If you're with someone with a Defined Mind, for example, and they're experiencing some mental anxiety, you can experience a LOT of mental anxiety. If you're sitting next to someone who's longing to quit their job and travel to a distant land, you can start wondering whether that's something you should do!

Your impressionable mind can leave you vulnerable to identifying with other people's thoughts, concepts, opinions, judgments and worries.

Our Open Centers can reflect our greatest potential, as well as our greatest confusion.
Your mind can either panic or bliss out in an encounter with emptiness. Your mind can either feel uncomfortably flooded by or passionately bathed in a world of thought.

If you have an Open Ajna, you might fall into the common trap of negatively comparing yourself to people with Defined Ajnas with their air of certainty. It's likely that you wish you experienced more mental certainty yourself.

You might wonder why you have trouble sustaining a consistent thought process when you're alone. You might feel totally sure of something one moment, and then suddenly, question the whole kit and caboodle—if you haven't lost the train of thought all together.

While some people with Open Ajnas tend to devalue the nature of their own minds, some go in the opposite direction. (The 'direction a person goes' will likely depend on familial and cultural conditioning.) These people become total intellectuals, studying everything under the sun, collecting reams of information, and spending their whole lives striving for and claiming mental certainty, even when they don't actually have it.

Despite their efforts, they rarely feel that sense of peace they're looking for. Though others might not see it, they can feel very anxious deep down, and suffer from a deep fear of being alone.

If you have an Open Ajna Center, your ticket to peace and freedom in this life, is to stop identifying with your thoughts, and to surrender to the magic of not knowing something…until suddenly, you know.

The more easily you can say, "Actually, I don't know," the better.
Give it a try. "I don't know."
Let those words roll right off your tongue.
Get *really* good at saying that. You won't regret it.

When you let go of trying to make sense of your life with your mind, of having to be absolutely sure of anything, you can share so many ways of thinking with others, and be totally free of prejudice and mental judgment.

One of the great and final perks of being delightfully non-attached to your thinking, is that you get to develop your natural psychic abilities! Your Open Ajna Center makes you a natural mind-reader. It enhances your capacity for empathy. It also helps you discern between people who are mentally clear, or confused and confusing!

## *THE PULL OF YOUR OPEN THROAT*

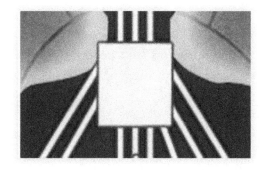

The Throat Center is the home of verbal communication, manifestation through action, metamorphosis, and the essence of Emergence.

The Throat is not a motor; it's more like a gear box, and very complex. It has 11 Gates (Gene Keys), each translating into a different voice. Biologically, the Throat is associated with the Thyroid and the Parathyroid glands.

One could say that all metamorphic processes must be initiated through the Throat Center. In other words, this Center brings change into our lives. If we don't honor our *Inner Wisdom Keeper*, the Throat is the place where things begin to break down.

Your Throat Center is Open, and so what you talk about and *how* you talk about it are greatly influenced by the people in your surroundings.

When you're on your own, you have the potential to feel very comfortable, just being silent. As soon as you're with other people, your Throat Center can come under a great deal of pressure to speak. Whatever's there—in yourself, in the room—simply has to come out.

Because of your Throat's sensitivity, you can end up sitting at a dinner party and talking more than anyone else! You can even end up with a sore throat or indigestion, just because of the conditioning coming in to your Throat from the outside.

People whose Throat Centers are Open can feel a deep need for attention. Many have felt unseen in their lives. They often want to share something valuable and contribute to the conversation, and can feel particularly frustrated when they don't feel in control of what ends up coming out of their mouths, or *when* it comes out.

Open Throat beings can end up blurting things out, dominating conversations, speaking without being invited, or during inappropriate moments. They can feel insecure about their ability to express themselves, and spend a lot of time rehearsing what they're going to say, instead of allowing for spontaneous self-expression.

Some have trouble understanding why, around certain people, their words flow out easily, effortlessly and articulately; while around others, they either can't make a peep or can only produce gobbledygook.

If you have an Open Throat, just knowing that you're actually designed to speak in a variety of ways, and at different times, can be a great relief. You're not supposed to be a consistent and predictable communicator.

That said, you communicate best when you're given space.

When your Throat is Open, your thyroid system can be strained by your environment. Depending on their Definition, certain people can literally put your metabolism under pressure. This isn't necessarily a bad thing, as long as you're not allowing that pressure to force you into speaking when you're not really needing to or control your speech with too much rigidity and self-judgment.

If your Open Throat is working too hard all of the time, it can throw off the delicate hormonal balance of your thyroid, and you can end up dealing with all sorts of metabolic issues. You can also get sore throats, tonsil problems, and more from straining your voice too much.

Since the Throat isn't as much about manifestation as it is about speech, it's also important that you refrain from over-doing. Children with Open Throats shouldn't be pressured to be total 'doers.' They need some **Be** time, too.

Don't get me wrong. With your Open Throat, you can accomplish a great deal. There should also be time for you to rest, and enjoy your own relaxed, silent company.

Keep in mind that your actions can be deeply conditioned by the people around you. This is such a key revelation for you.

This means that you don't ever need to be in a hurry to speak or act. If you're feeling pressured to speak or act before you're ready:

- Give yourself permission to slow down.
- Get quiet.
- Return to the basics of your design.
- Make sure that any decision you make about what to do or say, comes from your authentic decision-making process, whatever that is.

Your most natural state is Silence. You're designed to be silent until the moment calls for you to speak. Usually these moments of opportunity arise in relation to someone else's communication or invitation.

The healthiest place for you to have important conversations is a public place where you can be private, like in a restaurant or café.

When you're in a public aura, the Circuitry in your Throat Center gets 'hooked up' or connected to other parts of your design. You may find it much easier to say what you want to say in these kinds of environments. It also helps that you're surrounded by all kinds of people who have absolutely no expectations or agendas for you, in relation to what you should say or how you should say it.

Though children with Open Throats typically need time to learn how to articulate and adjust to customary verbal patterns, they can end up with incredibly versatile, spontaneous voices, and a true gift for mastering languages. Open Throat beings can easily pick up on all kinds of accents and dialects.

Many of the world's greatest singers and voice artists have Open Throats. These are usually the singers with a very big vocal range. Cher, Elvis and John Lennon all have (or had) Open Throats. Some of the world's most moving speakers have undefined Throats. Whether you like Bill Clinton's politics, he's a great example of that.

Bob Dylan, on the other hand, has a Defined Throat. He's got one voice that he sings with. And what a voice!

An invitation:

The next time you're in a group of people, see if you can relax as much as possible. Drop into a silent, receptive place. Do your best to wait to be initiated to speak by others. While you're waiting, notice any pressure you feel to speak—whether it be to say what you believe, what you're thinking, or fill in an awkward silence.

No matter how strong the impulse to chime in, practice restraint. Don't jump into the conversation. Again, notice any thoughts and feelings that arise when you're not participating in the conversation in an overt way. Are you feeling invisible? Unseen? Without value? Do you feel awkward? Embarrassed? Like you're going to explode? Get really good at recognizing how the pressure to talk manifests in you.

Once you've got a little 'speech pressure recognition' under your belt, I invite you to turn your attention towards what happens when you *are* talking. Pay attention to whether others are actually listening or interested in what you're saying.

- Are you are getting the attention you long for?

- Do you feel heard?

- Respected?

- Invisible?

- Overlooked?

- Like you're not getting through?

Do you often feel like you have to say what you were just saying again, but louder, just to get through? Do you go quickly from feeling 'too little' to 'too much'?

You might use your voice (or way of life) to attract attention, or end up disappearing all together.

You don't need to do either of those things. For you, it's all about trusting your aura, your natural capacity to attract the right people to you at the right time. The more you do this, the more you'll be able to enjoy being with people, whether you're talking or not.

Over time, you're likely to discover that your aura is talking all of the time, no matter what's coming out of your mouth!

You're also likely to discover that it actually feels so much better to be initiated into talking, as opposed to forcing it with your will. There are few things as lovely as having someone turn to you, and genuinely ask for your contribution.

When someone extends the invitation, it doesn't mean you have to talk. If you're not in the mood, you don't have to utter a peep. If you *are* in the mood, go to town!

# THE PULL OF YOUR
# OPEN G- IDENTITY CENTER

At the heart of every G-/Identity Center, whether Open or Defined, lives the mysterious Magnetic Monopole—the purely-attracting magnetic core of our designs.

Whether you hold the Magnetic Monopole as a metaphor or scientifically proven fact, I invite you to think of it as the magnet responsible for bringing together your body and mind/soul, for attracting everything and everyone you need into your life, and for pulling you through space.

The Magnetic Monopole is what Human Design calls the *Driver*—the living phenomenon within you that holds 'you' together, and gives you the experience, or the illusion, of being a separate entity: one person, separate, unique and apart from all other beings.

As the home of the Magnetic Monopole, our G-Center illuminates our individual identity in relation to the whole.

Since one could say that Love is the ultimate unifying force in the Universe, the G-Center is also the home of Love—love of the self, love of the body, love of the other, and love of humanity. From a transpersonal perspective, this is the Center where we have the potential to experience Oneness, a dissolving of the small 'self' into the All.

The other main purpose of the G-Center is to give us our correct trajectory, or direction, in life.

At its highest expression, our Identity is nothing more, or less, than the moving embodiment of Love.

People with a Defined G-Center are said to have a 'fixed' identity. I've never been a fan of the word 'fixed.' I prefer to see areas of Definition as 'specializations' or 'strong potentials.' Someone with a Defined G-Center has a specialized potential for love, direction in life, and way of being. One could say that their basic character, sense of morality, and internal culture are relatively consistent, no matter where they are or who they're with.

They may not know this about themselves if their Definition is largely below the surface, or they've experienced a great deal of conditioning away from their true nature. They can certainly feel as lost as the rest of us! Deep down, they are designed to have a very particular 'self' that they bring with them wherever they go. They have a strong potential to know who they are, and to inspire direction in others.

If you have an Open G- or Identity Center, you're not designed to have such a strong 'identity,' or a specialized direction in life. You can change, quite dramatically, depending on who is defining your G-Center at any given moment, and how they're doing it.

You are deeply sensitive to your environment and location.

Fortunately, if you can free yourself of oppressive conditioning, you are actually designed to **enjoy** this aspect of yourself—to let go of the need to know who you are and where you're going. You're not here to play just one role in life. Or to experience just one kind of love. Or to move in just one direction.

You're here to play many roles, to experience many kinds of love, and to move in all sorts of directions.

As you move through life, taking everyone and everything in, you have the potential to offer others such a tremendous gift. You can reflect identity, love and direction back to people, in such a way that helps them to feel more stable, confident and solid in themselves. You can help to bring out and celebrate the true nature of those with Defined G-Centers. You can help them drop through their conditioned identifications and reactions, and get to know themselves. You have such a gift for seeing, appreciating and celebrating diversity.

In a way, we could say that you are no one, and you are everyone. All at the same time. It's just not in the cards for you to 'know exactly who you are.' That's not actually what your life is about.

Most of us are conditioned to want to be what we aren't, so most of us with Open G-Centers (I include myself in this group), really want to know who we are. And who to love. And where to go.

Our whole life, in fact, can turn into a desperate search for a 'fixed' identity.

"Who am I?"
"Where am I going?"
"Will I ever find love?"
"If I do, will I be able to hold onto it?"

These are the kinds of questions we can spend our whole lives trying to answer. While we're busy trying to answer these questions, we can miss out on countless, fabulous and completely unexpected opportunities.

This makes sense. Not only in the mainstream, but in New Age or alternative spiritual environments, we're taught that it's essential to know who we are, what we want, and where we're headed.

Unfortunately, this leaves many people with Open G-Centers thinking that something is terribly wrong with them, because they're not designed to know (or even focus on) what they're 'supposed to do' in life, because they don't feel in control of their lives. This makes them especially vulnerable to losing themselves in whomever they're with.

If they haven't learned how to tap into their own *Inner Wisdom Keeper*, (or how to honor the process of their unique Authority), they can end up assuming the identities, directions and approaches to love of other people, without even realizing it. They can end up living other people's lives, latching onto things, people and jobs that give them a false sense of identity, security and inner solidity.

The truth is, if you have an Open G-Center, nothing is wrong with you at all.

In fact, you're wonderful! Your sense of self is beautifully flexible. Because you have the capacity to 'get' or identify with so many different kinds of people, ways of being and loving, you can embrace anyone. And whoa, do we need people who can do that on this planet.

This doesn't mean you have to be and do everything, or spend your precious time with everyone. It does mean that you get to play a variety of roles in this life, with all kinds of people, and you get to enjoy a flexible, playful and expansive sense of identity and capacity for love.

Please understand. I'm not saying that there is no direction to your life. I'm not saying you'll never find love or be able to sustain healthy, loving relationships in your life.

I'm just saying that you don't have to obsess or worry about these things too much. Your people, your right environments, and your direction will find you. Your direction in life will be deeply influenced by others.

You're designed to be guided by others. It is through the directions that others expose you to that you discover whether that direction is right for you.

Take me and Human Design as an example. Believe me, Human Design was the *last* thing I ever thought I'd be involved in. It wasn't until a dear friend of mind told me about it that my life began to change in ways I could never ever have imagined (or consciously pursued). I didn't go out hunting for Human Design. It found me, and wow, did it find me! Just as so many other things, people and places have found me since that time in my life.

This is the magic of the Open G-Center. I invite you to start thinking about those things, people and places that have grabbed you from the side and taken you for a ride. These are the kinds of unexpected experiences that have the power to launch you on your right path, if you let them. Once you've had enough of them, you can begin to trust in that Magnetic Monopole inside of you. Even though your G-Center is Open, that potent magnet is still working just fine. No need to overthink it.

Something to keep in mind: Once a direction has been genuinely activated in you, and your body has given you its blessing (through your Authority), you're free to stick with that direction as long as it feels right—

for a moment, a season or a lifetime. Your job is to honor what is alive in you, and always to remain open to inspiration, from wherever and whomever it comes.

You're likely to experience a plethora of directions in life, and you can become particularly good at recognizing the great ones, for yourself, and others.

## A Golden Rule for people like you

**If you are in the wrong place, you're likely with the wrong people.**
**If you're with the wrong people, you're likely in the wrong place.**

Environment is so important for you. You can feel deeply grateful to the people who get or introduce you to a wonderful environment—whether it be a country, town, restaurant or work station. In a way, people with Defined G-Centers who connect you to wonderful places are here to serve you. You never have to worry about where to go, because they'll show up just when you need them to show you the way.

It's wonderful to feel and express gratitude to those who influence your path in positive ways. Just because someone leads you to something valuable (e.g. a person, place, job, etc.) doesn't mean that you owe them your life, or your infinite loyalty. This is a common trap that some Open G-Centers fall into.

You may be led somewhere by someone and only be meant to stay there for a short while. That's OK.

Of course, you don't have to accept every direction, place or relationship that you're led to. That's where Strategy and Authority come in. It's always your job to choose once the opportunity arises. You don't have to drive yourself crazy pursuing opportunities, environments or roles that your mind has you convinced will finally give you that stable, reliable identity.

Similarly, it's not your job to chase after love. See if you can work your trust muscles and allow love to come to you, in whichever form it takes. Once love arrives, trust your *Inner Wisdom Keeper* to show you whether this particular love is right for you, and for how long it's meant to last.

To the extent that you can:

- Embrace the adventure of your life.
- Stay open to surrendering to any and all inspiration that comes from 'outside of you' (even if you're a Manifestor!).
- Joyfully release the idea that you're supposed to have some strong, unwavering identity.
- Embrace your natural gift for seeing, and ultimately teaching about, the eternal dance of life and our ultimate interconnectedness.
- Celebrate your ability to grasp the nature of Love itself, and that fact that Love and Oneness are the only directions that matter for humanity.

There can be such a tremendous relief when you truly embrace your Open G-Center. The more you can practice letting go of having to know who you are and where you are going, the more amazing you'll be at hopping into anyone's shoes and offering them deep, accurate and loving guidance.

## THE PULL OF YOUR OPEN EGO/HEART

The Heart Center, also known as the Ego Center, is an energy system within the body. It's considered to be one of the body's four motors. It is the Center of the Will, Willpower and ultimately, Surrender.

Though it looks small and simple, compared to some of the other Centers, it's actually extremely powerful and complex.

Whether Open or Defined, this Center is all about living on the material plane, feeding the ones we love, and living in harmony with others. It is about bonding and bringing babies (both human and creative) into the world.

This Center houses our will to survive not only as individuals, but as families, tribes, communities, and society as a whole. It is responsible for the creation of culture and society, and it's designed to express its care for humanity on the grass roots level.

Ultimately, it is home to our deepest longing to make a meaningful contribution to the world and help our whole planet thrive. It is through the Ego/Heart Center that we learn how to truly feed and nourish each other—physically, emotionally, intellectually and spiritually. Ultimately, it's where we learn about Universal Love, Valor, Resolve, Awakening and how to Surrender to Divine Will, as opposed to our little wills.

Just like all Centers, the Ego/Heart Center has the potential to express itself from the highest to the basest of frequencies. When overcome by divisive and fear-based conditioning, as it has been for thousands of years, this Center can become a collective hub for oppression.

If your Ego/Heart Center is Open, the pressure to conform to cultural norms is going to be extra potent. This is the Open Center that's going to get you to do whatever it takes to stay in the tribe, even if it means throwing your authenticity (or sanity!) under the bus. This is the Center that says, "Stay connected to your family and community, no matter what! Who cares if what you're doing doesn't make sense, feel good, or seem right deep down. Do it anyway. Or else!"

The Ego/Heart Center was mentioned earlier as one of the four motors or energy Centers in the Bodygraph. The energy associated with the Center is devoted to the survival of group bonds. It's here to make sure that the family, the community, the tribe, the society makes it. It therefore makes sure that products are sold, childcare is provided, protection is hired, etc.

People with Defined Egos (only about 35% of the planet) are born with a strong need to feel materially secure and to involve themselves directly in these life arenas areas.

Defined Ego/Heart beings have the potential to exert—and infuse their auras with—a great deal of will power. They intrinsically feel a strong need to make a contribution to the family and larger community.

Most people on the planet have Open Ego/Heart Centers. Despite the fact that they're in the majority, they can be particularly vulnerable to the Defined Egos of the world, to those who naturally transmit their will power into the space around them.

Open Ego/Heart beings absorb the impact of energetic will power. Without realizing it, they slurp up external pressures to perform well, prove themselves, *im*prove themselves, and to keep their commitments.

If you have an Open Ego/Heart Center, when you're around someone with a Defined Ego/Heart Center, you don't just take that energy in. You amplify it.

You're likely to be highly attracted to this energy. Somewhere deep down, unless you've dedicated your life to non-attachment practices, there's likely a part of you that's always longing for more will power, courage, discipline and follow-through. When this part of you takes over your decision-making process, it can lead you to handing over your authority to people with strong wills. It is in this way that the Open Ego/Heart Center can become a breeding ground for co-dependent relationships.

## Take this commonly used example

Let's say that you, an Open Ego/Heart being, decide that you want to lose weight. You find a diet coach or nutritional therapist who specializes in helping people like you. This particular therapist has a Defined Ego/Heart Center, unbeknownst to you.

The moment you walk into the room, you take in the therapist's will. You don't only take it in, you take it to a whole new level, amplifying and reflecting it back with gusto.

When in the presence of the therapist, you feel an enormous sense of empowerment, like you can do anything. You become convinced that you'll lose the weight and follow the plan, from A to Z. You make a commitment to the plan.

As soon as you leave the office, the surge of empowerment you felt starts to fade away. Before you know it, you're chomping on a Twinkie. You feel awful about yourself. You judge yourself as weak. You feel guilty and ashamed for making a promise that you're not keeping.

You go back to the therapist and apologize. The therapist is forgiving and encourages you not to give up. You begin to feel your hope and power return to you. You recommit, only to experience the same humiliating defeat.

As you repeat this painful pattern, time and again, your self-trust plummets along with your self-esteem. A sense of shame, inadequacy and hopelessness builds inside of you. You stop believing that you can be helped by anyone. You're convinced that there is something irreparably wrong with you.

### The truth is that there's absolutely nothing wrong with you.

Just understanding how your Open Ego/Heart works can offer you immediate relief from this kind of slippery, self-berating slope.

The Open Ego/Heart's basic message to you is:

There is nothing wrong with you. There's nothing to fix. Nothing to improve. Nothing to prove. You are beautiful, wonderful and good enough precisely the way you are. When you're not 'under the influence' of a present or past Ego field, you actually know this to be true!

There are few things more beautiful—or needed in our materially-obsessed, spiritually-starving, Western-influenced world—than the wisdom of an Open Ego/Heart Center.

When people like you dare to embrace your beautiful Open Ego/Heart, you can provide our suffering planet with the healing, sanity balm we need the most.

Keep in mind: just because you have an Open Ego/Heart Center doesn't mean you can't ever get anything done, or you're completely incapable of making and following through on commitments. My husband has an Open Ego/Heart Center, and he's been happily committed to our marriage, to being a father, to various career choices for years.

What having an Open Ego/Heart *does* mean, however, is that whatever you do, and whomever you decide to do it with, is not meant to be driven by willfulness. Your 'doing,' your acts of devotion, are designed to emerge naturally and organically out of you, not to be pushed or forced out.

One of the most common traps you can fall into is the Comparison Trap. Constantly setting yourself up against those who seem to effortlessly will projects, careers and relationships into being can be a real source of suffering.

Ironically, most of those people are probably Open Ego/Heart beings too, similarly lost in a self-improvement trap, and suffering as a result. When you're gripped by the self-bashing bug, you're not likely to focus on that sad fact. You'll be busy trying to convince yourself that you should be more of a go-getter.

That's not what you are, and thank the Good Lordess for that!

Remembering the beauty of your Open Ego/Heart will likely require practice and constant reminding. Given the world we live in—where we're constantly bombarded with images, offers, classes, commercials, bells, whistles, diets and dogmas, all carefully designed to push and manipulate us into proving and improving ourselves in countless (usually irrelevant, empty and unfulfilling ways) —the arts of self-acceptance and knowing one's own true value are two of the hardest to master.

When you find yourself on a comparison trip, beating yourself up for not having what 'they've got,' or being as fast or as disciplined as they are, I invite you to take a deep breath.

Ahhh…

It's actually not healthy for you to be consistently willful, super competitive or achievement obsessed. You might partner up with strong-willed people now and then, and benefit as a result. As a whole, competitive environments aren't ones you should hang around in all too often. It's not recommended.

When you spend too much time trying to prove yourself, you actually put too much pressure on your heart, stomach and gall bladder. Think heartburn, ulcers and heart attacks. Not that you'll get these, but let the possibility that you will, be a little incentive to help you stay clear of common Ego/Heart Center traps!

Here are the kinds of thoughts you need to be on the alert for:

- "I better do this because if I don't, I won't be worthy. I'll be a failure."
- "I have to be and show that I'm in control. I have to be brave."
- "I have to pump myself up, so I feel good about myself. Only then will others recognize my value."
- "I have to be loyal, no matter what."
- "I have to make and keep promises, so that others will see how trustworthy I am."
- "I'm not a good at anything unless I prove it first."
- "If I don't produce or have something measurable and impressive to show for my efforts, my life has no worth."

If you can manage to witness these kinds of thoughts without totally identifying with them, you're well on your way. Over time, you will come to understand that no matter what anyone else is doing, you are absolutely worthy, lovable, good enough and A-Okay.

On the other side of this realization is the treasure of the Open Ego/Heart. Your wisdom. You carry within you the potential to understand the nature of the Ego, its shadows as well as its ultimate potential. One of your life purposes, in fact, is to help heal our narcissistically wounded culture, to facilitate a process where we all get to drop our individual wills in service of Divine Will, the will of Universal Love.

Once your actions are no longer determined by your Open Ego/Heart conditioning, you may find yourself becoming extremely knowledgeable about the nature of Will, as well as the material plane. You may get quite good at setting firm, healthy limits with shadow-laden Egoic fields. Having an Open Ego doesn't mean that you don't have a spine. The opposite is true. It's just that your spine is here to protect you (and the rest of us!) from yucky 'never good enough' influences.

As you learn to set healthy limits with narcissistic influences, you're likely to experience greater ease when it comes to making and spending money, and providing for your family and community.

Your successes won't be driven by your own willfulness. You can master your life on the material plane best when you're ***not*** forcing, disciplining or willing, when you've dropped the achievement game all together.

### A final reminder

Try to avoid making too many promises, or at least making more promises than feel comfortable. When you do make a commitment, especially the kind that can really clutter up a life, see if you can skillfully leave yourself a way out. For example, if someone's invited you to a party, give yourself permission to say, "I'm really wanting to make it to your party, but I'd like to check in with you that morning to make sure I can." If you put too much stress on your Heart, it can actually break.

# THE PULL OF YOUR OPEN SACRAL

According to Human Design, if you have an Open Sacral Center, this means you don't have consistent, reliable access to your life force energy.

Unlike Generators (Generator Flowers), your body isn't supposed to be continually buzzing with energy. It's not necessarily hungry to use itself up to a point of satisfaction or exhaustion. It doesn't always speak to you with sounds that you can trust to be your truthful responses to life or your decision-making authority. You don't need it to.

When you have an Open Sacral, at least when you're on your own, you can truly discharge and rest. You can unplug from the craziness of the world and enjoy the gentle art of Being. You can actually space out, and love it!

If you try to keep going and going like a Generator, you're likely to exhaust yourself, and not in a good way. Demanding staying power isn't healthy for you.

You're here to live a more energetically balanced life. You need plenty of time to rest. When you make a contribution to the world, you're designed to do it in a way that makes the most of the energy of the people around you! That's right.

Though you have energy, (as all people do, regardless of their designs), you are not here to over-rely on your own energy. Instead, you are here to *understand* the nature of energy and how it works, and to guide others in the most efficient use of their energy.

Mystically speaking, you're here to allow energy and Life itself to flow through you, to allow Spirit to do its work through your sacred body temple.

Let me be clear. When we say you don't have reliable, consistent access to your energy, it doesn't mean that you have no energy or that you are not energetically available to life. You do, and you are.

There are few things that your body wants more than to share its resources with others, and to reap the harvest of a life well-planted and well-lived.

It's just that you're not here to do all of the work yourself. You need energetic supporters, and you need rest too.

The challenging thing is that we live in a world that's filled with Generators. Over 70% of the human population is either a Pure or Manifesting Generator.

Since you're always Open to Sacral conditioning, you're likely constantly surrounded by, taking in, and then amplifying the buzzing energy of Generators. You're also absorbing their frustration, anger and dissatisfaction—especially when they're not happy with the work they're doing, not living according to their own true nature, and feeling like slaves.

While you may be someone who is exceedingly interested in how life energy works, you're not meant to do all of the hard work with your own life energy.

Because of your Sacral Center's Openness to conditioning, you run the risk of working harder and longer than anyone. Your mind, the spokesperson for your Open Sacral, can be quite good at convincing you to ignore how tired you are and to push through.

Open Sacral beings aren't called "super slaves" for nothing! If there's one thing they struggle with the most, it's knowing when enough is enough.

Your Open Sacral Center makes you extremely sensitive to the energy of others. Your Sacral is happiest when surrounded by the right people. Too much of the 'wrong people' can sap your power and burn you out. This can lead you to run on the energy you've borrowed from the 'right people,' which can burn *them* out! You don't want that.

Your Sacral is Open. It is not biologically equipped to handle a consistent stream of energy pumping through your body. If you work too hard for too long without a break, your body can break down or collapse from exhaustion.

Once you learn when to call it a day, your Sacral Center becomes the portal to your creativity, sexuality and wisdom.

## A word about sexuality

You may find that you're particularly fascinated with relationships and sexuality. Keep in mind that given your Open Sacral Center, your sexuality—even fertility—can be easily 'conditioned' or influenced. When you engage intimately with someone, you are literally receiving their life energy into your body, like food, or fuel. This is why it's so crucial that you learn to be healthfully selective when choosing a sexual partner.

Another thing is that because of your Open Sacral Center, you might be tempted to over-identify with your sexual experiences, or to generalize about all sexual experiences based on the ones you've had.

Teenagers with Open Sacral Centers can benefit greatly from learning that their sexual experiences will depend on and reflect the quality of their partners. They can be deeply influenced by the people they choose to be intimate with.

This is true for you, too. Each chemistry you experience with another human being will be unique. Different partners will bring out different expressions of your sexuality.

One person might inspire you to become totally promiscuous. Another experimental. Yet another, completely asexual. Being selective, careful, and making sure that you connect with people who bring out the kind of sensuality and sexuality that makes you feel good in your body, and about yourself, as opposed to filling you with guilt, shame or self-judgment, is so important.

Knowing that if you don't feel particularly sexually empowered or alive with one person, this is likely saying much more about that person and the chemistry between you, than about your own potential! There is nothing more innocent and beautiful than an Open Sacral. It's a window that reflects the nature of sexuality itself.

## *THE PULL OF YOUR OPEN SOLAR PLEXUS*

The Solar Plexus, or Emotional Center, is the home of humanity's feelings and yearnings. It is ultimately the place where we can experience the greatest Serenity and Compassion.

Whether Defined or Open, this Center is going through tremendous changes in all of us, as it transitions from being a 'motor' to a Center of pure Awareness. As this Center becomes increasingly aware, our capacity for experiencing Unity, Communion and Interconnectedness will expand in ways we can't even imagine.

While this Emotional Center has tremendous potential for chaos, pain and destruction, it also holds the ticket to planetary peace. All depends on how graciously, compassionately and consciously each of us works with our emotions. The future of our planet is up to us!

If you have an Open Solar Plexus, you are an incredibly sensitive, empathetic person, who can really feel how others are feeling. You may even sense what they feel before they do (although your mental analysis of their feelings might not be accurate!).

You have the potential to patiently witness and surf rising and falling waves of emotions, within and all around you. You can soak up the highs and lows of life, enjoying the pleasure, needs, desires and passions that others bring out in you, without identifying with or holding onto any of it. You can become someone who is deeply wise about emotions; you can be a true barometer of the emotional health of the people around you.

There are many people who've always thought of themselves as 'super emotional' or 'overly sensitive.' When they are introduced to their Human Design, they discover that their Solar Plexus is Open. I was one of those people!

Statistically speaking, and ironically, the majority of people sitting on the couches of therapists and psychologists are people with Open Emotional Centers, not Defined ones.

You could say they're continually surfing up and down on the emotional waves of the people around them. They're not just going along for the ride; they're magnifying and identifying with every emotion washing through them. They then make decisions based on those feelings, whether the feelings belong to them or not.

The Solar Plexus also houses humanity's guilt, blame and shame.

When you have an Open Emotional Center, you run the risk of carrying around way more than your fair share.

Wherever you are Open, you are going to be receptive to and reflective of your surroundings. When you are Open, your emotional state will depend a great deal on who you're with, and how they're feeling.

Since about half of the population is emotionally Defined, chances are pretty good that you had at least one family member who had a Defined Emotional Center. Probably more. Growing up, you took in, amplified and reflected back the emotional life of the people with Defined Solar Plexus, and/or the emotional chemistry/Definition that is usually generated when groups of people come together.

When you have an Open Solar Plexus, you are not as genetically equipped to comfortably handle the energies that come in through your emotional Center. When you're exposed to emotional feelings that aren't pleasant, you can become exaggeratedly disturbed, not to mention physically uncomfortable.

In Human Design, we say that if you have an undefined Solar Plexus, much of your life is spent trying to protect your stomach. All of your efforts to feel happy, or to resolve or process emotional material, are sourced in this basic, underlying need to keep your belly safe from overload.

There are two common ways that people with an Open Solar Plexus tend to cope with this kind of discomfort. One way is repressive and the other reactive. Both ways have one goal—to get rid of unmanageable feelings as quickly as possible.

One way people attempt to get rid of emotional discomfort is to avoid confrontation at all costs. They essentially hide—from others, and from themselves. They essentially repress their emotional life.

Many of these sensitive beings learn from a very young age to 'make nice' and people-please people. These 'smoothing out' behaviors help them prevent painful emotional escalations, and, even more importantly, avoid the resulting flood of feelings that would otherwise leave them feeling helpless and overwhelmed.

Children with Open Emotional Centers often become the peacemakers in the family. They go to enormous lengths to keep everyone calm—including suppressing their own feelings, needs and truth. Their deep fear of what could happen if they 'rocked the boat' can cause them to develop self-destructive addictions (e.g. eating disorders), lie to themselves and others, or run away from people and relationships all together.

The other common way Open Solar Plexus beings cope with emotional discomfort is reactive in nature. Instead of stuffing down feelings, they act them out. They externalize the incredible pain they feel by rebelling and reacting stronger, louder and more angrily than anyone else.

Some of these kids become so angry that they end up medicated or in some form of therapy. As adults, they can feel emotionally out of control or deeply manipulated. They tend to be punished for their volatile reactions, so they can suffer from a deep-seated fear (and actual experience) of rejection.

Most of us Open Emotional beings use both repressive and reactive coping strategies, depending on the situation. We may repress, repress, repress, and then suddenly react. We may also react, react, react, only to discover that beneath our destructive behaviors lie deeply repressed feelings of sadness, grief and shame, just begging to see the light of day.

Wherever you fall on the repression-reaction continuum, if you have an Open Solar Plexus, you probably store a great deal of old pain in your emotional body. This is likely true whether you're aware of this or not.

Understanding your Open Emotional Center, which can take some time, can give you such incredible relief. You can begin to understand how emotional states can change in the blink of an eye. One moment, you might be sitting peacefully on your own, and the next, (as soon as someone enters the room), you feel terrified, upset or furious. Whew!

You're actually designed to be pretty 'calm, cool and collected' (as my grandfather used to say) when you're on your own. I encourage you to see if this is actually true for you. Realizing that this was true for me was quite the pleasant epiphany!

We all live inside of a bustling, evolving cosmos, and never truly 'alone.' Planetary transits can impact our emotional lives just as people can. There will be days and times in your life when you'll be emotionally conditioned by the stars. This conditioning will likely feel different, in that it won't be quite as 'specific' or intense as it can be when interpersonally activated. It'll still be there.

If you have 'hanging' or colored-in Gates (Gene Keys) coming out of your Open Solar Plexus, there will be certain emotional themes that are naturally familiar to you. Although you may need a person or a transit to bring these dormant themes to life, you do have a built-in, specialized way of experiencing feelings, yearnings, hope and despair. You could say your design has a preferred style of feeling nervous and of experiencing compassion. When you're truly living an authentic, full-hearted life, it has a favorite way of emanating Serenity.

If you have no Gate activations in your Open Solar Plexus, think of yourself as having infinite potential to feel, express and reflect back the full-spectrum of human emotions. Depending on the amount of maturity and witnessing capacity you bring to your emotional life, you can either reflect the best parts of humanity's emotional potential or its worst parts.

To stay healthy as an Open Emotional being, you need alone time. When you're on your own, you have the precious opportunity to clear out all of that emotional conditioning that you take in on a daily basis.

I also recommend that you try to avoid making emotional decisions. In other words, don't decide to do something based on how you're feeling in any given moment.

It's not that the feelings you are experiencing are never your own. There are Human Design analysts who disagree with me here, but I believe that we all have feelings, regardless of the state of our Solar Plexus.

It's just that more often than not, your feelings will be clouded, distorted or amplified by the feelings of those around you.

You are meant to make your decisions when you're feeling 'calm, cool and collected,' not 'frantic, fire-y and excited.'

## A little experiment

When you're with someone, and you begin to feel a rising emotional discomfort, give yourself permission to leave the room, if only for a few minutes. Return to your own aura. Slip back into your own skin, and notice what happens.

If you're involved in conflict with someone, and you get a knot in your stomach when you're with them, see this as a sign that you're not ready to engage. Give yourself time to cool off. If the other person is emotionally Defined, or the two of you create an emotional charge through your chemistry, chances are they'll also benefit from being given a little extra time to cool down. You'll be doing both of you a favor.

Even if someone with emotional Definition is transmitting their feelings into the room, you are likely amplifying them—making them seem bigger and scarier than they were ever experienced or intended by that person.

Your greatest responsibility is to work with your own reactivity, and to get to a place where you can witness whatever is moving through you with relative equanimity, compassion and non-attachment.

Over time, you can learn how to avoid the confrontations that aren't meant for you. Similarly, you can learn to have—even enjoy—the confrontations that you are meant to have and grow through. You can learn the art of being true to yourself, without running away from your own emotional experience or the people you care about.

Coming to terms with the deep sensitivity of your emotional system will help you learn these arts.

## Think of the Serenity Prayer

*God grant me the serenity to accept the things I cannot change;*
*the courage to change the things I can;*
*and the wisdom to know the difference.*

You can't change your sensitivity. You will always be Open where you're Open.

You will probably always feel some discomfort when you're in an emotionally stimulating environment. That said…

- You can learn to release yourself from over-identifying with those feelings. You can learn to let them swim through you, without getting hooked.

- You can learn to make sure you have plenty of time to yourself. You can offer yourself opportunities to come back to center, cool off, and sift through what's yours and what isn't.

- You can come to enjoy all of the pleasures that emotionally Defined people and transits bring into your life—the sexuality, sensuality, food, passion, excitement, romance, and music. You can do this without losing yourself in it all.

- You can learn to wait to make your decisions until you feel calm and clear, ensuring that your true self is making those decisions—not some petrified, desperate or reactive person who's willing to do anything in order to avoid a conflict or provoke one.

- You can be an essential part of the change this planet needs so much. You can do your part.

So many of the world's problems arise out of the emotionally-charged dynamic between the Open and Defined Solar Plexus.

We have Emotionally Defined people who are not waiting out their wave, not waiting for clarity, before they express themselves.

We have people with Open Emotional Centers taking the undigested emotional energy of the world, making it way bigger than it is, distorting it, and intensely expressing it, as if it were all their own.

Imagine a world where we all slowed down, where we all began to grasp the way our emotional lives operate, and actually took responsibility for our part in the dance.

When it comes to the Solar Plexus, I don't recommend that anyone accept what they hear about themselves as fact.

- Experiment with it.
- Notice how you feel when you're on your own.
- Notice how you feel around different people.
- Notice how long it takes for you, once you're alone, to go back to neutral—if you ever get back to neutral.

Eventually, if this information truly speaks to you, you might want to start dabbling in the daily transits, to get in touch with the larger celestial influences at work. For now, just play with what I've shared here, and see whether anything interesting or useful comes from it.

## THE PULL OF YOUR OPEN SPLEEN

The Spleen Center represents your body's consciousness. It is the home of our Intuition, our Depth and Integrity. It is humanity's primary awareness Center, the oldest one we have. Whether our Splenic Centers are Open or Defined, we share an instinctual and existential awareness with all other forms of life through this Center.

Because your Spleen is Open, it has a double potential—to be a place of victimization and fear and to be a place of tremendous wisdom and sensitivity.

In Human Design circles, people say, "There is no one more sensitive than someone with an Open Spleen." There is certainly truth to that statement.

If your Spleen is Open, think of your immune system as a sponge. Wherever you go, whomever you're with, your Spleen is soaking up the general level of physical health and well-being of your environment.

There's actually a joke about people with Open Spleens, and it contains a profound truth.

"Open Spleens make great doctors but lousy nurses!"

An Open and receptive Spleen makes a natural and powerful barometer. It can literally read the health of others. Its greatest potential is diagnostic in nature, as opposed to soothing. Because it can soak up ill-health as easily as it can good health, spending too much time with sick people (like nurses do) isn't always the best idea. Better to come in, do some potent diagnosing, or laser healing, then graciously bow out.

Quick and dirty healing, I say!

Many people with Open Spleens don't consistently feel good. This can amplify their natural aptitude for feeling fear.

If you've got an Open Spleen, a fear for survival and a heightened sense of alarm may play a big role in your inner life, even though your rational mind doesn't always understand why. You can actually fear for your survival just for not doing something you don't feel like doing, or contemplating leaving an unhappy relationship, or quitting a horrible job.

You can feel an exaggerated sense of fear when you need to say 'no' to someone. What if they don't like you anymore? What if they decide to leave you all together? If that happens, how will you make sure that you're safe, healthy, and able to protect yourself in the future, without them?

These kinds of fears are very human. We've all got them. When your Open Spleen is on overload, they have a real potential to keep you in unhealthy and unhappy relationships for too long.

Human Design is ultimately about the chemistry between people.

Whenever you are with someone else, you are going to receive their 'nature' or Definition through your Openness, and vice versa.

Anyone who walks into your life and defines, or influences, your Spleen is likely to give you the feeling of being safe and secure, even if this is not true in reality or the long run.

This is especially important for you to understand.

Think of anyone who is stuck in a relationship with an abuser, and is tragically convinced that their safety lies with the very person who's putting their life at risk. Think of anyone caught in a self-destructive addiction, who is desperately using a substance, a screen, a relationship, their work, gambling, people-pleasing, or any number of behaviors to self-sooth, numb out, run away, cover over, collapse away from, or avoid feelings of discomfort—like grief, shame, anxiety, depression, loneliness, abandonment, rage, emptiness.

These are extreme (though common) examples of what a neglected and wilting Open Spleen can lead to. They show how, more than anything, the spiritual work for an Open Spleen being is learning how to be comfortable with discomfort.

There are few practices more difficult, but more rewarding.

Of course, your experience of the Open Spleen doesn't have to be so extreme.

You might just feel some fear or anxiety when you don't feel good physically. You might also feel overly concerned when you feel a rumbling in your belly, or notice a blotch on your skin.

You might feel this way because, at a very deep level, you don't take your health for granted.

The wonderful thing about having such a sensitive and responsive body, and about not taking your health for granted, is that you're primed to become an incredible expert in the realm of health.

Many people with Open Spleens learn about self-care from a very young age. Some of the healthiest people I know are people with Open Spleens. They've got self-care practices that put the rest of us to shame!

As mentioned earlier, Open Spleen beings can grow into wonderful diagnosticians. They also tend to do really well with natural, alternative treatments and healing methods.

If you've got an Open Spleen, the truth is that fear is one of your greatest, most empowering teachers. More than anyone, you are here to process and learn from fear. To do this well, you must first learn to see fear as your ally, not your enemy. You must learn to simply be with fear, without impulsively or compulsively trying to avoid it.

In your own personal life, it's important that you begin to understand and track how you absorb and magnify the fear around you.

Each fear you learn to be with, thus master, will make you stronger. You can even reach a point in life where you are fearless.

First, you need to honor your fears, without trying to suppress or fix them.

It is actually through learning who and what doesn't feel good, that you can learn who and what does—in the truest sense of the word.

The kind of conditioning pulls to notice are:

- the pull to 'feel good right now' (to reach for the 'quick fix')
- the pull to feel safe and protected
- the pull to be liked (thus safe and protected)
- the pull to do whatever it takes to survive financially (even if you really don't like what you're doing)

## Golden Rules for the Open Spleen

*Avoid making spontaneous decisions, no matter how tempting!*

Pay good attention to your health. Your body is speaking to you.

Your Spleen is always out looking for the quick fix!

Quick fixes are rarely what you need. No matter how innocent they seem on the surface, they can be addictive.

When it comes to your Open Spleen, time is always on your side.

## *THE PULL OF YOUR OPEN ROOT*

The Root Center represents our body's drive to survive and our soul's impulse to evolve. Out of this Center comes a tremendous amount of fuel and energy, pushing its way up and out of us, getting things started and keeping us on our growth edge.

Through your Open Root, you're designed to take in a great deal of pressure and stress from your environment. When your Root Center is conditioned or influenced by other people, you're likely to feel certain pressures. Unless your Root Center has no activations (colored in Gates/*Gene Keys*), specific 'pressure themes' will spring to life in your Root when you're around certain people, or in any crowd, through a burst of adrenaline.

Depending on your specific design and who you're with, you might feel a physical pressure to be productive, to begin something new, or to focus on something very deeply. You might feel a building pressure within you to provoke the spirit out of others, or to desire a new life experience, even if you have no clue what that experience should be!

All of these pressures can be wonderful, when you're following the guidance of your *Inner Wisdom Keeper*, honoring your unique Strategy and Authority, and slowing yourself down enough. They can contribute to your blossoming.

When you're hastily making decisions to relieve the pressure and stress coming in through your Open Root, this Center will begin to wilt, and you may run into trouble. A neglected (wilting) Open Root can leave you in a very vulnerable place. It can make you move so fast and take on so much work that your health and immune system will suffer. It can make your relationships suffer too, since you'll be leaping into them impulsively, not mindfully.

The great irony of the Open Root is that the harder you work to get things done, in order to relieve yourself of pressure and stress, the more work you end up having to do!

People say, "Oh, that person handled that task so well and so efficiently. Let's give'em even more to do!"

It'll never end!

That's the good news and the bad news.

The demands of life will never go away. This is a stressful world we live in. So, you might as well give up the hope that the stress will disappear. It's time to release the illusion that as long as you work harder and faster than anyone else, you'll ultimately be rid of the pressure. You won't.

Deep inhale and deep exhale!

Once you give up this illusion, you can begin to learn to pace yourself. You can become extremely wise about the Art of Timing. You can become fabulously selective about what jobs, relationships and responsibilities you take on, and how quickly you get things done.

With your Open Root, you have the potential to be an extremely efficient person. Getting things done well and quickly is an innate capacity that you carry.

The trick is to make sure that you're doing what's essential, what feeds you, with the people who appreciate your valued efforts, and for a cause that speaks to your heart.

Lastly, make sure that after your hard work, you give yourself time to go back to 'zero,' to release the pressure, to experience your beautiful potential for inner stillness and deep relaxation. You've got that gift too!

# MY 'MOTOR' CENTERS ARE OPEN. SHOULD I SURROUND MYSELF WITH DEFINED MOTOR PEOPLE?

If you've got a lot of Openness in the 'motor department,' there are certainly benefits to hanging out with—or collaborating with—people who've got juicy motors running 24/7. This doesn't mean you're a limp, lifeless, energy-depleted being when on your own. You are absolutely whole and complete, just as you are. Even if no one is around, you are a living, breathing being, with a sacred and essential role to play in this world.

A few things to keep in mind when it comes to the Blossoming Bodygraph's Motors or Energy Centers

**Each Energy Center has a unique quality.**

**Root:**

> The Root, for instance, is all about adrenalized pressure. Its initiating energy rises up from the base, showing up as a hunger, a need, or a thirst, a drive to find meaning, experience change, launch a new venture, or find something intriguing enough to fully engage one's attention. It's all about our human momentum to grow and develop.
>
> People with Defined Root Centers tend to emanate an inner drive for life itself. They carry a strong and specifically designed evolutionary impulse within them. They're designed to have a specific impact on the world.
>
> If you've got an Open Root, being around such people can enhance your own inner more receptive and flexible drive in wonderfully unexpected ways. If you're not consciously cultivating the delicate (and essential) art of pacing, it can also stress you out!

**Sacral:**

> The Sacral Center is a whole different animal or motor. While connecting with someone's defined Root might get you going by awakening your hunger for life, it won't necessarily *keep* you going. People blessed with buzzing Sacral Centers (Generators) are consistently connected with the flow of life itself. This makes them particularly good at keeping things going once they've been initiated.
>
> Though all Generators are different, they all have consistent access to a creative motor that is built to experience satisfaction through being put to work and kept busy and engaged. Their natural energy is designed to flow into the world in a particular way.
>
> If you've got an Open (thus receptive and interactive) Sacral Center, and you're looking for collaborators whose engines are specifically designed to build, create and maintain, Generators sure

do come in handy. This is especially true when Generators are designed to genuinely respond to the kind of activities that match your passionate vision. If you're looking to unplug and relax from our buzzing world, you might want to withdraw into a quiet sweet spot every once in a while, and enjoy some Sacral-free (and frustration-free!) time.

**Solar Plexus:**

As shared earlier, the Solar Plexus isn't just a motor; it is an Awareness Center (in-progress). To the extent that it still operates as a motor, however, it is quite a different kind than the Sacral Center, which is relatively steady. Unlike the Sacral Center, the Solar Plexus isn't designed to 'put-put' along like a happy engine. It's designed to operate in a wave-like pattern. Though there are different kinds of waves, depending on the person's Definition, waves tend to move back and forth between experiences of hope and despair, or high energy and low energy.

If your Solar Plexus is Open, being around someone with a Defined Solar Plexus can bring a sense of depth, richness and juiciness to your life, and any project you're engaged in. This is especially true when the person you're with has learned to take conscious responsibility for their emotional life, by taking their time, trusting in their slow, deep truth-metabolizing process, and communicating with sensitivity, compassion and serenity.

My husband is a Manifestor with a highly Defined Solar Plexus. When he's being true to his nature, everything he creates is infused with an emotional richness and depth. I have an Open Solar Plexus. When we work together, my work often deepens and becomes much more evocative as a result. His presence in my life can be a tremendous gift.

**Ego/Heart:**

Similar to the Solar Plexus, the Ego or Heart Center is not a 'steady' motor. Instead of moving through a wave, however, it goes back and forth between being 'on' or 'off.'

The Ego/Heart Center is best known for running sprints, not marathons. When someone has this Center Defined, and it is turned 'on,' this person can bring a tremendous amount of willpower to any situation. If they've cultivated a healthy relationship to their Ego/Heart Center, their desire to contribute something valuable to the world, their capacity to follow through on their promises, and their knack for synergistic collaboration can do wonders for any project you're working on.

They may need to relax after a big push. If your Ego/Heart is Open, it doesn't mean that you aren't a great collaborator. You can actually be especially good at assessing your own and others' needs, recognizing valuable contributions, and coming up with win-win situations for everyone. If you can release yourself from competitive pressures and too much responsibility, if you can let go of needing to prove yourself, you're likely to get the most out of your Defined Ego/Heart collaborators.

I wouldn't worry too much about any of this. If you've got some Open Energy Centers, you don't have to go around looking for people with Defined motors, or work hard at staying away from them. I'd trust your Strategy and Authority (your *Inner Wisdom Keeper*) to help you recognize good relational fits, and cultivate a great sense of timing.

Regardless of your specific Design, what probably matters more than having *high* energy people around you, is having the *right* energy people around.

You want people in your life who are using their energy in ways that are healthy for you, that uplift and support you, and make you feel seen, heard, mobilized, and received. You also want people that just naturally bring out the good-heartedness, creativity and generous spirit in you.

(For an alternative view, see **The Motor Controversy** in the "Observe the Flow" Petal.)

## CAN MY ANGRY THOUGHTS BE FELT LONG-DISTANCE?

"Can we impact each other, even when we're not in physical proximity?" is a fascinating esoteric question.

If I were to attempt answering it from a Human Design perspective, I'd say, "Yes, totally."
I'd also say, "But let's hold this one lightly!"

It is truly amazing how connected we are to each other. Research studies show that if enough people meditate on peace at the same time, violence all around the globe can go significantly down during that period of time. Our thoughts and attitudes, when combined with energy, intention and un-conflicted action can be so very powerful, even magical.

We can only assume that when we're having powerful thoughts and feelings (like angry ones), they're also being sent out into a collective field of consciousness, whether we're aware of those thoughts or not. One could say we're all living in a giant bowl of Thought soup, to which we're all contributing, reacting, or responding to—consciously or unconsciously.

Depending on where we are in our own growth journey, and how well we've learned to 'receive energies' without over-identifying with them, we can respond in two ways: we can swallow whole everything that enters us through our Openness—amplifying and acting out without any mindfulness or heart-fullness.

Or, we can also allow incoming energies to wash through us, without clinging or pushing away. We (consciously or just energetically) witness what's entering us with a loving, compassionate presence—without being 'taken over' or swayed away from our wise Center.

To remain grounded in our *Inner Wisdom Keeper*, we don't even need to know exactly what's happening, or why. We don't need to know from where or whom a particular energy is coming—although learning to track energy can be a good practice, especially during the beginning phase of our Human Design experiment.

My point here is that we are all recipients of a constant stream of 'positive' and 'negative' thought patterns, moving towards and swirling around us in the collective field of consciousness. Even those of us with all Centers Defined are more Open and receptive than not. This phenomenon applies to all of us.

We're **all** constantly 'under the influence' of both personal and collective thinking, but it doesn't mean that we're all going to be impacted by these thoughts equally.

It is not our Openness, but our **relationship to our Openness**, that will ultimately determine the impact any given thought-form (or wave of energy) that is sourced 'outside of us' will have upon our system.

Think of Ghandi and his ability to keep an open, peaceful and strong heart-mind, even in the face of brutal and angry 'judgments,' not to mention literal, physically violent attacks.

On a more personal note, I'd venture to guess that the more intimate we are with someone, the more 'direct a line' our thoughts and feelings have with each other. In other words, our whole 'bodies'—physical, emotional, astral, etc.—are hyper-primed to care about what our loved ones think and feel. We're built to be as particularly tuned into their love and compassion as we are to their rage and judgment.

If you're angry at your partner, or they're angry at you, you're both likely to feel that somewhere, somehow on an energetic level.

The intensity with which you experience the other's thoughts and feelings might be influenced by the state of your Solar Plexus. If yours is Defined, and theirs is Open, for example, they might be more vulnerable to receiving, amplifying, distorting and/or reacting to whatever angry thoughts/energies you may be transmitting.

This doesn't mean that your thoughts will inevitably destroy or harm them in some irreparable way. It's important not to get rigid about these things.

Much depends on how you witness and hold your own process—whether you're on the 'sending' or 'receiving' end of this kind of an exchange.

If you find yourself overcome with angry thoughts about someone, your job isn't to repress your anger because you're afraid your thoughts will have a destructive impact on someone you love.

Your job may actually be to allow yourself to lean into, explore and find a way to give safe expression to the anger you're feeling. You're likely to find that if you do this, you'll be making room for the softer feelings that often lie beneath anger—like sadness, vulnerability and a deep longing. When you give your loving attention, first to the anger, and then to all that lives below, your heart will just naturally re-open to the person you love (whether or not you're meant to be together for the rest of your lives).

If you find yourself in the position of being an anger 'receiver,' I encourage you to first honor what you're sensing. Even if you're amplifying or distorting what you're picking up, it can be important to validate the fact that you are indeed picking something up (and that you're probably not crazy).

See if you can find a way to love yourself inside of that experience, without necessarily holding onto a victim stance, or blaming the other for 'doing something to you,' or being fully 'at fault' for how you're feeling.

You may find that the other is thinking or expressing something that you've also been feeling, but haven't allowed yourself to feel. You might realize that you're also having angry thoughts. You might also discover something completely different, which can shed light on your current relational dynamic.

When we're able to hold our emotional experiences with a degree of curiosity and a whole lot of acceptance, we usually uncover something valuable, clarifying and ultimately healing.

No matter our designs, we're **all** receptive and sensitive beings!

## *LIFE WITH AN OPEN G-CENTER*

My G-/Identity Center is totally Open, not one activation.

Learning to let go of the search for a stable identity, to surrender to externally-inspired directions, to embrace my capacity to reflect—not direct—people, and to enjoy the totally unpredictable ride that is my life…has been an exciting, terrifying, grief-inducing and releasing journey for me.

My original encounter with Human Design is an obvious example of my Open G Center at work.

Human Design entered my life from total left field, through a dear and deeply inspiring friend, Val Tate. Never in a million years would I have intentionally sought out this system. Yet, I'm so grateful it found me. I'll always remember stumbling upon a strange, angular-shaped, mechanical-looking chart sitting on Val's kitchen countertop, so many years ago. If my intuitive belly hadn't felt intrigued enough to ask her, "What the heck is this?!" that day, I might not be writing these words.

As touched on earlier, my G-/Identity Center has equipped me with a profound ability to reflect people, not direct them. Let me give you an example of what I mean by that.

Take religion and spirituality.

My mother always had a strong Jewish identity. She also has a highly-Defined G-/Identity Center.

She wasn't religious, so to speak. She did however fully embrace the cultural-social-activist aspects of Judaism, and had a deep love of tradition. Jewish customs were (and still are) a very big part of who she was and how she chose to parent her children.

My mother was also a teacher. (She was actually born on the Incarnation of Education.) Her entire adult life was dedicated to educating children in a way that would enhance their identity, worldview, and positively impact their direction in life.

It was very important to my mother that she instill in us (my sister—with a Defined G, and me with a totally undefined G) a strong sense of Jewish identity. She observed all of the holidays at home. She brought us to synagogue, sent us to Sunday school, Hebrew school, Confirmation school, and encouraged us to participate in all sorts of Jewish-related experiences, events, travels, summer immersion events, and social-service educations—all with the intention of making that Jewish identity (that had meant so much to her and her ancestors) stick.

While it stuck somewhat more successfully to my sister, it just didn't stick with me.

This is not to say that I don't have a deep appreciation for many of the gifts I received from my Jewish upbringing. I fully embrace the humanistic values embedded in so many of the teachings and experiences I had. I hold my experience of Jewish culture largely responsible for my love of learning and inquiry, my relational and psychological orientation, my deep desire to serve and empower the oppressed, and my self-effacing and neurotic sense of humor! I also believe that my ability to see and appreciate the beauty of all beings, regardless of their cultural background, came from my family's love of humanity (which, ultimately, transcended their allegiance to Judaism).

I still never really 'took' to the identity part. Even as a young child, I couldn't get behind what struck me as an embarrassingly immature God, or the 'chosen people' concept. I figured out pretty quickly that beauty, wisdom and 'Spirit' could be found in all people, in all religions—just as easily as ugliness, rigidity, fear and corruption.

When it comes to Identity, people with wide Open G Centers like me are a bit like Reflectors. We absorb and appreciate the potential beauty of all of ways of being. We can reflect the Love we find in all of its different forms. Specific 'identities' tend to slide off of us like they might a Reflector's Teflon aura.

(There are actually so many identities I could be speaking of here, aside from religious. I don't, for example, identify as 'U.S. American,' Human Design teacher, artist, author, etc.)

Interestingly, when I became a mother myself, I was faced with a dilemma.

- How do I impart a deep love of spirituality to my child?
- How do I share my sincere appreciation for my own Jewish heritage?
- How do I do this in a way that feels authentic to me?
- (In other words, if I could hardly get anything to 'stick' to myself, how in the heck do I get something to stick to someone else?!)

While I pondered this question, I watched my Danish husband (whose G-Center is Defined) easily and effortlessly impart a strong Danish identity to my daughter. Though Danes don't tend to be religious people, there is a secular Christianity that permeates the culture.

Just being around her father, basking in his obvious enthusiasm, made her want to know and experience the customs and traditions of his culture. I watched the positive associations build in her.
Before I knew it, I had a Christmas tree in our house, Christmas songs blasting on the radio, and meaty dishes I'd never have made myself (given my vegetarian leanings) cooking in the oven.

While I loved seeing my daughter so happy, and rejoiced in the depth of her connection with her father, I felt sad.

Why wasn't I able to transmit the rich traditions and gifts of my own Jewish heritage to my daughter? I felt like I was letting my mother, my grandparents and my 'people' down. I was depriving my daughter of her ancestry, of a unique golden thread that was meant to be a part of humanity's spiritual tapestry.

In an attempt to impart a Jewish identity in her, I tried all sorts of things.

I brought my daughter to Jewish Renewal (super progressive and inclusive) services and ceremonies. In an effort to keep what I loved and let go of the parts I felt uncomfortable with, I creatively modified all sorts of Jewish customs and holidays.

I even founded an ongoing spiritual parenting group where a group of us explored our own and each other's complicated and diverse relationship to spirituality and religion. We met regularly and shared the practices with each other that we found meaningful and heart-opening. We experimented with co-crafted and multi-cultural celebrating rituals together.

As much as I tried, I seemed incapable of planting a Jewish identity seed in my daughter. I couldn't feel or exude the specialized enthusiasm, and neither could she. It just wasn't something I could do.

Even if I could do it for a little while, I couldn't sustain it.

What I *could* do was expose her to people (her grandparents, dear friends of ours, etc.) who were so genuinely full of enthusiasm about their Jewish identities that she could absorb those feelings from them. Because I was simultaneously exploring Human Design, it was fascinating to see how those people with

Defined G-/Identity Centers seemed to be more effective when it came to imparting Identity. I felt almost viscerally the power of their own identities, and how grounded they were in them. It was so inspiring.

The less I tried to be who I wasn't, the easier it was for me to appreciate what I could offer my daughter.

One thing I could do really well was listen to, honor and reflect her own emerging identity, without attachment or pressure. I could express sincere curiosity about who she was, what she was coming to believe, or not believe, how she was naturally connecting with Spirit, or religion, or the people in her life who had a much more solid or 'specialized' relationship to these sorts of things.

Over time, I made peace with this with my Open G/Identity Center. I stopped blaming and judging myself for not being able to consistently feel and impart Identity.

I've also come to appreciate my Open G.

My natural ability to not only appreciate, but experience, diversity makes me a wonderful mirror. When I'm with people, and am able to reflect back to them what I see, sense and hear, they often discover their own wonderful identities in my presence. This is not because I'm transmitting anything spectacular, or showing them the way. It's just because being in my open, non-attached presence allows them to experience themselves without having to worry about my having some agenda for them. They are free to discover who they are.

Some years back, I participated in a Native American Full Moon Ceremony.

After the ceremony, the teacher invited me to walk 'The Red Path.'

To both of our surprise, I kindly responded with, "I love the Red Path, but my heart belongs to the Rainbow Path."

## INSIGHTS FROM OPEN Gs

Since we're all different, I'd like to share a how a few others have experienced life with an Open G/Identity Center. A big 'Thank You' to the *Designed to Blossom* participants represented in this section, for their generosity, openness and insightfulness.

### Participant One

"Something important that I have learned recently from Human Design and from my sessions with Rosy is that I have an Open G-center. The Open G, in my opinion, makes us relate to everyone and anyone, from any culture, any belief, etc. It is a beautiful gift to have an Open and receptive G Center, but it can also be confusing if we are not aware of it.

Looking back at my intimate relationships, I could always take on what the other person desired in a woman. I know that this sounds strange, but what I mean is if they wanted a good girl, who was nice, and traditional, I could be that person. But, of course, since I am not a traditional girl in many ways, the nice and 'good girl' parts that were attached to that identity, usually from their culture, were also not applicable to me.

For example, in certain cultures, a nice or good girl is one who does what society expects her to: follow the line, stay at home, most definitely not drink alcohol, be shy, be quiet, not think too much, love to cook, love to be the typical girl who defers to the man and other elders, be pretty, love to dress up, get their nails done, hair done, etc. You get the point.

But this was not me, like *ever*! I hated doing my hair and nails, I loved to go out drinking with my friends, I was not shy in most cases, I thought way too much, read way too much, only stayed at home if I wanted to, loved to cook but not so everyone around me has delicious food, but to make healthy food for myself (and anyone who wanted to be healthy too).

Basically, I was almost the complete opposite of what they wanted me to be, so invariably I took on this identity of their ideal woman. But sooner or later, the actual me would emerge. It would cause me so much grief not being myself all the time that I had to pretend, not as if I was doing it purposely to fool him (my partner), but more like I was doing it out of a need to be that person he thought I was.

And why did I get attracted to men who wanted those particular kinds of girls? Well, because my mom always wanted me to be that kind of girl. She hated the way I actually was, and constantly compared me to my sister, who was the perfect girl in every way. (By the way, only recently have I found out that my sister envied me for being so different, and felt sad for herself for being forced into the 'good girl' mold.)

So, in my 20s I was desperately trying to have the good-girl identity my mother wished for me. That process continued with my current boyfriend, and we had so much trouble because I confused him with being the good girl one minute and then the open-minded, devil-may-care girl the next!

Now I have learned that I will never know whether I am meant to be with this man for the rest of my life, unless I show up authentically to him. Since I was encouraged to start being more myself with him, I have been doing it so far. And the more I am myself, the more he is sticking around, understanding the real me, and liking me for me!

The goal changed from not wanting him to see the real me and then maybe leaving me, to allowing him to see the real me, and then deciding if he wants to stay or not. So far, he is still with me and I am so happily myself now. I am at the point where I am accepting some of those good girl aspects into my life (the ones that feel right for me), but not all of them. I still don't know if it will work out with this man, but either way, the goal is *not* to keep him at *any* cost, but to have him stay with me only if he likes the authentic me.

It's funny, knowing about my Open G-center has allowed me to be more 'me' than ever before."

## Participant Two

"I have an Open G/Identity Center. My life and identities have been episodic—like chapters in a novel—many, many identities. At this point in my life, I am feeling freer about my identity—more in the flow—not trying to define myself as much as I once did. This whole *Designed to Blossom* Course is so pivotal in letting myself be who I authentically am.

I felt pretty confused for a lot of my life. I'm thinking now it was the Open G-identity Center. At this point in my life—reflecting on all the phases I've gone through—I am so appreciative for all the experiences and identities I've had. I've had a very colorful life, as my friend says. It makes for good stories, too!"

## Participant Three

"I have an Open G/identity as well. I was a child who had to take care of my parents. I learned early on to match what was needed. I also had the ability to see things others couldn't see. There was no space to be me and have a 'self.' It has been a long journey for me to get to know my 'self.'

As you can imagine, I had to go through a lot of guilt, fear, anger and loneliness. When I realized that I`m not my story, but a spirit, something in me changed, and I found my true "Self." My story and childhood also gave me the gift of being able to go along with all kinds of people. I have always been accepting and open to other cultures and ways to be in life. This could be the gift of the open G-/Identity. I guess. Actually, I don't like to be put into boxes!"

(That last line is my one of my favorites! Perfect for the Open G!)

# *DO OPEN SACRAL BEINGS HAVE SENSITIVE TUMMIES?*

In the Human Design system, each Center has biological associations. (This information is covered thoroughly in the *Designed to Blossom* Course.) The Sacral Center—though we call it the gut, or "belly"—is actually associated with the ovaries and testes.

Often, when an Open Sacral Center is flooded with energies (or a Defined Sacral Center is frustrated or being misused), it's not the stomach that'll necessarily suffer, but the gonads! (That's not to say that one can't experience symptoms like nausea and constipation in relation to one's menstrual cycle.)

According to traditional Human Design sources, the Center that is directly associated with the stomach and intestines is the Ego/Heart Center.

When the Open Ego Center becomes too caught up in trying to prove and improve itself, or when the Defined Ego Center doesn't allow itself sufficient time to rest, our stomachs can break down from the pressure.

Given the somewhat narcissistic and contagious nature of Western culture, many Western bellies are under more pressure than they should be…pressure to do more, be more, produce more, power through more, etc.

While the Ego/Heart Center is associated with the stomach, the Throat Center is associated with metabolism.

The Spleen brings in the entire state of our immune system.
The Solar Plexus is connected to the whole nervous system.

One could say that all of the Centers, each representing organs and biological systems in the body, can impact the state of our bellies. Nausea can even be caused by inflammation of the liver (G-/Identity Center) or migraine headaches (Ajna).

Our bodies are highly sophisticated, intricately communicative, living organisms—where things are far less compartmentalized than they seem on a map, like a Bodygraph. Our Centers are always talking to each other, influencing each other, etc. They're all hooked up by an intelligent, interconnected network of Channels.

I write all of this, and I'm not even mentioning the advanced sub-school of Human Design, called PHS (Primary Health System)!

Students of the Primary Health System (PHS) go very deeply into the Body (the Design or Red aspect of the Bodygraph). PHS offers us a way to understand our body's nature as well as its digestive style. This system emphasizes the importance of learning what, when and where we eat, as well as how we've been conditioned to take in nourishment, and how we can benefit from freeing ourselves from that conditioning.

According to PHS, we each have pre-dispositions when it comes to taking in nourishment. Some of us are meant to eat one thing at a time. Some in the dark; others in the light. Some in silence, some in noise-filled environments. Some of us do best when we touch or prepare our food before we eat it. Others need to look at what we eat before it enters our mouths. The list goes on and on.

When we honor our digestive pre-dispositions, we can better receive and make use of the nutrients we take in. Our bodies work more harmoniously. We experience more energy, a more keen and productive brain, and…fewer digestive/belly issues.

The opposite is also true. When we eat how we're taught, as opposed to how we're designed, we can experience more belly problems.

PHS is considered advanced Human Design knowledge, and is not necessarily something to explore at the beginning of one's experiment, if ever.

It's important not to let Human Design—and its infinite buffet for the curious intellect—become yet another distraction or source of conditioning pressure for you.

Usually, making it a practice to trust and follow the guidance of your *Inner Wisdom Keeper* (Strategy and Authority) is more than enough to get you in the right place, with the right people, eating the right things. Keep engaging in the experiment of trusting yourself, have some fun, take some risks… and see what happens.

(For an alternative perspective on this topic, check out *How are the Centers Related to the Physical Body?* in Petal Three.)

# OPENNESS, SHAME AND HUMILIATION

We all have physical bodies with particular constitutions.

We have nervous systems with particular sensitivities.

We have our own 'souls' or essences with particular gifts and lessons to learn.

We have our own personal histories—with triumphs and traumas.

From a Human Design perspective, we have areas where we are more open to the world around us, more susceptible to conditioning messages, than other areas.

We're all more Open and receptive than we are Defined. Even though there are those who may seem more sturdy or solid because of their Definition, we are all still vulnerable to conditioning…just as we're all able to receive nurturing from those around us.

Our Openness is a wonderful thing. It's what makes us receptive, relational, flexible and adaptive.

All forms of conditioning—even the seemingly positive and genuinely well-intended—can lead us away from our true nature, or can make it more difficult for us to honor our uniqueness.

In order to survive (either emotionally, physically or both), we human beings learn from the moment we arrive to seek out and satisfy the approval of the people around us.

In most cases, we learn very early on that if we want to belong, if we want to be accepted, respected and valued, (if we want to be fed, clothed and sheltered!), we need to be or act in certain ways. These 'ways' must ensure our place in the 'tribe'—the family, the peer group, the school, the religious community, the nation, etc.

Any time we become aware of the fact that we're not living up to the expectations of the people we depend on for our survival, we can experience shame or guilt. Any time someone sends us the message, directly or indirectly, that we're disappointing them in some way, we can feel these painful feelings.

Just how deeply we take in these kinds of messages, and how much damage they do to our internal sense of who we are, is going to depend on a lot of different factors:

- How 'Open' we are.

- How strongly and violently the message is delivered.

- How frequently and pervasively we receive a particular message.

- How much the message is counterbalanced by more loving, accepting and honoring messages that we've also received and internalized.

- How much nurturing and support our 'true selves' have received.

The list of factors goes on and on.

What matters here is that we understand that everyone is conditioned, and that everyone is susceptible to experiences of shame and humiliation.

Another important piece is that while the conditioning messages we receive often enter through our Open Centers (or our Open places), we are often shamed for our Defined qualities, for our true nature.

Many women I know who have Defined Ego Centers were deeply shamed for being too strong-willed or powerful when they were young. They received conditioning messages saying, "Good girls should be feminine, obedient and soft; not stubborn, strong-willed and unruly."

Even though they have Defined Ego Centers, they can still experience the painful impact of negative conditioning in relation to that Center.

Sometimes when a Defined Center is shamed or judged, its expression becomes distorted. It takes on a 'shadow' form, usually reactive or repressive.

Many women with defined Ego/Heart Centers end up turning their strong will against themselves, instead of using it as a path towards self-empowerment and service to the world.

When we look at Jungian psychology, and we talk about the Shadow, it can be helpful to remember that the Shadow doesn't only refer to human qualities that are obviously shunned by society, (i.e. anger, jealousy, vindictiveness, vulnerability, etc.).

A Shadow can just as well be our Light, our strength, our talent, our joy, our capacity for ecstasy.

What makes something a Shadow is not the quality itself, but the fact that the quality has been forbidden, cast out, forced to split off from our conscious identity.

'What gets shamed' depends so much on the culture (family and society) in which we grow up. The qualities that are valued, the behaviors that are rewarded, are entirely different depending on what culture we come from, even our birth order.

You could have a sensitive boy raised in an ambitious macho culture shamed for his artistic nature, an ambitious boy raised in a more socialistic, homogenous culture shamed for his driven nature, a scientifically-minded girl raised in a conventional culture where girls are expected to be service-oriented and pleasing, shamed for her intellectual rigor; or a highly nurturing and imaginative girl raised in a culture where self-sufficiency and outer success are valued, and shamed for that.

We have people who are gender fluid or identify with a different gender than the one their biology represents, and they can be shamed for not fitting neatly into the gender box.

In the end, there are many factors that help to determine whether harsh conditioning messages become intrinsic parts of a person's identity ("I am bad"), or not:

- the extent to which a person is shamed
- the way in which a person is designed
- the way in which a person is taught/conditioned to take in and process negative messages
- other factors that are likely more spiritual/soul-oriented in nature
- all the ways trauma affects our lives.

Some people can be intentionally and dramatically humiliated, and not feel a drop of shame or humiliation.

Others can receive the slightest drip of criticism, and it can send them into an out-of-control shame spiral. (I know that one personally.)

It can be easy in Human Design circles to say, "Oh, I've got 7 Open Centers, so I'm much more vulnerable to conditioning than someone with fewer." While there can be truth to that, it's not the whole story. The whole story has much more to do with our experience of, and relationship to, our Openness, than how much Openness we've got.

Some people I know with many Open Centers have an incredible core strength that allows them to transmute their sensitivity into wisdom and clarity. Somehow, they're able to take in a whole lot without being flooded, or over-identifying with what's coming in.

Some highly-Defined people I know—because of their specific backgrounds—experience enormous vulnerability in the few yet potent Centers where they are Open. Sadly, the accumulated strength of their Definition becomes a horrible self-berating force.

## HUMAN DESIGN AS A 'BOLOGNA-DETECTING' DEVICE

In Human Design, we associate the Spleen with good intuition. A highly-Defined Spleen can provide a person with a natural 'bologna-detector.' Splenic beings can sniff out a healthy situation, just as they can smell something rotten.

You don't however have to have a Defined Spleen to be able to detect whether someone is being straight or trustworthy. Some of the most intuitive and truth-detecting people I know have Open Splenic Centers, though they may not rely on this Center for the bulk of their decision-making.

One of the many things I love about the *Gene Keys* and Integral Human Design is their acknowledgement of the evolving and multi-dimensional nature of the Design itself.

Any Design aspect—Defined or Open—can be experienced and expressed through a wide range of frequencies. You could have a highly-Defined Spleen and be completely hopeless at tuning into and trusting your intuition. You could also have a totally Open Splenic Center, and have spent your entire life studying and mastering the art of Intuition.

Any part of your design can enhance your bologna-detecting antennas if you are consciously working with your conditioning, and relying on your *Inner Wisdom Keeper* for decision-making.

- An Open Ego/Heart Center can help you sense whether, when and under which conditions someone is trustworthy or not.
- An Open Solar Plexus Center can help you assess a person's level of emotional maturity and authenticity. You can then choose to enter relationships with those who rise above reactivity, and respond to whatever is happening with honesty, transparency and compassion.

- An Open Ajna can help you recognize those intellects that have something valuable to offer you and the world. You can become quite good at weeding out the bologna-blasters, and appreciating the minds that easily embrace paradox and use their intelligence in service of the heart.

I encourage you to pay attention to your own truth-detecting gifts. What helps you know what and whom to trust?

You can then weave in the themes of your Open Centers. Enjoy the contemplation.

Even if you have no Open Centers, you are still here to learn how to discern between the 'real' and the 'fake,' the valuable and the discard-able, the love-enhancing and the fear-mongering, etc. We've all been given the exact Designs we need to be the best Truth-Detectors we can be.

If you watch the news for more than 3 minutes, you'll see that it is exactly this kind of discernment that we need to cultivate, more than ever!

(For a relevant exploration on Authority, check out *Our Multi-faceted & Universal Intelligence* in Petal Five.)

## *ON THE NEED FOR ALONE TIME*

I'm often asked whether there's a correlation between the amount of Openness in a design and the need for alone time. In the most general sense, I would probably say 'yes.' People with a lot of Openness in their Bodygraphs can feel flooded by the energies, pressures and stimulation of the world. A very 'Open' Generator, for instance, would likely respond positively to the right experience of solitude.

Generators with lots of Openness aren't the only ones who can benefit from alone time. Opportunities to unplug from the collective buzz can be wonderful for people with Open Sacral Centers, just as stress-free vacations can be experienced as pure medicine for those with Open Roots.

Our sensitivity doesn't only reflect the quantity of our Bodygraph's Open Centers, or the particular nature of the Open Centers we have. We all feel and experience our Openness differently. Someone might have only one Open Center in their entire Bodygraph, and be extremely sensitive in that area. They may need plenty of alone time in order to release the pressures or energies they've been taking in from just that one place. Someone with no Open Centers at all might need alone time to spend time with their thoughts, emotions or to practice a skill.

Other aspects of a design can point to a need for alone time. People with a lot of Line 1's, or 2's in prominent positions, for example, can need time alone to investigate, be introspective, or simply enjoy their natural impulses without having the feeling that someone's looking over their shoulder. Some People with a Line 6 in their Profiles may need 20 years of 'alone time'!

Certain Channels and types of Circuitry can give people this same tendency. For example, the Channel of the Prodigal (33/13)—even though it's part of a Collective and in many ways social Circuit—often brings with it a deep internal need to withdraw from the world and reflect upon one's life experiences, before re-emerging to share about them.

Individual Circuitry—one that goes on and off according to an intrinsic pulse, is deeply creative and at times melancholy—can create a need for withdrawing, diving deep, being creative, and then returning to the world with fresh, new energy. (More about *Circuitry* in Petal Three.)

People with Single Definition (where all of their Defined Centers are connected through Channels, without any 'missing' Gates) may find themselves enjoying their alone time, without necessarily feeling a need to find other people who can give them an experience of feeling whole and complete.

If you go deeper into the Design, beneath the level of Gates (and into the realm of Variables), you'll find that there are certain people who do particularly well in cave-like (or secluded) environments, or people with a certain depth of receptivity that might make them easily overstimulated by the world and in need of time to withdraw and space out, without the pressure to focus, strategize or constantly produce.

We all have different relationships to our designs, and to the world around us. Finding the just-right balance between self-connection and other-connection, between touching base with our own truth and inner core, and opening up to (and learning how to benefit from) the influences of the world around us is a spiritual practice.

Many of the examples I share here are 'positive,' in that they reflect people's healthy and understandable needs for being alone.

Having too much alone time can also be a reflection of a person's fear, shadow or 'Not-Self' being in the driver's seat. I know a woman with a 4/6 Profile, for example, whose life would have been so much more wonderful had she been encouraged as a child and young adult to reach out and connect with a network of friends. Sadly, she was conditioned to be a loner, and it took her many years to unleash her social potential, which for her was deeply connected to living out her life purpose. I leave you with two questions:

- What do you experience in terms of your need for alone time?
- What have you learned about your own just-right balance?

# Support Your Life: Petal Five

*Your Inner Wisdom Keeper's Unique Truth Compass*

SUPPORT
YOUR LIFE!

In Petal Five of the *Designed to Blossom* Course, we explore one of the most central aspects of Human Design, our *Authority*. This is the place we turn to for Truth—the part of us that we can trust to make our decisions in life, and to honor our own right timing. Just as we don't all belong to the same flower family, not everyone has the same kind of Authority. When we are in touch with our own unique truth-detecting system, we can make the most of the gifts we receive from the outside world without losing ourselves, or our ground, in the process. We can enjoy our Openness, without getting caught by it…or over-identified with it. We begin to liberate our *Inner Wisdom Keeper*.

Here in the *Designed to Blossom* Resource Book, we'll be exploring Authority from a multitude of perspectives, thanks to many generous students and clients who have brought their questions, frustrations, and insights to me over the years. We'll start by acknowledging our multi-faceted intelligence and the importance of restoring the mind to its proper place. We'll then hear a few voices from our Splenic Authority pool and take a look at the sometimes 'hard-to-grock' Self-Projected Authority. Finally, we'll look at some Authority-related challenges, such as when we don't resonate with our Authority, when honoring it freaks us (and the people we know) out, and when it's especially difficult to trust it (even during those moments when we're receiving Human Design advice!).

## OUR MULTI-FACETED & UNIVERSAL INTELLIGENCE

Although this Petal is dedicated to the exploration of Authority from a traditional Human Design perspective, I'd like to start you off with a lovingly heretical perspective.

No matter how you're designed,
your *Inner Wisdom Keeper* is wildly intelligent and resourceful.
It is connected to the whole of life.
It is far greater than your Authority, as defined by Human Design.

When we begin our Human Design experiment, we are encouraged to rely on a particular Authority, or perceptual orientation, based on the Definition in our Bodygraph. Accessing and honoring this Authority can be incredibly empowering as we learn to approach the decision-making process with increased autonomy and freedom.

Embracing our Authority, however, doesn't require that we ignore or discard the many other ways we can access our knowing. Regardless of the Open or Defined states of our Centers, we all have intuitions, feelings, emotions and gut responses. We all have body-intelligence and cognitive capacities. These are all at play when we enter any decision-making process.

Years back, when Richard Rudd was having one of his contemplative deep dives into Human Design, he had a fascinating revelation about Authority, the G-/Identity Center and its Magnetic Monopole. (As described in the Designed to Blossom Course, the Magnetic Monopole is an 'attractor field' that draws each of us along the line of our destiny.) Richard would say it "connects us into the living geometry" underlying all of life.

It doesn't matter whether our G-/Identity Center is Open or Defined. We all have a Magnetic Monopole, and its job is to unite our soul with our body, as well as our 'self' with our right life. Deeply connected to the second Gate (or *Gene Key*) in the G-/Identity Center, this magnetic aspect of our nature is designed to pull us along in life. When operating at its best, it connects us with the right place, the right people, at the right time.

As explained earlier, Integral Human Design takes the original blueprint of the Human Design Bodygraph and adds to it a *Spectrum of Consciousness*, described through the living language of the *Gene Keys*. Each element of the Bodygraph (e.g. Gate, Center, Circuitry, etc.) can be experienced and expressed through a continuum of frequencies—ranging from the most fear-based (*shadow*), to the most service-oriented (*potential/Gift*), to the most awakened (*essence/Siddhi*).

The second Gate or *Gene Key* lives deep inside the G-Identity Center. The 3 frequency bands associated with this Gate or *Key* are Dislocation, Orientation and Unity. Through Richard's sustained contemplations, he found that deep in the heart of this second Gate, lives a potential *universal* Authority—a way for any of us (regardless of the Definition of our G-/Identity Center, regardless of our knowledge or lack thereof about Human Design) to access our *Inner Wisdom Keeper*. Our ability to connect deeply with the potential and essence of this Gate can make it possible for us to make clear decisions that are intrinsically authentic, and in harmony with the whole of the cosmos.

According to Richard, it's all in the frequency. When we are driven by fear and caught in the shadow frequency, our decisions inevitably disconnect us from the whole; we end up dislocated from all of life. When we open our hearts to life, we just naturally orient ourselves through our decision-making process towards our highest potential, which can't help but serve Creation.

By truly connecting with the essence of this Gate, by surrendering to our own divinity and the natural direction of the Magnetic Monopole within us, we open ourselves up to being graced by a direct experience of Unity and Oneness. We no longer allow our emotions, reactivity or minds to direct us or tell us what to do. We only do what is in the Tao of our True Nature, which is connected to all of nature. This is why, as Richard wisely points out, so many mystical teachings guide us with the most simple directive of all: follow your heart.

# RESTORING THE MIND TO ITS PROPER PLACE

Genetics will always draw you to those who are different from you. Your Open Centers (Channels and Gates) will lead the way. They will speak to you through your mind, convincing you to choose people and situations that will fill up your Open Centers. This can be wonderful, because there are few things better than positive conditioning. People who are different from us don't only make great baby-making partners. They make great teachers and nurturers. They can nourish us in ways that bring out our true Self.

If we're not living our Strategy, let our genes take over, don't know or honor who we truly are (a marriage of body and soul, a combination of mind and body), we can't benefit from difference. Our genes will do their thing, and they won't be picky. They won't be asking questions on our behalf, "Say, does this person who has a Defined Spleen, this person who I feel protected and safe whenever I'm with them, actually keep me protected and safe, in reality?" "Are they capable of respecting, loving me in the way I really want? Or are they more of a drug?" These are not questions that keep our genes awake all night. All our genes want is someone different. They're not assessing the quality of difference.

Our minds may indeed be interested in these questions. In fact, they can get completely caught up in asking and trying to find answers to them, to the point of ignoring our bodies or trying to pretend that our bodies don't exist. Chances are, if we're relying on our minds to make our decisions for us, we'll end up in trouble. We'll only be getting half of the story, and that half will be very muddled up and confused. We might also be getting two halves of the story, constantly vacillating between each other. "Well, there's this…but there's also that."

In a way, you could say that our minds are often acting out opposing agendas. On the one hand, they're unconsciously representing our genes (trying to convince us to stay where we shouldn't because we can make good babies there), and consciously fighting what our genes want (trying to get us to rise above it all and fight our bodies' impulses, so we can hang out with people and in places that make 'spiritual' sense). Our minds are in a continual ping pong tournament.

Until we can restore our minds to their intended position (researcher/computer and Outer Authority, or authority for others), and our Authority to where it belongs (in the body, as a result of the sacred union between body and mind, the whole picture), they will almost always be able to convince us to go when we should stay or stay when we should go. Worse, they will keep us paralyzed somewhere in the middle, between countless rocks and hard places.

It is when we begin to trust our unique design, when we allow the parts of us (that are actually us lots of the time) to make our decisions, our mind transforms into a fabulously loyal, wise, witnessing and discerning servant and caretaker of our soul's 'vehicle.' That's when it can surrender to who we are and where we're going, without having to worry about controlling the ride.

# A FEW VOICES FROM OUR SPLENIC AUTHORITY POOL

Here's what a few *Designed to Blossom* Course participants had to say about life with Splenic Authority.

### Participant One

"Defining myself as Splenic was SUPER liberating, because I was carrying around this horrible notion of myself as being fickle, a changeling (also related to the Open G-/Identity, I think, taking on any and many identities), and these labels were weighing me down because I kept thinking, if only I could be 'normal' and steadfast like everyone else! But I was so happy to know and let it sink in that I am Splenic and can change. Strangely enough, the more I understand this, the less apt I am to be fickle...weird, huh?"

### Participant Two

"I used to think of myself as fickle too, so I was also happy to hear that the Spleen could change from one moment to the next. It's hard to explain to people why you're saying 'no' sometimes. 'My Spleen said so' doesn't work so well. Lol! I've started to become more aware of the feeling of 'that's not good for me.' Especially when related to things being said out loud. Sometimes I have to speak a decision out loud to get a good response. I kind of get a drop in energy, or a feeling of sinking energy when things are a 'no go,' or an empty feeling. Sometimes it's strong and other times just slight. It's been challenging to listen to that little voice, versus my logic. Or whatever sounds good. But I'm learning to trust it. And I'm great at detecting lies."

### Participant Three

"I feel it (my Splenic Authority) in the ways I make quick decisions about what I want to do...when an offer comes and I feel a 'yes,' I go. I like to think of the Spleen's intuitive qualities as there to help me keep moving towards synchronicities."

# A BIT ABOUT SELF-PROJECTED AUTHORITY

If you have Self-Projected Authority, you have a lot of Openness. You are deeply interactive by nature. Though you have your own feelings, drives and impulses rising up from within you, much of the time, they are not *only* sourced from within. They're also a result of your receptivity and capacity to take in what's going on around you. Whatever is going on inside of you is likely reflecting a combination of sensation, intuition, will, emotion and pressure.

Many experimenting with Human Design find it helpful to track our Openness, and to learn the difference between what arises from within, or comes from without. We often find that externally influenced inner experiences tend to feel more random. Physical, emotional and mental states can escalate in certain environments or around certain people, and then dissolve as soon as we are back in our own space.

Practicing healthy restraint and cultivating a witnessing capacity is especially important for those of us who have a lot of Openness, and who've tended to feel flooded, and then over-identify with (and act on!) every little thought, feeling and impulse that has moved through us.

That said, learning to witness our internal experiences without immediately acting or reacting is an important practice for all human beings. Think how safe and sane our planet would be if more of us learned to do this.

Self-Projected Projectors can feel confused about how their Authority works. Because they often feel a lot going on inside, they wish they could rely on it. Sometimes they feel so much going on inside that they're tempted to check out. Some feel the additional pressure to track every little internal movement, to a point of mental overwhelm.

Remember that Authority only matters when it comes to decision-making. Just because you're a Self-Projected Projector, and you may not be able to consistently rely on your gut instincts in order to make your own decisions, this doesn't mean that your gut is never speaking to you. Just because you aren't supposed to rely on your in-the-moment intuition for decision-making doesn't mean that you don't have an intuition, or that you can't ever tap into it.

Some of the most intuitive people I know have Open Spleens, and plenty of Open Sacral beings get very strong 'gut hits.' It's just that for you, the sensations and signals coming from your Sacral gut, Root, Solar Plexus, Spleen and Ego/Heart Center are going to be impacted by where you are, who you're with and what's going on in the stars.

Your true Authority lies in your heart, the place where love and joy reside. For you, Truth North has a direct line to your heart, especially during those moments when you're feeling particularly 'at the whim' of the world. (When I say 'heart,' I'm not talking about the Heart Center, but the G-/Identity Center.)

Your Authority is designed to help you naturally gravitate towards anything that enhances your experience of love—love for your body, for another person, for humanity, or for your beautiful self. The love that guides you doesn't have to be romantic, just as the joy that lights your way doesn't have to be 'happy.' The love and joy you're meant to trust goes much deeper than romance and happiness. It has the power to cut through overwhelm, ground you and drop you right into your core, no matter what's going on externally.

# I DON'T GET THOSE GENERATOR SOUNDS

Not all Generators experience the Sacral voice in the same way, with "uh huh's" and "uhn uhns." The whole point of Human Design is to honor our uniqueness, and help us find what works for us through a living experiment.

I know Generators who experience their Sacral 'yes' as a subtle pulling in a given direction. Others feel an increase of energy or feel their bodies simply moving into action. Others find themselves singing, whistling or humming or get a little giddy. Others feel a calm and focus coming over them.

I know Generators who experience their Sacral 'no' as a subtle nausea, a scratchy throat, a resigned sigh, a withheld breath, a sudden allergy attack, a low-level or free-floating irritation, a guttural grumble or moan, a tendency to get angry at their loved ones, a growing feeling of being trapped, pressured or resentful.

Some Generators find other decision-making techniques (that are designed to help people bypass the mind) to be useful in their experiment, either as gut validators or supplemental resources. These include muscle testing, embodied movement, art journaling (no words, just images) and that exercise where you stand up straight, someone asks you a 'yes/no' question and your body naturally leans forward (yes) or backwards (no). Embodied enactments and exercises like 'Stepping over the line' and 'Acting as if' can also help us access our body's truth as well. The possibilities are limitless. Chances are, if you're energetically drawn to a technique, you enjoy doing it, and it's leading you to make empowering decisions, your Sacral Center is giving its blessings to the technique.

# I'M SAYING NO MORE AND IT'S FREAKING ME (AND EVERYONE ELSE) OUT

Most people, as they go deeper into their experiment, find that they start to set more limits in their relationships. If they've struggled with setting boundaries throughout their life, this process can feel scary, uncomfortable, and in the beginning, a bit out of control.

Over the years, I've had many opportunities to grow into my name. One of the most important lessons I've had to learn as a 'rose-in-training' is to embrace and use my thorns. They are there for a profound purpose—especially when we're (finally) learning to courageously open our soft, delicate petals and share our gifts and essence with the world.

Given the extreme selfless conditioning I received growing up, and my genuinely caring nature, learning how to say 'no'—in a self-loving, assertive and effective way—has been, and still is, a daily practice.

There have been times in my life when it just hit me over the head…the extent to which I was losing myself in my relationships, or giving my energy away to those who didn't truly value it, or not saying 'no' when I really needed or wanted to.

Usually it's been some extreme life situation (i.e. a sickness, a sense of burn out, some really uncomfortable—and very familiar—interaction with someone which left me feeling utterly invisible, used, disrespected, etc.) that has awakened me to the old pattern, as if I were waking up from a bad dream.

During these potent moments, I've emerged with a new level of vigilance and self-preservation instincts. I've acted in ways that may have felt a bit odd and shocking to those who had grown accustomed to my selfless, understanding, overly-accommodating ways.

Sometimes I'd feel a little shocked by their shock…but mostly I'd feel guilty, like I'd done something wrong—either by setting the limit, or by having led them on by never having set the limit in the first place. I'd do a little back-peddling, or over-compensating in an attempt to minimize the damage. I'd usually feel resentful again…and say 'no' with more vigor than the situation might have called for (because again, I was saying 'no' to years of feeling like a slave).

I share this just to lend some normalcy to any shaky, surprising, shocking, scary, wobbly part of the process you may be going through. It's totally OK if it feels a little awkward, if you go a little back and forth, if not everyone (including you) knows what exactly to make of you and how you're behaving while you're growing healthfully into your thorns.

During these times, humor comes in very handy. Those people in your life who really love and get you will rejoice in these changes, even if the transformative process is a little bumpy. They will also be able to laugh with you. My guess is that your real friends will be deeply inspired by you too.

# TRY NOT FOLLOWING YOUR AUTHORITY

As someone with the 3/5 Profile, I have a very deep appreciation for the trial-and-error learning process. I don't even think it's possible to truly understand what it feels like to live authentically, if we don't at times go against the grain of our Authorities, or give into pressures, or get swept up by another's enthusiasm, or attempt to please someone, or lose our way.

How else are we going to know what our way is, what it looks and feels like, what its boundaries are? How else will we know how a good fit feels or how a bad fit feels? It's all wonderful grist for the experimental mill.

When we approach our life with a curious, permission-giving, always-ready-to-learn attitude, each decision we make (even the ones that are technically 'wrong') has the potential to become right.

A *Designed to Blossom* participant once shared about an experience, where she signed up for a course, not because her Authority gave its blessing, but because she got swept up in the enthusiasm of a dear friend. After some time experiencing the course for herself, she could feel that it just wasn't for her. Despite moments of self-doubt, guilt and a sprinkle of shame, she finally allowed herself to drop the course, and felt great relief when she realized that the friendship could survive her 'no.'

Had she not overridden her Authority, she wouldn't have felt as motivated to honor it the next time such a situation rolled around. She wouldn't have gained important insights into the kinds of situations that tend to throw her off-center, like when someone she loves is excited and invested in her saying 'yes,' or when she herself has a genuine wish to go on a journey with someone she cares about. She wouldn't have had the opportunity to practice saying 'no' to someone she cares about, or to learn that everyone survives.

In the *Designed to Blossom* Course, I actually recommend that Generators go on a major 'should' binge and see what happens. Since every Human Design student is learning to free themselves from the power of shoulds, I'll share the invitation here.

## GO ON A MAJOR "SHOULD BINGE!"

Take a day to totally push yourself to do all sorts of things you really don't feel like doing, with people you don't feel like being with. Really push, initiate, pursue, keep pursuing, regardless of whether you feel a flow or received or resisted. Ignore your body's signals as much as you possibly can. (For Projectors, ignore whether you've been invited or not, or whether you feel genuine love for the activity, or genuine connection with the person, or not. Manifestors, respond all you like. Reflectors, just do it. Don't wait.)

See what happens!

There is so much to be learned from this experiment. It's not always clear-cut. It can take a long time to get a feel for how your own response system (or Authority, for other Types) works.

Some people—when they try to ignore their body's clear messages—end up having obviously horrible days and learn how important it is to trust their body's yes's and no's.

Others realize that they have no idea what their bodies are telling them, so they don't even know whether they're ignoring their bodies' messages or not. They learn that they need a lot more practice at simply understanding and communicating with their bodies.

Others have particularly confusing days—where some 'pushed-through' actions don't feel good at all, but others feel surprisingly good. Someone might really not feel like going to a party, or a dance class, but once they're there, they have a great time.

It can really take time to learn how to discern between resistance that comes from fear, and the genuine 'no' arising from our *Inner Wisdom Keeper*.

Sometimes our bodies actually have energy to do something, but our minds have us convinced that doing it is dangerous or wrong. We can experience an internal holding back that could easily be confused with a lack of our Authority's blessing or Strategic harmony.

When we decide to take a day where we push ourselves to do things we have resistance to, we can also learn something about the source of the resistance. If we genuinely enjoy something we pushed through, chances are that there was a genuine response (or rightness) in there somewhere. We may be dealing with an area of our life where our genuine energy (or love, or rightness, or truth) has been habitually suppressed. This can lead to a very juicy inquiry…and further experimentation!

Similarly, sometimes our bodies seem driven to do something, but really, it's just an addictive pattern, driven by fear and/or survival coping strategies that have been operating in our lives for a long time. In these cases, the true response is overridden by the habitual behavior.

Patience and compassion and experimentation are key here.

# TRUSTING OUR AUTHORITY IN
# PAINFUL INTIMATE RELATIONSHIPS

Should I stay or should I go?

*"Should I stay or should I go?*
*If I stay there will be trouble.*
*If I go there will be double.*
*So come on and let me know.*
*Should I cool it or should I blow?"*
~ the Clash

When we are struggling inside of painful intimate relationships, the task of accessing our true Authority or *Inner Wisdom Keeper,* can be especially difficult. If we stay, we wonder whether we're allowing ourselves to be victimized. If we leave, we wonder whether we're refusing to take responsibility for our part in a painful dynamic, and blaming someone else for our problems.

Human Design can be so helpful when it comes to situations where there are no clear-cut answers to our questions, no templates to follow, no success-guaranteeing action steps. Honoring our Strategy and Authority can give us incredible guidance, as we navigate our way through this tricky and painful terrain, one micro-decision at a time.

Even when we're deeply grounded in our Human Design experiment, when it comes to our most intimate relationships, it can still take time before we have the clarity or courage to full-heartedly stay, or full-heartedly go. So much is at stake, and there are few places where our deepest conditioning has this much hold on us.

Because of this, I'd like to share some additional thoughts for you to take or leave, should you ever find yourself in a painful and confusing relational predicament, and having a hard time accessing (or trusting) your *Inner Wisdom Keeper.*

There can be a very fine line between seeing someone clearly,
holding that person responsible for their actions and impact,
and blaming them.

It's not always easy to tell whether a relationship has enough mutuality and maturity in it to be 'stay-worthy.' It can also be challenging to predict what can and will happen when we do our inner work.

Sometimes, we enter our Human Design experiment, or go through an inner transformation, and our outer world changes for the better. We can begin to respect ourselves at a deeper level, and suddenly, people begin treating us with greater respect…without our even asking for it. Even those we never dreamed could or would ever change suddenly act in ways that seem miraculous.

Other times, our Human Design experiment leads to a profound change on the inside, but nothing seems to change at all on the outside. Our parents are still our parents. Our critics are still our critics. Our partners are still angry all of the time.

Because of all of the de-conditioning work we've done, however, we may not be as deeply influenced by what the people around us think, say or do.

Perhaps because of additional psychological or spiritual work, we can more successfully see through arising relational dynamics. We can see the fear and hurt driving our partner's behavior, and we feel genuine compassion for them. We're able to remain connected to the truth and love-ability of who we are—even in the face of hurtful or unhelpful conditioning pressures. The 'negativity' just slides off, in the places where it used to stick.

Sometimes the fruits of our experiment show up through our growing capacity to set limits, to express our anger, or to leave a conversation or situation that isn't healthy for us.

Sometimes it's only when we dare to say 'no,' leave, or set a limit, that the outer world begins to change for the better. We might decide that we're finished doing all of the emotional work in the relationship, so we leave. Finally, our ex-partner might decide to give this crazy Human Design thing a try, or goes into therapy and starts doing the inner work necessary to make a healthy relationship possible in the future.

## And then...

Sometimes, we think we've mastered our design, or we've gone through a deep inner transformation, but we haven't. Or at least, we realize that we've got more work to do.

Maybe we've figured out how to leave bad situations, but we keep winding up in new versions of those bad situations. Same story, different characters.

Maybe we've figured out how to stay, no matter what. We can process relational dynamics until the cows come home, but nothing's really transforming. No one's really growing.

It's when we keep ending up in the same situation (e.g. with the same kind of partner, experiencing the same kind of reactions, repeating the same kind of repression, beating ourselves up and feeling victimized over and over again, etc.) that we usually wake up and take a new level of responsibility for our experience.

This is when we realize that there's no easy fix and 'no way around it.' We can only go through it!

Even if the people around us are walking *Not-Selves*, and screwing up left and right, there's no one out there to blame. At least spending any more of our precious energy and time blaming people isn't really going to solve our problem.

As Pema Chodrin writes, "Nothing goes away until it teaches us what we need to know."

*But what is it that we need to know?*

Sometimes we need to know that it's safe to feel our feelings—even the dark, painful and uncomfortable ones.

Sometimes we need to uncover what it is that we get out of being in whatever relational dance that we're in. Without this discovery process, our subconscious will continually sabotage our *Inner Wisdom Keeper*.

- Are we using our current problem as a distraction from our life purpose, a protection for someone we love, a way of avoiding failure…or more likely…success?
- Are we looking for evidence to prove an old belief—that we were once told, that we internalized—that no longer serves us?
- Are we indirectly expressing our anger at our parents, early caregivers or partners by securing our misery, by depriving them of our joy?

The list of possibilities is endless.

Sometimes we need to become aware of something we've been hiding from ourselves. A truth. A feeling. A need. Something that continually thwarts our attempts to honor our Strategy and Authority.

Sometimes we need to learn how to stop overthinking and just do something. We need to be willing to try something different, to do something new, to break the rules (even Human Design rules), and see what happens.

Sometimes we need to grieve the loss of an old dream…to come to terms with the fact that someone we hoped would change, someone we hoped would finally see, love and respect us for who we are, will never change. That they'll never ever be who we've wished they could be, or believed they had the potential to be.

Sometimes we need to learn how to discern between 'good hard' and 'bad hard'—between constructive labor and unconstructive labor.

…Between a relationship where, as an old *Designed to Blossom* participant wrote, both partners have the "necessary amount of awareness, desire and determination" to transmute a painful dynamic into a deeper intimacy and relational resiliency…

…And a relationship that just doesn't, no matter how badly we wish that it did.

Human Design offers us a powerful way to understand the unique chemistry of each relationship. Connection charts can shed light on how we're designed to bring out different parts of each other. Some relationships may have more potential to bring out our best or worst, than others.

That said, even relationships blessed with the most fabulous potential can have serious problems, for so many reasons. Relational problems can't always be fixed by an intellectual understanding of how our designs compromise each other or have too many electromagnetic connections. Even if we've heard we've got 'nowhere to go,' this doesn't mean we're ready to go anywhere.

We're often attracted to people who are like our parents, early influencers, or our siblings. The more intimate the relationship, the more likely it is to reflect the best and worst parts of our own growing up. Though at the start of our relationships, our partners may not seem very much like our original family members, it usually doesn't take long before they start to look and act a *lot* like the significant people from our past!

No matter how much we've mastered our own Human Design practice, stuff is bound to come up.

What matters is what we do with the stuff,
and more importantly,
what we're able to do with it.

**Here are three relevant questions:**

- What's the Commitment of each partner?
- What's the Capacity?
- What's the Consistency?

Sometimes having just one—or even two—of these three C's isn't enough to make a relationship work.

Someone can be really committed to working things out, or living their design, but not have the capacity, for a multitude of reasons.

Someone can be perfectly able to process emotional material and work through conflict, but not be committed enough to do the work that's required.

Someone can have the capacity AND the necessary commitment, but they don't show up consistently enough for the relationship to reap the harvest of hard work done over a long period of time.

In the end, we can only take responsibility for our own steps in the dance.

**A profound quote from a *Designed to Blossom* participant:**

*"Mutual healing and growth (evolutionary movement) take place, in my experience, when there is a shared dedication and more or less equal investment. Absolutely everyone deserves the chance to change and everyone does have that chance. Except we don't drive that car for anyone else but ourselves. If our well-being and joy within the context of an intimate relationship depend upon them changing the way they are—that is something to look at."*

In any given situation, there are limitless and profound life lessons for us to potentially learn.

- **How can we best learn what we need to learn?**
- **Where is the best place for us to learn?**
- **With whom do we engage in the healing and/or awakening process?**

I always come back to balance.

Even if it's true that we have low self-esteem, poor communication skills, and a tendency to get reactive when we're feeling angry, triggered or afraid, that STILL doesn't mean that we should stay where we are, with a person, no matter what. It also doesn't have to mean that we shouldn't give ourselves permission to leave until we've worked it all out, owned every shadow and retrieved every projection.

When a relationship or environment is really unhealthy (even if on an energetic level, it is a two-way street), expecting ourselves to work it all out within the relationship is like taking vitamins in a toxic swamp and expecting ourselves to attain the pinnacle of health.

Sometimes the best way to ultimately serve and heal a relationship is to go outside of that relationship in order to do the healing work.

Especially when we grow up in families where there wasn't a lot of positive, loving, empowering, nurturing going on, where we didn't have role models who could show us what love, acceptance, support and good communication look like, it can be so important that we do our healing in a different, more positive conditioning field…in a safe, protected environment.

Maybe, in addition to our Human Design work, we allow our *Inner Wisdom Keeper* to guide us to a counselor, or spend time with our good friends, immerse ourselves in a workshop, or join an intentional community for a while.

Whatever we do, what matters most is that we spend time with people we trust, people who see our innate goodness, who aren't threatened by our light, or afraid of our dark. During challenging relational times, we need people who can hold space for the full range of our emotional lives, and who can see and reflect back to us our beauty, and love us, even when we're not feeling all that love-able, and when we're gripped by fear or our shadow material.

It's when we spend enough time in healthy, loving environments, and when we've had the chance to receive and internalize enough positive nurturing messages, that we can then go back to those old triggering relationships and situations (if we want to!), with our *Inner Wisdom Keeper* intact, and experience them—and ourselves—differently.

> We can feel what we feel.
> We can see what we see.
> We can set limits when they're called for.
> We can leave if we have to.
> We can grieve if we need to.
> We can take our time.
> We can experiment.
> We can try and fail and try again.
> We can speak our truth in a way that is more easily received.
> We can feel the fullness of our own life cup.
>
> From this full place, we don't need to blame.
> We don't need to sacrifice ourselves either.
> We don't need to force an agenda.
> Or win an argument.
> Or convince anyone of anything.
> Because we know the truth of who we are.
> Even if we temporarily forget it...
> We know where to go and who to talk to...to be instantly reconnected with our unique Truth compass.

In the end, as we work the situation from a variety of angles, we find ourselves acting differently and appropriately to each situation. Each moment will be informing us of the right action.

As we act, we won't be coming from a place of repression or reaction. We won't be disguising our fears with an intellectual understanding of our Human Design.

We will simply take action. Natural, right-enough action.

Instead of blame or charge, there will be a natural movement towards—or back to—what is healthy.

# IS THE UNIVERSE PUNISHING ME FOR FOLLOWING MY GUT?

A wonderful *Designed to Blossom* participant was a highly creative Generator. Honoring her belly's positive responses as well as saying 'no' were usually easy for her, unless the situation was money- or survival-related. Sometimes she'd say 'yes' to a job that she didn't want, and then feel sick to her stomach. She'd take the job anyway, because of the financial security (and relief) doing so provided. She wasn't always sure whether the sick feeling she had was a signal from an unhappy Generator belly, or just a passing feeling. A few times she tried to take it as a signal, said 'no' to a job, but then ended up with no new job to respond to…and a whole lot of stress. She felt punished for trusting her gut.

This particular person had an Open Spleen, which exacerbated her survival fears. Of course, you don't have to have an Open Spleen to have money worries, or for survival fear to make it very hard to trust in your Authority. I'm a Generator with a Defined Spleen, and Lord knows I visit that place on a regular basis!

Here are a few questions to explore, should you relate to this situation:

## Where is there Flow?

When a certain kind of worry pattern continually gets in the way of a Generator's self-trust, it can be helpful to temporarily turn our attention away from the stuck place to where there's flow. Even if you only find one place where you've succeeded at honoring your belly, there's hope! Feel free to explore the following questions on your own or with someone you trust:

- If you are a Generator who's been feeling blocked in one or more areas of your life, where would you say you're *not* blocked? Where are you actually able to listen and honor your belly's wisdom? Include life arenas you tend to take for granted.

- When have you experienced flow in the past? Who and what contributed to that flow?

- Think of a time recently when you managed to say 'yes' or 'no,' even in the presence of fear or discomfort. What helped you to honor your belly?

- Who do you know that is particularly good at trusting themselves and honoring their truth in the arena where you find it most difficult? What helps them?

## Can you Respond Outside the Box?

Another helpful practice for Generators who feel stuck is to 'respond outside the box.' Many of us, when we're wanting to respond to life, don't even realize just how much we've narrowed our response playing field. We carry all sorts of assumptions about what kind of person, opportunity or experience will be in our best interest. Then we reserve our receptivity for whatever our mind has deemed worthy of responding to, and totally overlook all sorts of wonderful opportunities that don't fit the expected mold.

Expanding our belly's reach also means remembering that one response can lead to another. We may respond to a hanging out at a café, and them bump into an old friend who offers us a volunteer opportunity which leads to a fantastic paid job. If we're only open to responding to paid job offers, we risk missing out on exactly what we're needing and wanting.

I encourage you to widen your belly's gaze. Let the whole Universe talk to you. Be open to being surprised.

## Can You Give Yourself a Little Compassionate Self-talk?

When out of fear, you're extremely tempted to say 'no' to something you want or 'yes' to something you don't want, tell yourself something like:

"Hey, you (me). I know you're willing to do anything to feel some security right now. I get it. But will you do me a favor? Will you take a few breaths before you act? Let's see if we can wait just a bit, and simply hang out with the fear without doing anything yet. If it's OK with you, I'm going to reach out to someone who knows and loves you for a little support. I'll make sure it's someone who's good at helping you access your belly wisdom and who can come up with good questions for your Sacral Center. I'll also choose someone who knows what you're capable of when you're not terrified, someone who can remind you of what truly excites and sustains you, before you jump into (or out of) something, and make us both sick."

## Can you Get to the Heart of the Conditioning?

In this course participant's case, it was easy to see and feel the sabotaging power of her Open Spleen. The conditioning messages she had internalized through that Center in relation to themes of safety, security, money and survival were some of the strongest and most potent bullies she had. If you find yourself in a situation like hers where you're feeling particularly unable to honor your body's wisdom, and you know it, do an Openness exploration. Here are some questions to get you started:

- Which of your Open Centers is shouting the loudest? What is it saying?

- What are its most potent messages?

- Take some time to explore their origin. Who used to say this? Why? How did it impact you when you were younger and more vulnerable to that person's influence?

- If I could wave a magic wand and make that voice disappear (or guarantee you that everything would work out fine), would you be a 'yes' to this opportunity? Would you be a 'no'? Would you be a 'not yet'?

- Think of someone you admire who embraces a very different, more encouraging and empowering message in this arena. Who is this person?

- What would they say to themselves if they were in your situation?

- What would they say to you if they were by your side right now? Write it down and put it up somewhere. Look at it regularly.

## Can you Pay Extra Attention to your Body?

If you notice your body complaining when you make a decision, pay attention. When our bodies are used to our continually ignoring their signals and overriding their needs, sometimes the only option they have is to make us sick.

If you're in the process of making a decision and you feel sick, or get an ache or a pain, that's a great time *not* to make the decision. Your sick/yucky feelings are likely your body's way of saying 'no, thanks' or 'not yet.' Even if you've got a Defined Spleen and are normally capable of making spontaneous decisions, you may still need to wait, especially when fear is in the mix, and you're dealing with an area in your life where you have a history of difficulty accessing your *Inner Wisdom Keeper*.

Whatever your design, buy yourself time. Tend to your body. Restore calm in your nervous system.

## Can you Gently Remind Yourself that You're Still Human?

Human Design is a practice. It is an experiment that can take a long time to get the hang of. In the beginning of your journey, you're going to need to stretch your discomfort tolerance muscles. You may do this by delaying a decision, breathing into a feeling, or bringing mindfulness to the situation. Whatever works for you.

Even as you get better at trusting yourself, and you experience increased flow in your life, it's important to remember that you're still human. Feelings of fear, pain, sadness, anger, worry, despair and discomfort are all a part of the human landscape.

While you're learning how to honor your belly's wisdom, work on embracing your humanness too.

# *HOW TO STAY TRUE TO OURSELVES WHEN IN A HEATED DEBATE?*

Intellectually heated conversations have the power to bring people into their heads, and out of their Human Design experiment. One of the greatest gifts Human Design provides us is countless opportunities to notice what happens within us, and between us, when we get swept up by the mind.

I'm a great lover of the mind and its capacity to wrestle with complex topics and bring us to a place of self- and other-understanding. I have also experienced the damage bright minds can do to bodies, hearts and relationships when people feel under attack or misunderstood.

## An Invitation

If you are in a conversation (in person or online), and you sense what began as a healthy, mutually respectful inquiry is turning into a heated intellectual debate, slow down. Just for the moment, forget about the content of the discussion. Bring your full attention to what's happening within you.

- What's happening to your breath?
- Your sense of safety and connectedness?
- Are you shutting down?
- Are you reaching out for what you truly need?

Notice the more charged thoughts occupying your mind. The thoughts that don't have anything to do with the topic of conversation. Are any of them familiar? For example:

- "No one understands me."
- "I can't get through."
- "She must not like me."
- "I've done something wrong."
- "If I don't make it better, no one else will."
- "People are idiots."
- "Nothing works."
- "I can't be myself here."

Allow your own inner inquiry to move in the direction of your own conditioning and early life experiences. How might they still be impacting you and your relationships in real time? See if you can find a way to soften your heart. First and foremost, towards yourself.

- How can I be more kind to myself?
- More gentle?

- More patient?
- More understanding?

The gentler an atmosphere you can create within you, the easier it will be to be honest with yourself, and see the ways you may have gotten temporarily swept up in mental mania. Whether your Head and Ajna Centers are Defined or Open, you may discover places where you've been holding on too tightly to beliefs and opinions, or working too hard to convince others of something that may not really matter in the end. You may find places where you've been judging yourself and others too harshly, or abandoning yourself emotionally.

I think many people are drawn to Human Design because of its profound emphasis on inner and outer congruity. When we truly surrender to our *Inner Wisdom Keeper*, we find that more and more of the time, our thoughts, feelings, expressions and actions align.
Becoming a congruent, authentic being is a lifelong journey. It requires radical self-honesty and a deep sense of humility. Such qualities grow best in gardens of tenderness. When we judge ourselves too harshly, or hold ourselves up to rigid standards (whether those standards come from old parental or cultural conditioning sources, or newer ones, like Human Design), we can create a field within and around us that makes it very difficult for learning and growing. We use too much of our efforts and gifts defending ourselves against real and perceived attacks.

I often find that if I manage to slow myself down enough during a heated debate, my mind begins to serve the constructive aspects of the conversation, rather than sabotage them. It prioritizes process over content. It helps me share places where I feel triggered or vulnerable, and to get curious about the deeper experiences of others. Over time, as everyone's nervous system relaxes and we remember that we actually care about each other, our minds start coming up with creative, nuanced and paradox-embracing perspectives. Next thing you know, a seriously 'quagmired' conversation laden with emotional field mines becomes transformative, illuminating and healing.

## *TRUSTING OUR AUTHORITY WHEN IT COMES TO SLEEP*

Although our Bodygraphs change when we go to sleep, we still remain Open where we're Open. When we sleep very close to someone, and they are Defined where we're not, we are influenced by their energies in our sleep (and vice versa). An aura is said to extend about twelve feet all around the body, including above the head and below the feet. This means that if we're sleeping close to a wall, and on the other side of that wall our neighbor is sleeping, we can actually be taking in their aura, and they ours!

Because of this, some people (especially Open Sacral beings like Projectors, Manifestors and Reflectors) can have trouble getting the high-quality sleep they need in order to wake up clean and refreshed. Emotionally Defined beings can also benefit from waking up in their own aura, so that they begin the day with a good feeling for where they are on their wave, outside of others' influence.

Some Human Design enthusiasts feel strongly that sleeping alone is essential to returning to neutral, starting the day as oneself, and living an authentic life. Many people who have gone through a deep Human Design experiment agree. I know couples who have their own rooms. I also know families that sleep on their own whenever they're feeling off kilter or overstimulated. Because of some potent cultural norms around sleep, it can take courage (and relational sensitivity!) to experiment with sleeping on one's own, when you're in a couple.

I had a family bed for years (which brought about its own form of cultural disapproval) and still sleep with my husband, so I'm no evangelist when it comes to this one. However, if my Sacral responds to sleeping on my own, I do it. If Human Design is about anything, it's about freeing ourselves from worrying too much about what everyone else thinks, and living lives that work for us.

If you typically share a bed with someone, and your *Inner Wisdom Keeper* feels drawn to a little sleep experiment, go for it and see what happens.

(More on *Sleep* in Petal Seven: Moving Beyond the Map)

# *HOW DO I TRUST MYSELF WHEN SOMEONE GIVES ME HUMAN DESIGN ADVICE?*

Sometimes I find it really helpful, when trying to discern whether a piece of Human Design advice is a healthy one for me or not (at least in the moment), is simply to notice how it impacts me when I take it in.

- Do I find myself more relaxed, more trusting, more courageous, more inspired, more empowered, more myself as I receive it?

- Or do I find myself increasingly full of self-doubt, judgment, hopelessness? Do I feel essentially unseen in some way?

Even if the advice itself is wonderful, if I'm using it against myself, its essentially wise nature becomes distorted, and it becomes more damaging than helpful.

Sometimes tough love is just what I need to get off my insecurity-butt, move into action and honor my Authority. Sometimes it's what I need to finally let go of something that I'm not meant to act on at all.

Sometimes, tenderness and self-acceptance for myself and my creative process (even if it's not such a glamorous one!), is just what the medicine doctor ordered.

As always, it's a dance.

One thing Human Design teaches us is that our unique way of learning about anything (e.g. a system, philosophy, skill set, education, etc.), can be so incredibly different.

Some of us are designed to leap off the cliff and let our intuitions speak unhindered.

Others of us are designed to be more methodical and studious in our approach.

Some of us learn by doing and experimenting.

Some of us learn better by apprenticing or learning from the masters.

Others by getting a doctorate in the field.

We're all so different. That's what makes our individual voices so unique…and paths so multi-colored. Why shouldn't our learning approach to Human Design reflect our unique designs?

I encourage you to trust yourself and your own experience—especially when it comes to taking in a system like Human Design.

You can learn from ALL of your experiences, including those that result from having taken 'not the best' advice!

Whenever you can, follow your open, unburdened and playful heart!

# Open to Your Path: Petal Six

*Gain a New Perspective on your Purpose*

OPEN UP TO YOUR PATH!

In Petal Six of the *Designed to Blossom* Course, we explore PROFILE—an aspect of our Life Purpose, or the unique role that we, as beautiful unique flowers in a planetary garden, are meant to play out in life. Our Profile sheds light on some of the major themes we are likely to encounter in life, as we move toward living out our true purpose. We learn that, at least when it comes to Human Design, our Life Purpose is nothing that we have to go out and try to make happen. It is designed to unfold naturally, as a result of our living our lives authentically.

There are 12 distinct Profiles in the Human Design system. All Profiles have their own gifts, challenges and set of paradoxes. Each role or life path style consists of a combination of two numbers. One of the numbers (or Lines) represents your conscious Personality, or the more known aspect of you. The other represents your Design, your body, your genetic make-up, or the less conscious (in Human Design lingo) aspect of you. (For an additional perspective on the conscious and unconscious aspects of Human Design, see *The 'Black and Red' isn't so 'Black and White'* in Petal Three.)

Here in the *Designed to Blossom* Resource Book, we'll empathize with and reassure those who don't like their Profiles, remind all of us that we are not our Profiles, and then go through the 6 Lines, this time with even more of a *Gene Keys* twist than I was able to provide in the *Designed to Blossom* Course.

## I DON'T LIKE MY PROFILE

If you've had this thought, you're not alone. All Profiles have their shadows. They also have their blessings! In my experience, all Profiles give us exactly the gifts we need to work with and transform their inherent challenges.

Every aspect of your design (not just your Profile) can be experienced in ways that are painful and difficult, or in ways that bring about incredible healing, joy and creativity. Nothing in your design is static or one-dimensional. Every part of it is built to be highly responsive to the attitude you bring to it.

You are officially invited to embrace a loving, gentle and curiosity-rich attitude towards your entire design—Profile included.

# YOU ARE NOT YOUR PROFILE
# (THE SUM IS GREATER THAN ITS PARTS)

In this Petal, I will be sharing more about each of the 6 Lines, so that you can deepen your understanding of your Profile. Please keep in mind that *you are not your Profile*. Your Profile can only illuminate something about the role you're meant to play out in life. Frankly, there's nothing you need to do in order to make that role happen, other than be your lovely self.

While it can be helpful to break down the various elements in our design in order to understand them (and ourselves) better, this process has its limitations. In the end, it's all about the weave.

An understanding of one of your Profile Lines (on the Personality side) becomes more interesting when you combine it with the other Line (on the Design side). An understanding of your Profile becomes more illuminating when you weave it together with the particular Gates (or *Gene Keys*) that the two Lines are connected to. Your Incarnation Cross (consisting of the Profile Lines and their corresponding Sun/Earth Gates on both the Personality and Design side) finds its magic when explored together with the many other aspects of your multi-faceted design. Your design becomes much more alive and empowering when you explore it with YOU in mind, with your unique life experience, conditioning story, and your evolving relationship to your design and your journey.

*In other words, the sum is greater than the parts.*

# THE 6 LINES WITH A GENE KEYS TWIST

The *Gene Keys* and Integral Human Design provide incredibly rich and expansive perspectives on the 6 Lines and your Profile. I sprinkled some *Gene Keys* wisdom into the *Designed to Blossom* Course, using *Gene Keys*-friendly titles for the 12 Profiles. Here, I'm going to share a bit more about each of the 6 Lines, also from a *Gene Keys* perspective. Please know I'm only giving you a tiny taste. We're just scratching the surface. If your *Inner Wisdom Keeper* feels drawn to going deeper into *Gene Keys* or Integral Human Design waters, that's wonderful. I'll share how to do that in our final Petal.

Please don't feel too obliged to learn or memorize any of this. Trust that if something pops out or lingers with you, that there's something in it for you. Enjoy!

## LINE 1

• Element: Earth

• The First Chakra (Base)

• Biological associations: Our bones, the inherent structure of our bodies, our muscles

*This line is deeply connected to our experience of our Individual nature.*

Wherever we have a Line 1 in our design, we're looking at an area where we have the potential to be deeply introspective and investigative. We're looking at an area where we're primed to want to get to the bottom of things, to uncover the truth.

At its highest expression, this Line becomes the Mystic, someone who embodies a deep inner certainty that transcends the surface ups and downs of life.

At its 'lowest' or most fear-dominated expression, this Line shows up as a deep insecurity and a fear of our own potential. When we're gripped by this kind of a fear, our bodies can literally shake. We often need more information about ourselves and our situation. We need a loving self-confrontation—an opportunity to receive information from people who are capable of speaking to us directly, honestly, and from the heart.

In the realm of our more intimate relationships, this Line may show up as a tendency towards repression, towards hiding our thoughts, feelings and needs from others. We may find ourselves keeping secrets, sabotaging ourselves, or constantly running away from or avoiding potentially difficult or uncomfortable interactions.

When this Line is activated emotionally in a teenager, it might show up as secretiveness, a tendency towards self-sabotage, or a more confrontational attitude or persona—which is ultimately an attempt to escape from the deeper fears lurking within.

When it comes to freeing the spirit and healing this Line's relational wounds, the best medicine is self-love. We heal by being devoted to self-discovery and the Truth. We stop hiding from ourselves. We face our fears and stand up for ourselves. We dare to go straight into the core of our wounds.

We often find that beneath all of our fear is a free, creative and wild part of us that's just waiting to be seen, embraced and released. The more we allow ourselves to uncover the truth of who we are, and engage more courageously with our relational partners, the more our self-love grows, and the healthier our bodies become.

## LINE 2

- Element: Water
- The Second Chakra (Passion and Relationships)
- Biological associations: Our immune, lymphatic and reproductive systems

*This line is deeply connected to our experience of Relationship.*

Wherever we have a Line 2 in our design, we're looking at an area where we have the potential to be the objects of projection or project onto others. These are aspects of ourselves that call us to drop into a deeper level of being, relating and expressing without having to prove anything or be productive in any way.

At its highest expression, this Line becomes the Seer, someone who just naturally expresses pure inner light. We become deeply relaxed at the core of our being.

At its 'lowest' or most fear-dominated expression, this Line shows up as a tendency to provoke people, without necessarily realizing it. We may be in denial, or emit an energetic aggression we're not aware of. We may seem naive or superior. However we express our fear, we can wind up making unintentional waves. When this happens, more than anything, we need opportunities to simply **be** in relaxing environments, where we can let go of all agendas and be free from the agendas we're afraid others might have for us.

In the realm of our more intimate relationships, this Line may show up as a tendency towards denial or anger—turned against others or ourselves. We may find ourselves overwhelmed by or expressing powerful emotions that can appear aggressive.

When this Line is activated emotionally in a teenager, it might show up as a form of blindness, or a tendency to externalize one's upset through finding fault with others and blaming. Taking on a superior attitude can be a way of escaping from deeper feelings of inadequacy or guilt. Those with more introverted, repressive tendencies are more likely to turn their anger and blame in against themselves, and feel inferior. When it comes to freeing the spirit and healing this Line's relational wounds, the best medicine is to love another. We heal by coming out of our shells, out of our *selves*, and connecting with the people, animals and beings around us. The more we can relax and relate to others naturally and intimately, the freer we will feel in all of our relationships. We don't even have to mentally understand what's happening. As long as we're opening, relaxing, and genuinely connecting, whatever denial or anger was there will just naturally dissolve.

# LINE 3

- Element: Fire
- The Third Chakra (Energy and Experience)
- Biological associations: Our cardiovascular systems and belly

*This line is deeply connected to our experiences of Family.*

Wherever we have a Line 3 in our design, we're looking at an area where we have the potential to learn so much through our life experience, mistakes and all. We're looking at highly mutable aspects of ourselves that are built to make discoveries through a process of trial and error and continually and creatively adapt to our evolving inner and outer worlds. At its highest expression, this Line becomes the Mythical Fool, someone who playfully and lovingly combines wisdom, joy and humility.

At its 'lowest' or most fear-dominated expression, this Line shows up as a tendency towards pessimism or evasiveness. We may experience an upset stomach. We may seem unreliable to others, and even more importantly, not come through for ourselves. When we find ourselves resisting life, or avoiding people and uncomfortable situations, chances are we're feeling under too much pressure. We're feeling powerless. The first step towards reclaiming our joyous nature is to release the pressure valve, however we can. Any way we can give ourselves permission to be who we are will be most supportive.

In the realm of our more intimate relationships, this Line may show up as a tendency towards shame, greed (never-enoughness), and an ambivalent relationship to commitment. It is often our self-destructive tendencies, like addiction, that prevent us from healing.

When this Line is activated emotionally in a teenager, it might show up as a form of free-floating angst, or a tendency to complain—to others or about ourselves. Teenagers who act in frivolous ways are often trying to escape from deep-seated feelings of shame.

When it comes to freeing the spirit and healing this Line's relational wounds, the best medicine is to love— and experience love within the context of—one's family. We heal our self-destructive patterns by seeing them clearly, and by acknowledging our utter lack of control. The best thing we can do is to find a way to release pent up emotions through laughing, deep in the belly. The more we let go of control, and 'give it up to the Universe' with a sense of self-compassion and amusement, the healthier our relationship to our families—and money!—become.

# LINE 4

- Element: Air
- The Fourth Chakra (Love and Community)
- Biological associations: Our respiratory system, our lungs and chest

*This line is deeply connected to our experience of Community.*

Wherever we have a Line 4 in our design, we're looking at an area where we have the potential to have strong Convictions. We're also looking at those places in our lives where our connections to others play a larger role, where friendship and sharing are especially important.

At its highest expression, this Line becomes the Prophet, someone who walks the earth with an open, honest, friendship-bringing heart.

At its 'lowest' or most fear-dominated expression, this Line shows up as a tendency to think or perceive the world from a fixed or rigid place, to constantly seek reinforcement for the walls around our hearts, or to hide our true feelings and nature beneath a polished, less authentic surface. When we find our minds and attitudes narrowing, and ourselves getting too caught up in appearances, it's time to invite in some softness. As we soften, we gain the courage to be more honest with ourselves, to reconnect with our integrity, and even to experience our more romantic nature.

In the realm of our more intimate relationships, this Line may show up as a tendency to either feel rejected or to reject, and to put up a protective emotional wall. It is when we hide our true feelings, or pretend that everything is okay when it isn't, that we prevent ourselves from healing.

When this Line is activated emotionally in a teenager, it might show up as a form of inauthenticity or a false persona. Teenagers who 'give in without protest,' who reluctantly accept what is happening, no matter how they actually feel, are often trying to escape from the fear or feeling of being rejected. Deep down they're still reinforcing their most negative thoughts about themselves and the world around them.

When it comes to freeing the spirit and healing this Line's relational wounds, the best medicine is to become our own best friend, to allow our hearts to thaw out. The best medicine is to love—and experience love within the context of—one's family AND community. We heal our fear of rejection by simply being ourselves, by removing the masks that we wear and allowing others to see us as we truly are, and to come closer to us. The best thing we can do is be gentle with ourselves, and provide ourselves with the true acceptance we long for. The more we accept and express who we are, the more positively influential we become, and the more we can allow the nurturing and support of others to positively influence us.

# LINE 5

- Element: Ether
- The Fifth Chakra (Power and Projection)
- Biological associations: Our nervous system, our throat

*This line is deeply connected to our experience of the Collective, or Humanity as a whole.*

Wherever we have a Line 5 in our design, we're looking at an area where we have the potential to bring order and synergistic Organization into our lives and the world around us. We're looking at our ability to Lead and provide others with practical assistance and support. Leadership can look many different ways, depending on who we are. There is a potential here to radiate a certain kind of authority that can draw people to us and have a powerful impact.

At its highest expression, this Line becomes the Avatar, someone who emanates simplicity, and who leads from a place of deep listening.

At its 'lowest' or most fear-dominated expression, this Line shows up as a tendency to lose touch with reality, to misuse one's power, or to allow others to misuse theirs. We can find ourselves buying into hierarchical structures that don't serve us, or becoming tyrannical. When we find ourselves experiencing some sort of power imbalance or delusion, what we really need are simple, practical solutions that bring us back down to earth, and reconnect us with our hearts.

In the realm of our more intimate relationships, this Line may show up as a tendency towards guilt, and getting lost in a complex mental labyrinth that proves just how guilty we are, or just how victimized we've been by others. It is often our self-pity—and the fantasy that one day everyone will regret how badly they've treated us—that prevent us from our own healing.

When this Line is activated emotionally in a teenager, it might show up as a tendency to look for external reinforcement in order to justify or validate one's story or attitude. Teenagers who often feel sorry for themselves or identify as victims, are often trying to escape from deep-seated feelings of guilt.

When it comes to freeing the spirit and healing this Line's relational wounds, the best medicine is to allow ourselves to fully feel our disappointment, as well as our fear that we may have disappointed others. We heal our disappointment by forgiving ourselves, and continually rescuing ourselves from the quagmire in our own minds. Naturally, we find ourselves forgiving others as we soften our hearts towards ourselves. The more we can embrace our feelings and forgive ourselves, the more clarity we develop in general, the more we're able to pierce through delusions and see what truly is before us, and within us. This clarity allows us to have far-reaching effects, not just on ourselves, but society as a whole. Instead of feeling betrayed, victimized or misunderstood by society, we find ourselves recognized and utilized in a deeply empowering way.

## LINE 6

● Element: Earth of the 'next realm'—where we're all headed, evolving towards
● The Sixth and Seventh "Higher Chakras" (Education and Surrender)
● Biological associations: Our endocrine system, our meridians, our head

*This line is deeply connected to our experience of the Universe, the Cosmos, Spirit.*

Wherever we have a Line 6 in our design, we're looking at an area where we have the potential to be extremely Objective. We're looking at the aspects of ourselves that are Visionary in nature, that can maintain the big picture without getting lost in the nitty gritty—or not so relevant—details.

At its highest expression, this Line becomes the Magus, someone who is wise, accessible and in touch with humanity's future.

At its 'lowest' or most fear-dominated expression, this Line shows up as an aloofness or arrogance. We can seem or be inaccessible to others. When we find ourselves withdrawing from the world, or looking down on it, the medicine that shifts us out of that state is patience—with ourselves and the world.

In the realm of our more intimate relationships, this Line may show up as a tendency towards isolation, and towards disassociating or leaving the body. When we vacate the premises (either literally or emotionally) because we don't trust anyone, we prevent ourselves from healing.

When this Line is activated emotionally in a teenager, it might show up as a general feeling of being picked out and discriminated against, or a paranoia. Teenagers may appear overly sincere on the outside, but underneath, they are likely suspicious of others and their intentions. They can also be constantly second-guessing themselves and their own intentions.

When it comes to freeing the spirit and healing this Line's relational wounds, the best medicine is to break ourselves out of isolation, by first and foremost, including ourselves. We heal our loneliness by becoming embodied, by embracing life and whichever expression of the Divine resonates most authentically for us. The less we resist what is, and the more we allow for it (while remaining present), the more 'full' and free we become. Ultimately, our freedom allows us to fully engage with our lives, and to experience the kind of spirituality that embraces both Spirit and Matter, that both transcends and includes.

# Move Beyond the Map: Petal Seven

*Bask in uncharted, contemplative territory, and expand your family of supporters!*

In Petal Seven of the *Designed to Blossom* Course, Human Design is looked at as a blossoming field of study as well as a profound mystical exploration. I share about my own soul-searching journey from Jovian Archive to the *Gene Keys*, and how that journey contributed to my unique way of holding and teaching Human Design, my understanding of the core teachings of the *Gene Keys*, as well as the birth of *The Wisdom Keepers Oracle Deck*, a self-development tool that is being used and enjoyed by Human Design and *Gene Keys* enthusiasts all over the world.

Here in the *Designed to Blossom* Resource Book, I would like to share some of the challenges, and even more of the benefits that can arise out of a Human Design and *Gene Keys* synthesis. We'll look more deeply at the important role *shadow*, pain and paradox play in any individuation process, whether we are engaging in a Human Design experiment or walking down the *Gene Keys* Golden Path. We'll explore the arts of Restraint, Patience and Reverence, and find out whether Human Design can make us rich! At the end of this Resource Book, I will share ways in which you can deepen and expand your own journey, should you feel inspired.

## GENE KEYS TRICKLE DOWN; HUMAN DESIGN TICKLES UP!

I have had a profound experience of the 'trickle-down' effect of a contemplative path. If one sits with an essential inquiry long enough, it will penetrate and transmute every aspect of one's life. This is a deep truth offered by the *Gene Keys*.

Just as the *Gene Keys* have felt like a giant shower of golden light pouring down from above and into the cells of my being, Human Design has felt like a warm grass-roots practice, a healthy dose of the 'power of the small,' tickling at my toes, one conscious step at a time.

For some time now, these two practices have sung happily in my Generator belly. Not everyone feels this way. We're all so different. We need different things, at different times, often in a different order.

Some need to go as deep as they can possibly go into a system. Some simply need to be initiated with a system seed, and then move on. Some need to cycle through systems, going back and forth between them, returning when there is a special need.

As many transpersonalists say, "It is important that we don't confuse the map with the territory." Systems like Human Design are meant to carry us from one place to another. Once we arrive at our destination, they are built to dissolve. I resonate so deeply with that.

What I've found in my own life, as I've immersed myself in *Gene Keys* waters, is that my Human Design map hasn't dissolved. It's simply evolved.

While I resonate deeply with the vastness, flexibility and Love of the *Gene Keys* territory, I continue to find the specificity of the (increasingly Integral) Human Design map of myself very helpful as I navigate my way towards my ultimate 'map-free' destination.

Through Human Design, I've learned to track energy and how it moves—both out from me and into me, and between those around me. I've learned how to tune into whether/when I (or another) am being energetically seen, recognized, invited, engaged, repelled, etc., or not.

- Whether something is coming alive in me (or someone else), or not.
- Whether I am being respected as an authentic being, or not.
- Whether my energy (gift) is being used well, or not.
- Whether I am making choices to avoid uncomfortable feelings or pressures, or not.
- Whether I'm working too hard with my mind or fear-driven will power, or allowing heart-seeded commitments and relationships to rise up within me naturally, easily, effortlessly, or not.

Especially when I'm feeling flooded or overwhelmed, about to jump into a new life chapter or relationship, or when I don't have the time and space to delve into a deep contemplation, my Human Design practice helps me to temporarily hone in on the now in an exceedingly practical way.

For me, Human Design is an invitation to cultivate the art of micro-discernment. It's like a moving meditation map—one that ultimately trickles up from the infinitesimally small acts that make up each moment of my life.

The practice starts out small and narrow. Over time, it gets bigger and wider, until it's all about frequency, and the choices are just being made through me as I flow freely through my life and the increasingly wondrous environments I find myself in.

I like to see Human Design as a *choosing meditation*—that if taken to its zenith, doesn't require any incessant tracking at all.

While I don't think Human Design knowledge is necessary for everyone to benefit from the *Gene Keys* experience (or for everyone in general!), it's certainly helped me practically pace myself, and actually absorb the nourishing 'Slow Down' message of the wonderful 52^nd Gene Key, with its Gift of Restraint. It's helped me to gently remind myself to take one decision at a time, one new relationship at a time, one environment at a time, and remain true to my energy body.

# HUMAN DESIGN AND BEYOND

Some years back, I created a casual video series where I shared some of the ways I was integrating my Human Design knowledge with Richard Rudd's *Gene Keys* and the related Integral Human Design. I thought I'd glean a few wisdom pearls from that project and share them here, for your perusal.

## THE POWER OF LANGUAGE

Language matters. When we receive a Human Design Reading from someone, or are told who we are (and who we're not) through a Human Design lens, it matters how we—and our potential—are described. For many of us, even the tone of voice used by a Reader matters.

When we receive a Reading from someone who combines a cold, mechanical language with an over-emphasis on our design's shadow potential, we can end up feeling afraid, doomed, victimized or disempowered.

I am not advocating for an avoidance of shadow. As Carl Jung taught and as the *Gene Keys* teach, there can be no Gift without Shadow. There can be no true liberation without a deep understanding of where we've been imprisoned. I am not even saying that there isn't a time and place for tough love.

I *am*, however, advocating for love. I am encouraging the use of empowering, compassionate and creative language by those who transmit Human Design information as part of their service to others. What we say and how we say it impacts how people hear us, how deeply they allow the transmission to go, and how motivated they become to put what they learn into practice.

While the fear of being Not-Self or a 'bad Human Design student' can be a powerful motivator, few things penetrate or motivate as profoundly as love. People become courageous when in the presence of someone who not only genuinely wishes for their liberation, but can see them liberated, and can help *them* see themselves living in alignment with their highest potential.

This is why I appreciate the intention and gift offered through Integral Human Design. Werner and Laura Pitzal, together with Richard Rudd, worked tirelessly to deepen and broaden the language of the Human Design System, giving each element not one, but three names—each keynote reflecting one of the frequency Gene Keys' frequency bands (or tiers in a spiral): *shadow*, *potential* (Gift) and *essence* (Siddhi). This language supports the ultimate truth that all of us can change how we embody and express our designs.

### *Nothing is written in stone. Not even our DNA.*

## IT'S AN EXPERIMENT

Just as Buddhism does not demand blind faith, neither does Human Design. The only way to determine whether there is anything in this for you is to give it a try, and see what happens.

There are benefits to a radical approach to the Human Design experiment. I've been inspired by courageous Human Design enthusiasts who have transformed their lives through such an approach. I've been such a person myself.

Few people are ever truly liberated through a half-hearted process. Devotion, without doubt, brings rewards. When we consistently dare to honor who we are in the face of external pressures and internalized expectations, we strengthen our core being and free our authentic spirit.

That said, we don't have to be rigid to be devoted. A radical approach to anything (even an experiment designed for personal emancipation from external conditioning) can lead to fundamentalism. Fundamentalism dwells in the mental realms. It is belief-based, the opposite of what Human Design is meant to be.

A fundamentalist approach to Human Design may look embodied and feel empowering on the surface, but it is just another source of conditioning. A good way to detect whether you're falling into the Fundamentalist Trap is to see whether you and your community are experiencing a whole lot of intrapsychic, interpersonal or collective divisiveness. Divisiveness feels qualitatively different than healthy individuation/differentiation.

Your job is to find your own way, and to trust it. Should Human Design become a significant part of your life, whatever you learn from your personal experiment will become an important contribution to our evolving field.

Some people believe that until we discover our Human Design, we are only living out the Not-Self. I would like to put a question mark around the word 'only.' I would also like to invite us to take a more dialectical perspective. We have our pre-Human Design lives, our 'thesis.' We have our post-Human Design discovery lives, our 'antithesis.' Once we're sufficiently grounded in our Human Design experiment, enough for it to become second-nature, we have our fully integrated lives, our 'synthesis.' There is no need to throw any beautiful pre-Human Design babies out with the bathwater.

**Transcend and include, Baby!** (Thank you, Ken Wilber, for that wonderful phrase!)

## OUR BLUEPRINT IS LIVING

The Bodygraph is alive, responsive and multi-dimensional, not fixed, rigid and two-dimensional. It is a changing quantum field. Richard Rudd once called it, "the mantra given to us by the guru of our Higher Self." Our Human Design can point to the vastness of our potential for growth and development. It can point to what we'd look like when if we were fully awakened. But it is not who we are. The attitude we embrace while engaging in our personal experiment can profoundly impact the way in which (and the frequency through which) our design is expressed. I encourage an attitude of openness, permission, love, curiosity, honesty, integrity, courage, adventure, playfulness, compassion and a willingness to surprise yourself.

## THE BEAUTY OF OPENNESS

In the beginning of the Human Design experiment, there are few things more powerful and empowering than an awareness of our Openness. We learn how impacted we—and our entire identities—have been by the people around us, our environments, even by the transits. We realize that so much of our thinking, feeling and pressures towards doing don't even belong to us.

As we individuate, we learn that we don't have to own, identify with, take responsibility for, or act upon every single impulse, thought or emotion moving through us. We release ourselves from victimization and become increasingly grounded in our True Nature.

When we liberate ourselves from one form of victimization, we run the risk of falling into another form of victimization. Instead of over-identifying with *what's coming in* through our Openness, we over-identify with our Openness itself. We continually reinforce the fact that we are at the whim of others—their thoughts, their feelings, their stress, their frustration, their will power, etc. We get caught in the trap of Dualism. "There's Self; there's Not-Self." "There's me; there's you." "There's mine; there's yours."

There's a slippery slope between that kind of thinking and, "This is what **you** are doing to **me**!"

Over the years, I've come to lovingly hold a paradox, one which makes room for both essential empowerment paths. Take my Open Solar Plexus as an example. When I feel flooded or overwhelmed by emotional material, I first remind myself, "You know what, Rosy? This isn't all yours. You're not responsible for understanding and metabolizing every little bit of what you're feeling right now. See if you can be with it. Breathe through it. Witness it. But don't identify with it. Don't over-own it."

Once my nervous system has calmed down a bit, I actually allow myself to own it. I tell myself, "Rosy, it doesn't matter where these emotions came from, how much of them belong to you, or how much of them belong to someone else. As long as they're here, inside of you, they're yours. Welcome these feelings into your body-being like a friendly guest house. You'll likely learn something from their company. Maybe something good will come of your process, for you and others."

## DIFFERENTIATION AND ONENESS

Human Design is all about the art of differentiation. At its highest expression, it's a giant celebration of humanity, of the beauty and sovereignty of each unique shard in our collective diamond. Human Design encourages each of us to be, trust and accept ourselves for who we are, and let others be who they are.

At its lowest expression, (which often emerges when a hefty fear of the End Times is in the mix), it can sound a bit like, "Screw you, world! I'm going to be and do whatever the hell I want. My only responsibility is to myself. As long as I'm following my unique Strategy and Authority, I'm good. I'll survive. If you don't get that it's all a big joke—if you're foolish enough to buy into the Not-Self world, that's not my problem. I'll wave 'ta ta!' as you and the rest of humanity go off the rails, riding the Program's crazy train."

I like to remind myself that the ultimate purpose for the differentiation journey is Collective Communion. At first, we learn to ground, stabilize and protect our unique individuality. Once we've learned to honor our unique selves, we are free to come back together—not through old hierarchical conditioning patterns or oppressive structures, but through a highly synergistic self-organizing process.

If each of us represents a single cell in the larger planetary/cosmic body, it's always in the larger body's best interest to have as many healthy, authentic and aligned cells as possible whizzing around, doing our thing. We're living in a holographic Universe. Maybe I am different than you on the surface, and you're different than me. But inside of me is you, and inside of you is me, and inside of each of us is the entire cosmos. The 'Program' is quite a big illusion, but there's an even bigger one, 'Separation.' Let's not get too caught up in the grandest illusion of all.

## SLEEP

When I was pregnant with my daughter, I had a very strong and positive response to having a home birth and practicing *attachment parenting*, which included having a family bed. When I shared this with a Human Design authority at the time, they questioned whether this was a genuine Generator response, or my Not-Self in disguise.

Certain that sleeping alone was the only way to be oneself, and to support a child in becoming themselves, this Human Design expert suggested that my desire to co-sleep was influenced by my highly conditioned Open Solar Plexus. I was letting my fear of the baby feeling sad and alone, and my desire to avoid having a confrontation with my child, prevent me from teaching her how to sleep by herself. I was setting her up from the very beginning for a Not-Self life. They also said, if it turned out that my child had an Open Spleen (which she did!), co-sleeping would also condition her to be overly-dependent on my Defined Spleen.

Though I was shaken up by this feedback, I ultimately trusted my *Inner Wisdom Keeper* and did what felt right. So far, I'm happy to say that my 14-year-old daughter seems to be doing just fine.

Some years later, I shared about this experience with Werner Pitzal (the co-founder of Integral Human Design). I'll never forget what he said. "Why are we more afraid of being influenced by the people we love the most, than we are of the transits in the sky? Why should it be so scary to sleep in the auric embrace of your beloved partner, or beside your child who you're so clearly responding to nurturing?" Why should it be safer to be conditioned by neutrinos in the collective field than to be conditioned by the people that we love?

I found these questions profound, so I share them with you. Something to ponder.

## THE POWER OF RELATIONSHIP

When first discovering a system like Human Design, it can be fun to purchase a pre-written or pre-recorded 'Reading,' where you get to learn about the basics of your chart without having to participate in the process. Such a Reading, of course, can't take the place of connecting with a real person, someone who isn't just working off of a fixed blueprint, but is relating to you as a human being, at a particular moment in your life. If you have the opportunity to receive a LIVE Reading with a skilled and compassionate Human Design professional, I encourage you to do it.

I am a believer in the healing power of relationship. There are few things as transformative as working with someone over a period of time, who truly knows you, sees you and cares about you, someone who can love you through your most painful, shameful times.

If you are looking for someone to help you deepen your Human Design experiment through a long-term coaching or counseling relationship, remember that chemistry and trust are as important as knowledge. This person is not only going to tell you about your nature, they're going to help you explore your conditioning, some of it vulnerable and painful. If one of their biggest jobs is to encourage you to be courageously authentic in your life, make sure you feel that you can be courageously authentic with them.

If you are wanting to explore Human Design in a group setting (in-person or online), allow yourself to be selective. Allow your *Inner Wisdom Keeper* to guide you, as you choose which group to join, how much to participate, and how deep to go. There are all kinds of groups out there, many of them wonderful. They're not all necessarily going to be the right fit for you. Trust yourself.

There are so many ways to explore the *Gene Keys* and connect with the *Gene Keys* community. Since working with the *Gene Keys* inevitably includes shadow work, both personal and collective, I also recommend that you allow your *Inner Wisdom Keeper* to guide your decisions. Take your time. See what's out there. Gravitate towards the people, groups, retreats and courses that inspire you, resonate with your heart, and create a field of safety to explore deep material. A compassionate sense of humor is always a great quality to look for in a person or community! We *Wisdom Seekers* can take ourselves way too seriously. I'll include resources at the end of this book.

# A WORD ABOUT THE GENE KEYS

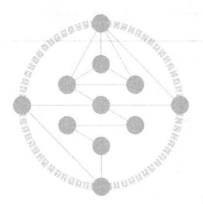

As I share in the *Designed to Blossom* Course, the *Gene Keys* are a body of knowledge here to help us transform our core self-beliefs, expand our consciousness and release our individual creative genius into the world.

*The Gene Keys: Unlocking the Higher Purpose Hidden in Your DNA* is also an actual book, a contemporary I Ching, written by Richard Rudd, a teacher of world mythology and award-winning poet. It is also a path of self- and cosmic-discovery. There are many, many offerings that have grown out of the *Gene Keys*, (including Richard Rudd, Werner and Laura Pitzal's Integral Human Design, which I've referred to throughout this Resource Book), as well as a worldwide community that is contemplating, experimenting with, refining, and sharing the wisdom of this living transmission.

64 universal archetypes lie at the heart of the *Gene Keys*. They correspond to the 64 hexagrams of the I Ching, the 64 Gates of the Human Design Bodygraph, the 64 codons of our human DNA, and the 64 Wisdom Keepers in the *Wisdom Keepers Oracle Deck*, another one of my labors of love.

Both Human Design and the *Gene Keys* are **massive** syntheses. Human Design, as you know, brings together modern science (quantum physics, biochemistry, genetics and neuro-gastroenterology—the science of the 'gut-brain') with some of our most ancient systems for understanding the universe and our own nature (the Chinese I Ching, the Zohar/Kabbalah's Tree of Life, both Eastern and Western Astrology, and the Hindu Chakra system).

The matrix of Human Design was revealed to Ra Uru Hu in the form of the basic Calculation, Bodygraph, Crystals, and the various layers of information lying beneath the 64 Gates or Hexagrams of the I Ching (e.g. Lines, Colors, Tones, Bases). Ra then interpreted this matrix, providing the rest of us with concepts such as Type, Strategy, Authority and the Rave I Ching.

You could say that the *Gene Keys* were drawn from the same matrix as Human Design, but distilled through the unique and vast prism of Richard Rudd, who ultimately brought the Golden Path to the world, an accessible, self-led contemplative journey.

As previously mentioned, the *Gene Keys* consist of 64 universal archetypes reflecting the original pattern of the universe. You could say that together, they form the holographic matrix of space-time itself, representing an alive and forever-evolving wisdom, existing everywhere and in everything.

Though the same eightfold geometry of the 64 has been discovered by many cultures, over thousands of years, Richard Rudd's *Gene Keys* are a unique universal language which weaves core aspects of Human Design together with psychology, sociology, mysticism, physics, biology, music and indigenous wisdom. The territory mapped by the *Gene Keys* is infinite.

There are several journeys that can be explored within the *Gene Keys* Golden Path map—the path towards purpose, towards love, towards true prosperity and more. Each path is a rich and beautiful way of understanding oneself, life and the universe.

For me, working with the *Gene Keys* has been a very different experience than working with Human Design.

- While Human Design empowers us through a spiritual practice of decision-making, the *Gene Keys* invites us to practice the art of **contemplation**.

- While Human Design is exceedingly practical, the *Gene Keys* are organically transformative.

- While Human Design shows precisely how our conditioning gets in the way of our True Nature, and gives us full permission to go against the grain, the *Gene Keys* help us learn how to be with the strong feelings that often emerge as we work to liberate ourselves from the grips of our conditioning.

- While Human Design gives us a roadmap for aligning ourselves with our True Nature, the *Gene Keys* help us understand and surrender to the beauty, depth and poetry of that nature.

- While Human Design shows us how to become authentic, liberated and empowered individuals, the *Gene Keys* inspire us to embody our gifts and serve the world—with deep breaths, grounded bodies, relaxed minds and softened hearts.

# EMBRACING PARADOXICAL TEACHERS AND TEACHINGS (HUMAN DESIGN & THE GENE KEYS)

Maybe it was my experimental nature (3/5 Profile) that made me especially willing to dive into both Human Design and *Gene Keys* worlds simultaneously. Or, maybe it was a divinely inspired intuitive-Generator gut. Or, maybe it's because I'm often swimming in paradoxical waters. Or, maybe it is the fact that I feel such genuine respect for both Richard Rudd and Ra Uru Hu and their work in the world.

I feel that there is plenty of room to explore and enjoy both teachers—both worlds, Human Design and the *Gene Keys,* even though they are so different, and even though there are aspects of these approaches/frames/paradigms that can seem mutually exclusive.

I have a dual appreciation for duality-oriented (Human Design) and nondual approaches (*Gene Keys*/*Integral Human Design*) to life.

Obviously, I've experienced the gift of Human Design in my own life, and probably wouldn't have bumped into and responded to Richard Rudd's *Gene Keys* work so strongly, had I not first entered in through the Human Design portal.

While I probably wouldn't have chosen Ra to be my best friend, I did (still do, though he is no longer with us in body) appreciate his down-to-earth, no bullshit, get-that-foundation-under-your-belt way…not to mention the tremendous amount of devotion and work he poured into creating the solid, wide and deep field that Human Design has become today.

I've also been involved in enough alternative environments over the years to enjoy the fact that Ra wasn't floating around on some fluffy cloud of self- and other-aggrandizement, completely divorced from reality.

Richard Rudd's written contributions to Human Design always resonated with me quite deeply. I have a special appreciation for the flexible-frequency focus of Integral Human Design and the *Gene Keys*. Just because we've been genetically imprinted and brought up in an environment, our lives and potentials don't need to be written in stone. While we each have our Gifts—genius, uniqueness, original blueprint, there are infinite ways in which these aspects of our nature can be expressed.

Richard Rudd and the people drawn to the *Gene Keys* have also felt more like kindred spirits to me, like the kinds of people I tend to surround myself with in my everyday life.

It's a dance, as always.

Sometimes the kind of tough love embodied by Ra Uru Hu is necessary (something I've certainly needed to learn about, as someone with an Open Solar Plexus and confrontation-avoiding tendencies). Often, I find that there are gentler ways of supporting a person's path of transformation, more loving ways of working with the shadow that don't require an over-identification with it.

In my life, I've found that there are few things more confronting ('tough') than having someone see your beauty and love you for who you are! An old Rebirthing teacher who was deeply inspired by the *Course in Miracles*, Binnie Dansby, taught me that in my late teens and early twenties. She always used to say, "Love is the greatest confrontation of all." So very true.

### How I know when Human Design is really working…

I can feel in my own body when Human Design knowledge is liberating people—when it's opening our hearts to ourselves, making self-acceptance easier, releasing us from the pressures of external conditioning forces.

I can also feel when it's being used to further a mega-brainy existence, or when it's becoming one more form of conditioning, filling people with new guilt trips and opportunities to prove themselves to an external authority figure—whether it be Ra, the Human Design analyst or coach, or someone else.

It's a very visceral sensation in my body.

Over and over again, I find that it's so much less about what we do and what we do it with, and so much more about where we come from when we do what we do, and how we do it.

# WHEN OUR GIFTS ARE ALSO OUR SHADOWS

One of my beloved professors from the California Institute of Integral Studies (Mark Fromm) taught us about the *Elegant Solution*. He said that most people, when growing up in imperfect family/cultural environments, find an elegant solution—a way to let out as much of their 'light' or true nature as they possibly can, without threatening their survival in the tribe.

In a very real (albeit upside-down) way, I consider most people's gifts (talents, etc.) to be aspects of their shadow material—in the sense that these essential light-infused qualities in us have been forced into the shadows of our existence, forbidden to fully bloom, because they were experienced as threats to our survival.

When forced to live in the dark, these otherwise lovely qualities come to take on 'shadowy' traits.

Following in the footsteps of Carl Jung, Richard Rudd teaches that all we need to do is shine the light of consciousness on a shadow for it to reveal its inherent gift to us, its essence. This understanding has helped me gain the courage necessary, over the course of my life, to revisit my shadows through a gentle process of contemplation.

It also reminds me of Marianne Williamson's wonderful quote:

> *"Our deepest fear is not that we are inadequate.*
> *Our deepest fear is that we are powerful beyond measure.*
> *It is our light, not our darkness that most frightens us.*
> *We ask ourselves, 'Who am I to be brilliant, gorgeous, talented, fabulous?'*
> *Actually, who are you not to be? You are a child of God.*
> *Your playing small does not serve the world...*
> *...As we are liberated from our own fear,*
> *our presence automatically liberates others."*

# *IS THERE A PURPOSE FOR MY PAIN?*

One of the most central teachings of the *Gene Keys* (and other mystical studies) is that everything we experience on the personal plane, no matter how painful or confusing, whether it was sourced from within us or someone else, has the potential to transform us and the world.

The attitude we hold towards our own suffering is what determines whether it ultimately serves us and humanity, or not.

- Do we push our pain away?

- Do we judge it?

- Do we try to get rid of it?

- Do we feel victimized by it?

- Do we hold others fully responsible for it?

Or…

- Do we allow it to be what it is?

- Do we embrace it?

- Do we fully feel it?

- Do we allow it to wash through us, open our hearts, unleash our humanity, fill us with compassion—for ourselves, and ultimately for others?

At this level, it doesn't matter where the pain is coming from, whether it's coming to us through our inherited genes, familial legacies, collective traumas, or Open Centers. What matters is how we meet the pain.

When we meet it like Rumi's 'Guest House,' with courageous surrender and mindful witnessing, our personal experience becomes a potent, transformative cauldron for the collective.

As we heal our own loneliness, we heal a piece of the loneliness plaguing all of humanity. As we love ourselves in our vulnerability, we help humanity embrace its vulnerability. We are, after all, so deeply connected.

As shared earlier, the *Gene Keys* were brought to the world by Richard Rudd, a mystic/poet/author/teacher who used to be quite involved in Human Design. He has been able to offer the *Gene Keys* as an incredibly powerful and relevant mythology that takes the most essential aspects of the original Human Design transmission to an entirely new level. It takes a more transpersonal, archetypal, multi-dimensional look at the 64 Gates or hexagrams of Human Design.

There are several 'journeys'—or sequences—one can go on when exploring one's *Gene Keys*. The first is very connected to what in Human Design we call the Incarnation Cross, and is about Life Purpose. The second (the Venus Sequence) is deeply centered around the themes of Love and Relationship. The third (The Pearl) is all about Prosperity. These (and more) are all to be found in the Hologenetic Profile.

Getting nice and grounded in your design is a wonderful place to start your journey…and to learn to accept, trust and honor yourself, as a uniquely lovable human being. Once you've got the map, you can move beyond it!

# CONFESSIONS FROM A HUMAN DESIGN LOVER (THE BENEFITS OF DRINKING HALF OF THE KOOL-AID)

Even though I've had moments of self-doubt, I feel strangely fortunate to not have dived so deeply into Human Design that it became my entire world. For one thing, I haven't come to see Human Design as the only way to become a liberated or awakened being. I haven't felt the need to shut out the people in my life who aren't living according to their designs. I haven't abandoned my mystical, communal and heart-centered orientation. I haven't become so obsessed with the infinite details of the Human Design system (a trap my Open Head and Ajna could easily have fallen into) that I lost the point of the experiment entirely.

In the end, everything has its shadow. A person can get so lost in the line-color-tone-base-transit-left-right tracking of Human Design. A person can get so obsessed about the right and wrong of each choice and the impact of each interpersonal or neutrino interaction that the world loses all of its magic.

High-frequency contemplators can become equally lost—so lost in the big Spiritual picture, so high up in the clouds that they don't notice what's happening right in front of their noses, or inside of their bodies, or between them and the people around them. The most sophisticated of them can find increasingly subtle ways to avoid having to deal with the lessons awaiting them in the oh-so-mundane world.

I raise my half-filled glass of Kool-Aid to the dance of integration!

(If you're interested in diving deep into this wormhole, please check out my book, *Walking a Fine Line: Becoming a Professional Wisdom Keeper in the Healing Arts*. This book was written to inspire professional Wisdom Keepers and communities around the world, and to invite an ongoing, nuanced and collective dialogue on professionalism in the alternative healing arts. More information about *Walking a Fine Line* at the end of this Resource Book.)

# REVERENCE AND PATIENCE
# (MY LIFE'S PURPOSE CAN'T UNFOLD FAST ENOUGH!)

There are places in our lives where Reverence comes easy. Who wouldn't take a look at a sleeping child, for example, or a glorious flower, or a magnificent sunset, and not experience at least a moment of heart-opening, breath-taking and awe-inspiring appreciation?

There are also those other places, like when we're spending time with relatives who aren't necessarily withholding their opinions or spreading the love. Or when we're interacting (and sharing the planet) with people whose worldviews, values and behaviors are so different from our own. Or when we're looking in the mirror at our own gloriously, imperfectly human reflection.

Or, when we're engaged in a creative process (like fulfilling our life's purpose!), and things aren't going quite as smoothly, quickly or neatly as our minds would like.

How hard it can be during times like these to practice the kind of joyful presence, respect and gratitude for life so beautifully captured by the gift of Reverence.

Sometimes, when we're feeling impatient with our life and the way it's going, when Reverence is beyond our reach, it can help to start with Mindfulness—the ability to be with and witness our uncomfortable experience from a place of calm, neutral presence. We relax, breathe deeply. We watch our thoughts without grasping or pushing away. We do our best to loosen the hold of judgments, agendas and time pressure. We practice kindness towards ourselves.

When I'm in one of my "My life purpose can't unfold fast enough!" states, I like to pull out my *Gene Keys* book and read one of my favorite passages about the Gift of Restraint:

*"To begin anything, you must first have a clear intention. The more selfless your intention, the more power it will have. If you begin with the right intention, then everything will follow, but you must resist the temptation to interfere with the process out of fear. The intention is the seed, and the seed contains all the necessary ingredients and properties that will be needed in the journey ahead. The seed even contains the specific fragrances that will attract the right allies at the right times.*

*It is also true to say that the greater the power, the longer it takes to germinate. The seed of a yew tree and the seed of a sunflower are similar in size. However, whilst the sunflower will grow to its full size within the space of a few months, the yew tree has depth and complexity and will begin at a different pace and follow its own timing. It may take 10 years just to reach the height of the sunflower, but it may live as long as 5,000 years. So it is with all human ideas and actions… We humans cannot see the details of the journey ahead; we have to trust in the direction that our intention takes, even if it does not make sense to us at the time. This is the power of Restraint—to allow your life to unfold without urgent demand."*

One of my all-time favorite quotes by Anais Nin is, "And the day came when the risk to remain tight in a bud was more painful than the risk it took to blossom."

This quote speaks so beautifully to the fear that so often holds us back from allowing ourselves to fully bloom. Whether we are afraid of not being good enough or our own success, our fear can easily cloak itself in tendencies towards procrastination and perfectionism. Sometimes, we must be willing to push through our fear and resistance, out of reverence for our gifts and our soul's yearning to share those gifts with others.

Sometimes (this is the delicate dance!), the biggest gift we can give ourselves is patience, trust and a profound reverence for the natural timing of our own growth process. We need to show a willingness to get out of the way, to sit back and watch—in wonder and awe—at the pure intelligence guiding each and every (visible and invisible) step of our unfoldment. We need to demonstrate an openness to the probability that our own flower's process is mysteriously—synchronistically—connected to the processes of our 'garden mates' and the Great Garden.

Here is a three-fold invitation for you—a way to practice Reverence towards yourself, and your own (creative/life) process, especially during those times when it feels difficult:

## Start with a little intention seed check-up

Whatever intention you're working with, make sure that there's a good chunk of love at the core of your seed. See if there's a way you can make it less about you (i.e. whether you're good enough or not), and more about the people or beings you just might help if you get out of your own way and share what you feel moved to offer. (Remember, it's not about being perfect!)

## Embrace your inner yew tree

Remind yourself, as often as you need to, that as long as you're planting seeds that have been sincerely sprinkled with love, there is an intelligence at work, in you, and all around you.

This intelligence is permeating every situation, guiding, gathering and patiently setting the pace behind the scenes. It is creating just the right conditions for your full and glorious unfoldment. Trust that this is happening, whether you know it or not, understand it or not, or feel like you have any control over it or not.

*Then take a deep breath and let go.* (Who knows? Your little seed might be growing something entirely different than you imagine, yet something equally magnificent. Seeds can be delightfully tricky that way!)

Chances are, you'll know when it's time to take a risk and bloom, because you won't be able *not* to (even if you're scared). Your right time will have arrived, and your whole being will be perfectly primed to meet it.

# WILL LIVING MY DESIGN MAKE ME RICH?

A *Designed to Blossom* Course participant (a Generator) wanted to know whether I could guarantee that living his Design would make him rich. He wanted an answer to the question, "Do I follow the money, or do I follow my passion? And, if I follow my passion, will the money follow?!"

From a Human Design perspective, this (very understandable!) question itself poses a problem, for it is mental by nature. The whole point of Human Design is to help us learn how to enter into a deeply energetic, embodied experiment, so that we can dare to allow something other than the mind guide us.

When a person truly practices self-honoring, however that looks for them, it can have a profound and pervasive influence on their relationships, careers and creative lives over time. I've often found, in my own life and in my clients' and students' lives, that a new more fulfilling life direction emerges in a non-linear way, based on a series of tiny decisions and micro-adjustments that the intelligent body-spirit makes—in each interaction, each situation.

For Generators, such a practice requires ever-increasing levels of self-respect, a willingness to learn how to set healthy limits and take impassioned risks, and a deepening understanding of the preciousness of our energy. For Projectors, it requires prioritizing relationship, trusting deeply in the aura, being highly selective when receiving invitations, and making sure there's always time to rest and relax. For Manifestors, it requires trusting their passion, honoring their deep need for freedom, resting between sprints, listening well to the people around them and caring for others by being clear communicators. For Reflectors, it requires practicing patience, having faith in their unique process, being highly selective around environment, and making sure that they've got reliable, good, empathic and neutral counsel.

Regardless of Type, a self-honoring practice also requires a willingness to look at our deep subconscious beliefs and conditioned attitudes, the ones that often drive our decisions, instead of our *Inner Wisdom Keepers*.

The results of our practice can surprise us. As we act with greater self-respect, jobs we've hated can turn into jobs we enjoy. We can find ourselves playing a new role in an old place. Or suddenly, a door opens, and we find ourselves making a living, or benefiting from a prosperous life circumstance, that we never could have dreamed up on our own or planned with our conscious minds.

The actual process of living in alignment with our nature is grounded and practical, but the way our lives unfold when we're living in this way is in many ways magical, and increasingly synchronistic…especially as we drop deeper and deeper into our hearts. (When I say 'heart,' I'm not talking about the Ego/Heart Center. I'm talking about that place where love resides.)

This is where a deep exploration of the Golden Path of the *Gene Keys* can come in. This journey of Self-Illumination can ground us in our purpose, open our hearts, and ultimately pave a path for us towards prosperity. Of course, the timing must be right for us to take this journey, and it's not for everyone. The more at home we are with our Human Design practice, the better we'll be at assessing whether such a journey is the right fit for us, and what the right timing may be.

In the Golden Path, we have the opportunity to explore the connection between our relationships (to self and others) and prosperity. Interestingly, it is through a process of healing, of releasing the pain of separation, of learning how to love and be loved, that we are empowered to step into our true life's purpose, and to be sustained by it.

# Final Words

I hope you've enjoyed the *Designed to Blossom* Resource Book and have managed to pluck out some juicy, inspiring and thought-provoking fruits along the way. As shared throughout this Resource Book, Human Design and the *Gene Keys* aren't meant to be fixed or static; they are meant to evolve and grow. They can't evolve, deepen or expand without people like you and me—doin' our thing, refining our *Inner Wisdom Keeping* practices and contributing as we go.

If you resonate with my way of holding Human Design and the *Gene Keys*, and would like a foundational, comprehensive and creative introduction to the Human Design system (with a *Gene Keys*-friendly twist), I invite you to check out **Designed to Blossom: A Foundational Course and Creative Workbook in Human Design**. It's available in print and as an e-book on Amazon.com. (For more information and to feel out the fit, feel free to visit wisdomkeepers.net and also read the testimonials at the beginning of this Resource Book.)

You are also warmly invited to check out my latest labors of love: **The Wisdom Keepers Oracle Deck & Inner Guidebook**, and **Walking a Fine Line: Becoming a Professional Wisdom Keeper in the Healing Arts**. These are also available on Amazon.com.

**The Wisdom Keepers Oracle Deck** is an empowering tool of self-acceptance and understanding, a playful way to embrace our shadows with love and uncover the gifts that only we can bring to the world. This deck makes a wonderful learning supplement for *Gene Keys* (and Human Design) enthusiasts. Given that the *Gene Keys* represent a vast body of knowledge and are intellectually rigorous, this deck offers people an additional way to glean its essence—one that is direct, intimate, relational and heart-opening.

***Walking a Fine Line: Becoming a Professional Wisdom Keeper in the Healing Arts*** is a warm invitation into an ongoing, nuanced and collective exploration of professional integrity.

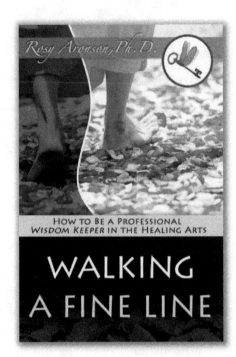

- If you are a professional Wisdom Keeper, *Walking a Fine Line* will inspire, support and stretch you. Sharing knowledge and techniques is only half of our task. Discovering how to share, with whom, when, how much, why, and where make up the other portion. *Walking a Fine Line* speaks to the wisdom, skill, art and balance we all need to live and serve those who come to us.

- If you are a seasoned Wisdom Seeker, this book will help you cultivate healthy boundaries and a discerning mind, so that you can successfully engage with professional Wisdom Keepers that best suit your needs.

- If you're just getting started on your Wisdom Seeking journey, this book will help you know what to look for, and what to look out for! It can help you assess your needs, clarify your wants and enable you to find the quality support you deserve.

Whether you live, work or learn in a spiritual or alternative learning environment, together—through a shared and honest inquiry—we can raise the quality of our collective service and grow as a planetary family of creative, caring individuals.

# Resources for You!

For all things *Wisdom Keepers:*

*wisdomkeepers.net*

For all things *Gene Keys & Integral Human Design*:

*Genekeys.com*
*Onedoorland.com/genekeys*
*Integralhumandesign.net*
*teachings.genekeys.com/integral-human-design/*

## More places to deepen your love of Human Design:

*Integral Human Design*
*Jovian Archive*
*Human Design America*
*Karen Curry*
*Kim Gould*
*Steve Rhodes*
*Richard Beaumont*
*Chetan Parker*

# ABOUT THE AUTHOR

**Rosy Aronson, PhD**, is an Artist, Blossoming Guide and ordained Spiritual Counselor with a Masters in Expressive Arts Therapy and a Doctorate in Intuitive Listening and the Creative Arts. In addition to the ***Designed to Blossom*** Foundational Course & Creative Workbook in Human Design and this Resource Book, Rosy has created the ***64 Faces of Awakening, The Wisdom Keepers Oracle Deck, The Wisdom Keepers Inner Guidebook, The 64 Faces of Awakening Coloring Book, Walking a Fine Line: Becoming a Professional Wisdom Keeper in the Healing Arts*** and ***A Tale of Serendipity, Part One*** of ***The Wisdom Keepers Adventure Tales Series***, to reflect essential healing archetypes that lie at the foundation of our universe. Her deepest intention is to provide empowering tools for people to awaken their *Inner Wisdom Keeper* and bloom into their authentic selves.

An avid permission-giver, pressure-dissolver and embracer of the unknown, Rosy believes we are literally designed to blossom, and the more each of us radically trusts, honors and expresses our True Nature, the more magic we can create together.

CPSIA information can be obtained
at www.ICGtesting.com
Printed in the USA
LVHW060325180420
653688LV00034B/1638